M000102599

Thinking the US South

Contemporary Philosophy from Southern Perspectives

✦

Edited by Shannon Sullivan

NORTHWESTERN UNIVERSITY PRESS
EVANSTON, ILLINOIS

Northwestern University Press
www.nupress.northwestern.edu

Copyright © 2021 by Northwestern University Press.
Published 2021. All rights reserved.

Printed in the United States of America

10 9 8 7 6 5 4 3 2 1

Library of Congress Cataloging-in-Publication Data

Names: Sullivan, Shannon, 1967–editor.
Title: Thinking the US South : contemporary philosophy from Southern
    perspectives / edited by Shannon Sullivan.
Description: Evanston, Illinois : Northwestern University Press, 2021. | Includes
    bibliographical references.
Identifiers: LCCN 2020041823 | ISBN 9780810143302 (paperback) | ISBN
    9780810143319 (cloth) | ISBN 9780810143326 (ebook)
Subjects: LCSH: Philosophy—Southern States. | Philosophy, American. | Southern
    States—Intellectual life—21st century.
Classification: LCC B946 .T45 2021 | DDC 191—dc23
LC record available at https://lccn.loc.gov/2020041823

CONTENTS

Part III. Southern Practices

ACKNOWLEDGMENTS

My thanks go to Trevor Perri, senior acquisitions editor, and two anonymous reviewers for Northwestern University Press for their support of this book and helpful suggestions during the revision process. I also appreciate the copyediting and formatting assistance that maggie castor provided as the manuscript was being prepared for review. Finally, I warmly thank the authors of the book's chapters and afterword, who took up my invitation to think critically and creatively about the South. I appreciate their hard work and their willingness to take some philosophical and existential risks as they wrote their essays.

Chapter 1, "The Southern White Worker Question," includes material adapted with permission from pages 196 to 203 of Linda Martín Alcoff's *The Future of Whiteness* (Cambridge, UK: Polity Press, 2015). Chapter 9, "Dumping on Southern 'White Trash': Etiquette and Abjection," has been adapted with permission from pages 25 to 39 of Shannon Sullivan's *Good White People: The Problem with Middle-Class White Anti-Racism* (Albany: SUNY, 2014).

This book is dedicated to my daughters, Samantha and Sophia, whom I love dearly, and to Jennifer, Michele, Julia, Maya, Gordon, Lisa, Ben, Joanne, Ruth, Emily, Erika, and my parents, Alex George and Bettye, for being there for me and helping me through hard times.

Introduction

Doing Philosophy from Southern Standpoints

Shannon Sullivan

What might it mean to do philosophy from Southern standpoints—and why would anyone want to do that? As many feminist, critical race, existential, phenomenological, pragmatist, and other philosophers have argued, knowledge is situated. It emerges out of contexts and practices that often are shaped by gender, race, class, sexuality, religion, and a number of other salient axes of lived experience. There is no placeless, timeless location from which to know the world. There is no generic, God's-eye point of view for human beings to occupy. Given this fact, do regional differences within the United States make a difference philosophically? If so, how? Put another way, if place matters, how does *this* place—the US South—matter?

This goal of this collection is to explore these questions, using the US South (aka, "the South") as an intersectional site for philosophical inquiry. The book's main thesis is that regional location and regional identities in the United States play an important role in epistemological, ethical, political, emotional, affective, ontological, and related matters. And yet, the philosophical significance of the South has largely been neglected or ignored. Some exceptions include feminist philosophy in which the South shows up peripherally as the authors examine issues of race. I am thinking, for example, of Linda Martín Alcoff's childhood in Florida as the daughter of a Panamanian father, Kim Q. Hall's experience of the Confederate flag growing up in a white Virginian family, and Ladelle McWhorter's love of her boots when she went line dancing in Virginia.[1] Lucius T. Outlaw (Jr.) also describes how being born and raised in racially segregated Mississippi was (and is) an important source for his philosophical thinking.[2] I was fascinated learning these things about Alcoff, Hall, McWhorter, and Outlaw as I was reading their philosophical work. These tidbits complemented a remark made to me years ago by Leigh Johnson (a Tennessean) about the need for a conference on philosophy and the South.[3] All this led me to wonder: what might a situated philosophy look like if its rootedness in the South was self-consciously central, rather than marginal to its significance? The ten chapters and afterword in this book are a beginning of an answer to that question.

But why the South in particular? I chose the South not only because I am a Southerner (of sorts: a Texan), but also because the South is not merely one region among others. In fact, in attempting "simply" to pinpoint it geographically, we already can see how the South as a productive concept is at play. Is the South the eleven states that seceded to form the Confederate States of America? No, because that would omit Southern states such as Kentucky and West Virginia. It also would include Texas, which is in the Southwest rather than in the South proper. (Texas was part of the Confederacy, an oft-forgotten fact.) Is the South all states below the Mason-Dixon line? Not exactly, because that would include Florida, which is geographically south but culturally different than the South even though it also joined the Confederate States of America. (Like Texas, Florida has a particularly complicated relationship with the South.) The point here, as with the book as a whole, is not to try to define the necessary and sufficient conditions for being part of the South but to illuminate some of the generative results of using the South for philosophical thinking.

The South is not solely a geographical location. It also is an idea. Sometimes it is a fantasy; other times, it is a nightmare. In any case, it is a prominent component of the US national imaginary. Witness the South as a nagging reminder of, if not an outright synonym for, chattel slavery and the Civil War ("the Old South"); as a marker of stupidity and backwardness ("rednecks" and "white trash"); as a symbol of progress ("the New South"); as a national embarrassment and even a literal joke ("You can tell a Southern virgin when you see a girl running faster than her father and brothers"); and above all, as a dumping ground for allegedly being solely responsible (guilt) for racism and white supremacy in the United States. The South also is a site of tremendous regional pride ("Some are born Southern; others just wish they were"), although whether that pride is a shameful sign of the incorrigible racism of the South tends to depend on whether you ask a Southerner or a Northerner.

Consider the controversial topic of the Confederate flag. The historical record is clear: the flag that today is "the Confederate flag" was not the flag flown by the Confederate States of America during the Civil War. It was a battle flag flown by Robert E. Lee's Virginia troops that became associated with the Confederacy many years *after* the South lost the war. In 1948, the prosegregation Dixiecrat party adopted the flag, which soon became a symbol of white support for racial segregation across the South. Various Southern states such as Georgia and Mississippi redesigned their state flags to incorporate the Confederate flag (Mississippi was the last state to change this design, signing legislation on June 30. 2020, to remove the Confederate emblem from its flag), and five Southern states (Florida, Mississippi, Georgia, South Carolina, and Louisiana) continue to legally protect the Confederate flag from desecration.[4] In the words of one historian, "the [Confederate] flag was and is a symbol of first, slavery, then of white supremacy, and ultimately of resistance to racial equity."[5] For this reason, South Carolina finally bowed to pressure in July 2015 to take down the Confederate flag from its state-house grounds in the wake of white supremacist Dylann Roof's murder of nine African American churchgoers at Charleston's Emanuel African Methodist Episcopal Church.

I wholeheartedly agree with the removal of the flag. What concerns me, however, is the way that the question of its removal—and of the meaning of the flag itself—often was and is reduced to the false dichotomy of heritage versus hate. According to that dichotomy, either the Confederate flag is a symbol of white people's supremacist hatred for people of color, and African Americans in particular, *or* it is a symbol of pride in and love for Southern heritage and ancestors. On the latter point, in the words of one white South Carolinian who protested the flag's removal, support for the Confederate flag allegedly is not about hating anyone but "about loving where you come from. . . . As the song says, if you don't stand for something, you'll fall for anything, and I stand for what my ancestors [who fought with Robert E. Lee] went through."[6] In contrast, a Showing Up for Racial Justice (SURJ) counterprotester at the same event claimed that "the people who believe this [flag] represents heritage were taught that in school. . . . It's terrible to say they don't know any better, but if that's what they were taught, that's what they believe."[7]

I will return shortly to the condescension that virtually drips off the SURJ protester's lips. First, I want to note that Southern heritage and hate are not opposed because Southern heritage *includes* hate. Its hate is complex—maybe hate always is—but at minimum it is complex because it combines hatred of people of color with hatred (or at least deep hostility and suspicion) of white Northerners, and both of those with love for white ancestors. That hate needs to be understood *as heritage*, however, not as hate *simpliciter*. It is something that provides a connection to family roots. It is one reason why none of us are isolated individuals but instead nourished (or poisoned, as the case might be) by ancestral soil. None of us are or can be root-free, so one's heritage cannot be simply tossed aside, as complex and problematic as it might be. It has to be reckoned with and worked through. This is complicated, some-times in traumatic ways. Family does not stop being a possible site of hate just because it is family, and hate does not change into something warm and nurturing just because it can be part of family. Despite this complexity—or perhaps because of it—telling someone to simply abandon their heritage will not work. It is like yanking a plant out of the ground and wondering why it soon shrivels up and dies. Granted, depending on the particular soil, remain-ing in it also could kill the plant. But if the plant could vehemently resist being yanked up by someone else, I am sure it would.

This leads to my second concern about the false dichotomy between heri-tage and hate. Southern heritage includes hate, but it is not reducible to it.

This reduction, however, is precisely what the question "heritage or hate?" performs: heritage equals hate, period. "Heritage or hate?" is almost always a rhetorical question, after all. In contrast, I think that one—*one*, not the only— dimension of the Southern insistence on heritage is an attempt to define being a Southerner without reducing it to being racist and white supremacist. It is part of a deeply felt love for being Southern and a refusal to interpret that self-love as wholly insidious. Can one love being a Southerner and not be a bad person? More pointedly, can a *white* person love being a Southerner and not be a bad person for that reason? Or to really get down to it, can only Black people legitimately love being Southerners? I hope the answer to that last question is no. The Confederate flag is an incredibly harmful and destructive symbol for white Southerners' love of being Southern, but it is not the love that necessarily is a problem—it is the racism and white supremacy. New symbols need to be created as focal points for these questions about being a Southerner. Merely damning the flag without discussion of all that it is being used to convey is not going to solve the problem, it is only going to make it worse.

The condescension of the SURJ protester is a case in point. I do not know if she is a Northerner, but the type of comment she made is characteristic of white Northern condemnations of the South. These go back at least to the middle of the nineteenth century when white Southerners complained about white Northerners' patronizing disdain for them. As Virginian Albert Bledsoe sarcastically described white Northerners' attitude toward the South in 1860, "in the overflowing exuberance of their philanthropy, they take pity of [*sic*] our most lamentable moral darkness, and graciously condescend to teach us the very A B C of ethical philosophy!"[8] Attitudes like that can lead white Southerners to reactively cling all the more tightly to the Confederate flag, if only to say "fuck you" to the North and its hypocritical dumping on the South. If doing that also means doing harm to Black people and other people of color via the flag, then some white Southerners are willing, perhaps even eager, to do so. That is devastatingly problematic, to say the least. Also problematic, however, is the forced or assumed combination of hating the North and hating people of color. Southerners need to create critical, creative practices and symbols through which we all, including white Southerners, can love the South (and despise the white North, if need be—that too is complicated and needs much more examination) that are separate from racism and white supremacy.

I began this introduction by saying that knowledge is situated. Another less fancy (more Southern?) way of saying that is to say, as I do above, that roots matter. They matter both personally *and* philosophically. However, the issue of roots—and soil, to continue the metaphor—is connected in troubling ways to issues of land. What does it mean to be rooted not just in particular families but also in stolen land, as all non-Indigenous people in the United States are? Moreover, the more that global interconnections increase, the more local roots tend to matter—for better or worse. Sometimes what a person is rooted in is nourishing; sometimes it is toxic; often it is a mix of both. Either way, it is not a viable option, personally or philosophically, for people to be completely rootless. So, what can we make of the particular soil out of which Southerners grow? Is it primarily backwards, even noxious, as most of the jokes about it seem to assume? What would the affirmation of Southern roots look like if it also reckoned with past and present settler colonialism in the United States? Is that combination even possible? Could the South ever be philosophically nourishing?

The chapters in this book respond to these questions in complex ways. The answer to any of them is rarely a simple yes or no. While the book focuses on the South, for example, it simultaneously is and must be about more than the US South. (I note that the book's authors and I will capitalize "the South" and "the Global South," as well as "the North" and "the Global North," when we discuss regions that are part of national and global imaginaries. We will use "the US South" and "the US North," rather than "the South" and "the North," when further clarification is needed. We will use lowercase "south" and "north" when discussing geographical areas or directions.) The US South, including its relationship with the US North, is situated globally as part of the Global North in relationship with the Global South. For this reason, the chapters in part 2, "Southern Borders," focus in particular on the US South in connection with the Global South. This connection, however, should not be read as restricted to those three chapters. It is relevant to the entire volume. Southern identities and Southern practices are formed in and through Southern borders that are not merely with the US North. They also are with the Global South. While the US South tends to be subordinated by the US North, the US South also is part of the Global North that generally dominates the Global South. Understanding the complexity of global regional differences is thus important to understanding national regional differences within the United States. We cannot adequately understand the US South without understanding the Global North, and we cannot adequately understand the Global North without examining its relationship with the Global South.

In addition, the book does not narrowly focus on race. While race rightly will be a significant topic in many of the pages that follow, the US South—including its complex relationship with the Global South—is about much more than race. It provides an important lens to see not merely racial but also class, religious, gendered, and inter- and intra-American differences, and to explore them in their intersectional relationships with each other. The results of doing so include discussions of a fresh, distinctive look at how identity is constituted; the role of place, ancestors, and (be)longing in identity formation; the impact of regional differences on (what counts as) political resistance; the ways that affect and emotional labor circulate; practices of boundary-policing, deportation, and mourning; issues of disability; racial and other forms of suffering; and above all, the question of whether and how doing philosophy changes if it is deliberately done from Southern standpoints.

The three chapters composing part 1 of the book focus on "Southern Identities," demonstrating the complexity of what the South is or might be. Linda Martín Alcoff opens the book with an analysis of race, region, and class. In her chapter, "The Southern White Worker Question," Alcoff notes the national hand-wringing that has occurred over the racism of working-class white Southerners. What is their problem, the left often agonizingly asks? Why does racial solidarity between working-class and more affluent white people always seem to win out over class solidarity with working-class people of color? The answer, Alcoff argues, is more complicated than we usually realize. To unpack that answer, Alcoff insightfully examines the US national political imaginary that regards the South as culturally backward. Engaging the work of Karl Marx and journalist W. J. Cash, Alcoff notes the economic and psychological reasons that lower-class white Southerners aligned themselves with the white gentry, but she also argues that a new feature of contemporary working-class life must be reckoned with—that the white working class no longer feels it has a say in the United States, which Alcoff argues is connected to the demise of unions. The result of this demise often appears to be a racial tribalism among white people, but racism and supposed white superiority are usually more unstable than they appear. Closing with the story of a white working-class former Klan member who changed his views about race after working politically and personally with a Black woman, Alcoff concludes that the future of the South is open and undetermined. It can be a site of both racial justice and white nationalistic politics, fueled in either direction by the denigration and economic deterioration of Southern white workers.

In chapter 2, "Southern Land: Indigeneity, Genocide, and Racialization in Whitened Lineages," Ladelle McWhorter critically examines the way Southern identity is felt, or assumed, to be tightly bound up with love for the land of the South. This attachment to the land rarely acknowledges that all non-Indigenous Southern people—of any race—were born and live on land that was stolen from Indigenous people. Some Southerners even think of themselves as "indigenized" to the land in a way that other US whites (Yankees) could never be or understand. Interestingly, this identification with the land intensified *after* the Civil War, when impoverished former plantation owners had to sell to speculators, forfeiting many acres of Southern land. McWhorter demonstrates how racialization, in this case of Southern whites, is a colonizing strategy, one that produces "white Southerners" who can be identified by their love for the land via the simultaneous erasure of Indigenous people from the story of the South's war with the white North. In turn, resisting racialization can be a way to resist colonizing strategies. And yet, as McWhorter agonizingly acknowledges, she cannot *not* be a Southerner, just as she cannot not be American or white. Writing with anger rather than guilt at the harm that racism, colonialism, and genocide have done to Indigenous people, African Americans, and the white working class—especially children—McWhorter grapples with what a philosophy of the South might be when it is formed out of historical awareness, contingency, and awareness of difference. As McWhorter insists, this will not be so much a full-blown "Southern philosophy" as it is a whirlwind over an abyss, formed as much in violence and exploitation as in love and wonder.

In chapter 3, "Between Socrates and Grandma: On Being a Black Southern Philosopher," Arnold L. Farr confronts the challenges that Black Southern philosophers face when engaging in critical self-reflection. Such self-reflection is a distinctive mark of the discipline, and yet it is a paradoxical exercise (at best) when it is expected of those who are routinely excluded from and made uncomfortable within the field. Socrates might have been killed at the end of his long life for practicing philosophy, but it is an entirely different matter to cultivate wisdom when one is socially dead at birth. Blending philosophy with autobiography, Farr powerfully describes a world that is hostile both to his Blackness and to his being a Southerner. These tensions and hostilities are heightened when Black Southern philosophers work from texts that generally are not recognized by white people as philosophical. "Grandma's metaphysics" is a case in point. Juxtaposing the wisdom that comes from Southern Black communities with the wisdom that is championed by academic philosophy, Farr argues that the beginning of Black Southern wisdom is figuring out how to ensure that one's natal death sentence is not carried out. Black grandmothers in particular provide holding communities and epistemic communities that are crucial to survival. Their metaphysics, which does not concern truth claims but rather provides the glue that holds Black Southern life together, is a type of religious attachment distinct to the Black South. Farr demonstrates how what once was a double source of self-doubt—being Black and Southern—became for him a tool for generating self-respect and advancing philosophical discourse.

Borders defining the US South are an important theme that runs throughout this book. The three chapters in part 2, "Southern Borders," concentrate on that theme by examining borders the US South shares with both the US North and the Global South. In chapter 4, "Are You a Yankee? Purity, Identity, and 'The Southern,'" Michael J. Monahan challenges notions of purity that often lie at the heart of identity. He begins by examining whether he might be a Yankee interloper in his childhood hometown, which is due west of Louisville, Kentucky, but in southern Indiana. Certainly, some of his fellow Indianans have thought so. This raises the question: What does it mean to *be* a Southerner? And what does it mean given that the North-South divide has interrelated global, regional, and local significance? Monahan thoughtfully explores how the Global North is defined in terms of relative wealth, food security, health outcomes, and political stability, while the Global South has significantly lessened indicators in these and other various social goods.

In the western hemisphere, the boundary between north and south shares similarities with the global distinction, but includes significant linguistic and cultural aspects. Finally, in the United States, the distinction shares certain of these global and regional features but is above all conditioned by the historical rupture of the US Civil War of the 1860s. Monahan works through these different ways of drawing North-South and Global North-South distinctions in order to better identify their similarities and differences. He convincingly argues that a key feature of these distinctions is their fundamental *relationality*: there can be no South without a North, and vice versa. This creates a paradigmatically *dialectical* relation between the terms, where neither can be understood independently of the other, and together they constitute a way of understanding the world that cannot be reduced to the sum of its parts. By working some of the movements of this dialectic in each arena and their relation to each other, Monahan challenges the pretension to purity that informs so much of the dominant modes of thought relating to each of these North-South and Global North–Global South divides. The global divide is directly linked to the distinction between the modern and the traditional. Situating the US conception of the North and the South within its regional and global contexts, Monahan demonstrates that there are many different ways to be Southern, both globally and in the US South.

In chapter 5, "Affective Economies from the Global South to the US South: Global Care Chains and Southern Sympathy Fatigue," Shiloh Whitney examines the complexities of affective injustice across the US North-South and the Global North-South divides. Drawing on sociologist Arlie Hochschild's work on global care chains through which dominant groups exploit subordinate groups' affective resources, Whitney carefully tracks how white members of the religious right in the US South attempt to "close the borders of human sympathy . . . to all the people who have cut in front of you." This means closing affective (and literal) borders to immigrants, people of color, and the poor, and yet this is done while simultaneously exploiting affective resources from the Global South. Considering affect to be produced through circulation in affective economies, Whitney analyzes colonial history, misogyny, and the feminism of privileged white women as affective economies of sympathy. All three of these phenomena share features with the sympathy fatigue found by Hochschild in the US South: they all are produced by a colonial economy that ultimately dumps affective labor southward. Juxtaposing the anxiety about sympathy exploitation in the US South with the exploitation of affective resources from the Global South, Whitney insightfully demonstrates how the Nixon-era Southern strategy of manipulating white people's fear of Black advancement has also become a kind of global Northern strategy. This would be a strategy in which US Northern whites join with US Southern whites to restrict their compassion and sympathy—and the resources that flow from those affective economies—to the Global North, and the United States in particular.

In chapter 6, "Altars for the Living: Shadow Ground, Aesthetic Memory, and the US-Mexico Borderlands," Mariana Ortega discusses the production of spaces of mourning in connection to memory practices—not for the dead, but for the living. In so doing, Ortega movingly examines the question of who deserves to be remembered—or rather, who does not deserve to be remembered, even when alive, even when there are altars for them. Using the photography of Verónica Cárdenas, an artist from the border town of McAllen, Texas—specifically her series of photos about detained undocumented immigrants at the border of Mexico and the US South-Southwest—Ortega calls for aesthetic memory as a way to honor all of the immigrants, both regionally and globally, who have become invisible as humans and hypervisible as alleged criminals. Presenting striking images from Cárdenas's *Traveling Soles* series, Ortega analyzes the photographs in the series as well as the spatialities that Cárdenas created in order to honor border-crossers, primarily Central American children who have been apprehended at the US-Mexico border and put in detention camps. As Ortega presents the photographs and the spaces they created, they become instances of spontaneous memorialization and altars for the living. The photographs in turn become *memento vivere*.

Is there any philosophical significance to distinctively Southern ways of living, moving, talking, singing, and so on? The four chapters in part 3, "Southern Practices," explore that intriguing question. In chapter 7, "'I Ain't Thinkin' 'Bout You': Black Liberation Politics at the Intersection of Region, Gender, and Class," Lindsey Stewart examines how the US North is assumed to be both the geographical location and the normative standard for Black liberation. In the form of oppositions between North and South, region also operates as a shorthand for gender and class tensions in Black political thought. The North is thought to be the place where Black people (men) can engage in strong political action against racism while the South is assumed to be a backwards place that requires Black people (men) to emasculate themselves. This shorthand plays out in the political philosophy of Iris Marion Young, for example, which serves as an example of how Black Southern women tend to be omitted in the (hi)stories that are told about political struggle for Black liberation. In Young's "ideal of city life," the North is normalized and Black Southern life is displaced in social political discourse. As Stewart powerfully demonstrates, a similar pattern of privileging the North can be found in the work of W. E. B. Du Bois. As a corrective to this problem, Stewart introduces Zora Neale Hurston's work on Black Southern life. Taking seriously Alice Walker's claim that "no one could wish for a more advantageous heritage than that bequeathed to the black writer in the South," Stewart argues that there are social-political resources that emerge in the dynamic intersection of race, region, class, and gender. Stewart's central example is what she terms "principled indifference," which is an indifference to white people and their concerns for the sake of protecting Black people's inner life and joy. Stewart's chapter concludes with an analysis of Beyoncé Knowles's performance of "Sorry" as a striking instance of Black female Southern indifference.

In chapter 8, "Black Ancestral Discourses: Cultural Cadences from the South," Devonya N. Havis challenges the notion that Southern Blackness is nothing but oppression and misery, which has long been the framework for depicting Black peoples and their cultures. This is not a framework from the distant past. It is very much alive and well today. It can be found, for example, in Colson Whitehead's Pulitzer Prize–winning novel *The Underground Railroad* (published in 2016), which also was selected for Oprah's Book Club and has thus received significant uptake from the general public in the United States. Havis begins by examining the alchemy of the tragicomic, which is important for understanding Black ancestral discourses as something other than immiseration. As she does so, she draws on ancestral archives provided by her father, who was a "possibility model" for the affirmation of Black community. Havis then astutely analyzes Whitehead's novel, demonstrating how what she calls "plantation logic" is still at work in the book even though it recounts a Black slave's journey to freedom in the antebellum South. With Havis's creative intervention, we can hear Blackness beyond the limited possibilities available when conceiving it as mere opposition to whiteness. On her account, to be able to hear the thick cadences and inflections of Black "cultural music" requires understanding the US South. This is why laboring to resist the framework of Black immiseration can be considered a philosophical practice in and of the South.

Chapter 9, "Dumping on Southern 'White Trash': Etiquette and Abjection," explores how intra-white class biases and antagonisms between North and South work together to support the alleged moral goodness of middle-to-upper-class white people. Rather than furthering racial justice, white people's moral goodness tends to interfere with it, dumping problems of racism onto so-called white trash. I begin with the etiquette of race relations, examining the forms of social control that distinguish Black and white people. In the United States, racial etiquette has been (and is) a habit that both exerts social control and enables social distance between white people and people of color. In so doing, racial etiquette also operates intra-racially, between classes of white people. Middle-to-upper-class white people tend to denigrate white trash, hillbillies, and rednecks as improperly white: loud, uneducated, uncouth, and too much like the Black people and other people of color that they are "supposed to" be completely different from. The distinction between so-called white trash and proper white people is also regionalized. White trash and Southernness tend to be conflated, as if merely being Southern makes a white person simultaneously too close to Blackness *and* guilty of the nation's ongoing racism. Challenging the idea that (white) Southern practices are synonymous with racism, my aim is not to let poor white people off the proverbial hook. I instead attempt to call out middle-to-upper-class white people's hypocrisy and call for their taking responsibility for ongoing racism, white privilege, and white supremacy.

Part 3 closes with Kim Q. Hall's essay "On Being Slow: Philosophy and Disability in the US South." In her chapter, Hall asks, what does it mean to be or to be perceived as slow? How does the slowness of some forms of disability relate in complex ways both to the perceived slowness of Southern people and to the ability to do philosophy well? Hall returns to W. J. Cash's influential *The Mind of the South*, discussed by Alcoff in chapter 1, in which Cash is unequivocal about what he perceives as the impossibility of philosophy in the US South. For Cash, the Southern mind's tendency to drift, along with its conformity, ignorance, intolerance, and paucity of imagination, make the region and its people downright hostile to philosophy. Cash's characterization of the Southern mind resonates with contemporary stereotypes of white, especially rural, Southerners as "dumb rednecks." While Cash focuses on "the Southern mind," Hall masterfully critiques the ableist logic that informs abiding assumptions about the extent to which Southern body-minds are fit for philosophy and whether the US South is hospitable to philosophy. From a Southern drawl to a presumed general dull-mindedness, Southerners are frequently stereotyped as slow. In addition to critically examining this stereotype, Hall offers a feminist queer crip reframing of what it means to be slow. Slowness is often perceived as evidence of a lack of capacity for reasoning and prosody presumed necessary for academic and philosophical success. In contrast, Hall creatively seeks to reframe slowness as a critical resource. Slowness has no value (or lack of value) in itself, and it can even be a mark of privilege in an accelerating world of global capitalism that demands speed from its workers. As Hall demonstrates, however, slowness also can be a tool for resisting oppressive assumptions about who is fit to do philosophy. In that way, it can be a resource for cripping philosophy in and of the South.

Finally, Lucius T. Outlaw (Jr.)'s afterword, "Philosophizings in/of/regarding 'the South(s)': A New Field of Discourse in US American Philosophy?," reflects on why academic philosophy in the United States has not paid much, if any, professional attention to the South. This question is especially acute for Outlaw given both the importance of the region to the United States and the fact that scholars and artists in many other fields have long given serious consideration to the South. It also is an acute question given the critical and creative scholarly work being done on the Global South (and Global North), which has a great bearing on the US South. The work of Portuguese sociologist and economist Boaventura de Sousa Santos is particularly illuminative and significant for Outlaw. Santos's writings break with the Western-centric tradition of critical theory, helping produce reconstructions of knowledge that would be extremely relevant to new understandings of the US South. Outlaw closes the volume with a call for additional scholarly work that plumbs the philosophical depths of Southernness and the South.

This book provides a rich variety of ways to develop, contest, and otherwise do philosophy from the perspective of Southern standpoints, but it merely scratches the surface. Ten chapters can only do so much. In particular,

I note that issues of settler colonialism in the South (and elsewhere) deserve more philosophical attention than this collection has been able to provide. So do the roles that religion and spirituality play—or not—in doing philosophy from Southern standpoints. With Outlaw, my hope is that the essays that follow will inspire additional intersectional work on the philosophical import of regional differences in the United States, and of the South in particular, in connection with the Global North and Global South. It might or might not produce something that could be called "philosophy of the South," but either way, we could learn a lot from it.

Notes

1. See Linda Martín Alcoff, *Visible Identities: Race, Gender, and The Self* (New York: Oxford University Press, 2006); Kim Q. Hall, "My Father's Flag," in *Whiteness: Feminist Philosophical Reflections*, ed. Chris J. Cuomo and Kim Q. Hall (Lanham, MD: Rowman and Littlefield, 1999); and Ladelle McWhorter, *Bodies and Pleasures: Foucault and the Politics of Sexual Normalization* (Indianapolis: Indiana University Press, 1999).

2. Lucius T. Outlaw Jr., *On Race and Philosophy* (New York: Routledge, 1996).

3. And there eventually was one, sort of. A SPEP session entitled "Philosophy in/of the South" took place in Memphis, Tennessee, on October 19, 2017, with papers presented by Linda Martín Alcoff, Leigh Johnson, and Lucius Outlaw, with Eduardo Mendieta as moderator. I thank all four participants and the SPEP audience for their critical insights and stimulating discussion, which were important for encouraging and shaping this volume.

4. Daniel Costa Roberts, "8 Things You Didn't Know about the Confederate Flag," *PBS NewsHour Weekend*, June 21, 2015, accessed March 29, 2019, https://www.pbs.org/newshour/politics/8-things-didnt-know-confederate-flag.

5. David Goldfield, quoted in Tyler Harris and Skye Allan, "Heritage or Hate? Scholars Add Context in Wake of Charleston Massacre," *UNC Charlotte College of Liberal Arts Exchange* (Fall/Winter 2015): 14.

6. Quoted in Bristow Marchant, "3 Years Later, Confederate Flag Casts Shadow Again over SC State House," *The State*, July 10, 2018, accessed March 29, 2019, https://www.thestate.com/news/politics-government/article214555950.html.

7. Quoted in Marchant, "3 Years Later."

8. Albert Taylor Bledsoe, "Liberty and Slavery: Or, Slavery in the Light of Moral and Political Philosophy," in *Cotton Is King, and Pro-Slavery Arguments Comprising the Writings of Hammond, Harper, Christy, Stringfellow, Hodge, Bledsoe, and Cartwright, on this Important Subject*, ed. E N. Elliot (New York: Negro Universities Press, 1969), 272.

Bibliography

Alcoff, Linda Martín. *Visible Identities: Race, Gender, and The Self*. New York: Oxford University Press, 2006.

Bledsoe, Albert Taylor. "Liberty and Slavery: Or, Slavery in the Light of Moral and Political Philosophy." In *Cotton Is King, and Pro-Slavery Arguments Comprising the Writings of Hammond, Harper, Christy, Stringfellow, Hodge, Bledsoe, and Cartwright, on this Important Subject.* Edited by E. N. Elliot. New York: Negro Universities Press, 1969.

Hall, Kim Q. "My Father's Flag." In *Whiteness: Feminist Philosophical Reflections.* Edited by Chris J. Cuomo and Kim Q. Hall. Lanham, MD: Rowman and Littlefield, 1999.

Harris, Tyler, and Skye Allan. "Heritage or Hate? Scholars Add Context in Wake of Charleston Massacre." *UNC Charlotte College of Liberal Arts Exchange* (Fall/Winter 2015): 14.

Marchant, Bristow. "3 Years Later, Confederate Flag Casts Shadow Again over SC State House." *The State,* July 10, 2018. Accessed March 29, 2019. https://www.thestate.com/news/politics-government/article214555950.html.

McWhorter, Ladelle. *Bodies and Pleasures: Foucault and the Politics of Sexual Normalization.* Indianapolis: Indiana University Press, 1999.

Outlaw, Lucius T., Jr. *On Race and Philosophy.* New York: Routledge, 1996.

Roberts, Daniel Costa. "8 Things You Didn't Know about the Confederate Flag." *PBS NewsHour Weekend,* June 21, 2015. Accessed March 29, 2019. https://www.pbs.org/newshour/politics/8-things-didnt-know-confederate-flag.

Part I

Southern Identities

1

✦

The Southern White Worker Question

Linda Martín Alcoff

In the days when there was a vibrant "old left," debates were collectively orchestrated around central topics identified as *questions*. There was "the Woman Question," "the National Question," even "the Jewish Question." Varied theorists took varied positions on these questions, and argued out their conclusions. As odd as it may sound today, the rubric provided a helpful means to coordinate what was sometimes a real democratic airing of views. Until, that is, answers to these questions hardened into party orthodoxy.

Since the election of Donald Trump in 2016, political scientists, sociologists, labor, and antiracist activists have been debating what I want to call, in this nostalgic vein, "the Southern White Worker Question." As with the earlier debates, this one concerns the relationship of Southern white workers, male and female—a specific social identity group—to broad class-based movements for social justice. The question that is being endlessly debated is, why does the racism of Southern white workers so often trump, so to speak, their class solidarity? Will they ever change? Most of the answers have been weak; some are insulting. This chapter sets out to offer a different approach that will hopefully contribute to a better account.

Before I begin, however, let me offer a disclosure: I am a Southerner, raised largely in the South by the white Southern part of my family. Most made a moderate income living off the land or the water in trailers or houses they built themselves. My uncles drove trucks, built bridges, cut hair, fixed engines, and lived off of government programs; my aunts grew vegetables, raised chickens, made the family clothes, and could cook any meat that ventured into the yard. I loved this family, and yet I continued to feel like (and was made to feel like) something of a foreigner because my father was brown and I immigrated from Panama. In my youth I got involved in political organizing against the resurging Klan, among other projects, and met real heroes and heroines from the civil rights movement, Black and white, who had worked together for years. I left the South at the age of twenty-eight, but

remain inspired by my Southern comrades who have continued the struggle
for justice.

The South in All Its Multiplicity

The South is both a *Place* and an *Idea*. As a place, the South was the area
within the United States that endured, and benefited from, the longest period
of slavery. In 1860, South Carolina was the richest state in the nation, and
two-thirds of the wealthiest families in the country lived in the South.[1] The
South has historically had the greatest reliance on the agricultural sector of
the economy, and most of the region's agricultural production is exported to
the rest of the country.[2] Industrialization has remained comparatively low
even today. Regular cotton planting has weakened the land, yet for landless farm tenants who must constantly move (about one-third of the farmers
in some areas), cotton remains the surest bet for survival. Both whites and
Blacks have always picked cotton: Johnnie Cash had scars on his hands even
as an adult from picking, and some of the white part of my family picked as
well. But only the Black public schools changed their schedules during picking season, even through the 1960s, so that children could go into the fields.

Eight of the poorest states in the United States are in the South. Given
the region's agricultural abundance, the high rates of poverty in the region
cannot be explained as the result of scarce natural resources: rather, today's
regional poverty is a problem of resource management. And resource management is always a problem of political policy: How are the natural and
labor resources managed, by whom, and toward what end?

As a predominantly agricultural region, the South has had a storied long-
term alliance between the white planter class (a sort of quasi-feudal landed
gentry) and the class of landless white workers and yeoman. This alliance
has been maintained postslavery, generating some interesting analysis, as I
will discuss here, about the way in which racial solidarity appears to regularly triumph over material class interests. The alliance is not entirely stable
nor is it uniform across the region, and it is important to correct the usual
story with the many examples of racially inclusive, worker-based progressive
struggles: the Free State of Jones County formed during the Civil War out
of disaffected white rank-and-file soldiers and freed slaves; the Gulf Coast
Pulpwood Association, which organized successfully across race lines even
in Klan-controlled rural areas; the broad justice coalitions of today, such as
the North Carolina Poor People's Campaign led by Reverend William Bar-
ber; as well as many progressive electoral campaigns that have put African
Americans in office. Such organizing histories are regularly ignored by journalists who would prefer to scapegoat and stereotype. Yet, while we need to
complicate the too-easy picture that is sometimes given of the race-based,
cross-class white alliance as permanent and indefeasible, there is no doubt

that it is a strong feature of Southern history and continues to affect national electoral outcomes and union organizing efforts. Thus, as a *Place*, the South has distinctive economic and political characteristics.

The South also constitutes a powerful *Idea* that plays its own role in the national political culture. In reality, of course, there are multiple ideas of the South: an idea of the South in the North, an idea of the South in the South, and various ideas of the South among diverse racial and ethnic groups. These various ideas about the South have significant influence within the national political imaginary of the United States. I am thinking here of Michèle Le Doeuff's sense of imaginary, as meanings that can operate below or beyond explicit articulation. Images, she writes, are functional for an unjust system because they "sustain something which the system cannot itself justify, but which is nevertheless needed for its proper working."[3] But the imaginary can sometimes work against a system when its "meaning is incompatible with the system's possibilities."[4] In other words, the imaginary holds things in place, but by doing so it contravenes the dynamism inherent to any system, even the system Le Doeuff is writing about, which is the history of European philosophy.

The South has long been regarded as a culturally backward place that has stymied the democratic possibilities of the country as a whole. Its own potential for cultural dynamism is kept in check by characterizing agents of change as carpet baggers; misrepresenting Southern history in school textbooks; and maintaining racism in the public sphere by subterfuge, dog whistles, and misdirection. The white, cross-class alliance is today maintained through invocations of voter fraud, Black-on-white violence, and welfare cheating that are used to justify all sorts of policies with racist effects, from voter suppression to police violence to a rejection of single payer health care. Le Doeuff's concept of the imaginary is helpful in explaining why the facts do not matter: because images play at will below the surface, outside the text, beyond explicit statements. The idea of dog whistles is that politicians make *intentionally* covert references, and we know this to be true.[5] But the idea of the imaginary is actually different than this: it is that commonly used metaphors, examples, and imagery convey meanings even without the conscious intent of the speaker or writer. One of Le Doeuff's examples is Thomas More's *Utopia*, in which he elaborates the idea of utopia using an image of a self-sustaining island economy. Self-sustaining islands cut out the need to factor in or theoretically elaborate relations with others outside of one's utopian space based on justice. It allowed European readers in the colonial period to hold onto the idea that internal social relationships can be rational and just while outside relationships can be based on barbarism, war, and exploitation. Thus, the island imagery tells us something about More and his influence that may have little to do with intentional misdirection.

In relation to the South, I want to suggest we have two imaginaries at play: the racist imaginary *in* the South that stalls progress, but also the national imaginary *about* the South as the key place that plays this counterrevolutionary role. It is the latter imaginary I want to address here. Of late it has taken the form of a "culture of poverty" thesis directed against poor whites, to suggest that it is their own inherited defects, willful ignorance, and unruly behavior that keep them poor.

The South is the site of what some refer to as the original sin of the United States, where there existed the most extended period of violent suppression of African Americans as well as other nonwhites during slavery and postslavery. This is not the only or the primary original sin of the United States, to be sure: the genocidal violence required to enact a settler society in an already populated continent is a central constitutive feature of the nation, as is the forcible removal of Indigenous groups to reservations with little arable land, and also the refusal to honor the terms of the Treaty of Guadalupe Hidalgo in 1848 that resulted in the impoverishment, denigration, and disenfranchisement of millions of former citizens of Mexico. It is critically important to attend to the multiple atrocities the colonial state and then the United States orchestrated that made this country "great."

Still, it seems that the South's imagined centrality to the original sin of slavery works as a form of functional abjection so that other parts of the country can avoid acknowledging their own historical debts to slavery as well as other forms of race-based subjugation. Locate the problem in the South, disavow and punish it: problem solved. On the one hand, such an argument is used by racist Southern apologists to deflect social criticism, but on the other hand, when one lives in the liberal northeast, as I do, Shannon Sullivan's analysis of "good white people" resonates daily, as good middle-class white liberals continually find racism everywhere else but in their own gentrifying real estate practices and abandonment of public schools.[6] Thus, targeting the South continues to serve as a means to avoid engaging with the systemic racism in the elite and middle-class lifestyles of the white, hip-hop-loving, professional creative classes, or the institutional racisms rife in most economic and educational institutions throughout the country.

The national dimension of the problem of racism is clear. In 2016, Hillary Clinton won the popular vote, but Trump, running on an overtly racist platform, won 2,600 counties to Clinton's 500 counties. Although Clinton won the largest cities, Trump secured an incredible 84 percent of the geographic United States, north, south, east, and west.

However, there is no question that parts of the South elect avowed racists, and that there are a host of politically generated problems, such as: wages lower than the national average; right-to-work laws in every state but Maryland since 1947; higher poverty; intentional withholding of health care by refusing to engage with Obamacare; and resistance to gun control (some Floridians proudly claim to live in the "gunshine state"). There are regionally specific causes and explanations relevant to these regionally specific problems, one of which is the particular history of white, cross-class solidarity. This has been the subject of analysis for decades.

Poor Southern Whites

In 1941, W. J. Cash, a Southern white journalist, published what became an influential study, *The Mind of the South*, focused on the white Southern imaginary.[7] Cash was brought up in Southern rural life, in largely white areas of western South Carolina. A few of his forebears had owned slaves, but most of his family were "yeomanry"—non-slaveholding small farmers. Cash's biographer tells us that, interestingly, in this part of South Carolina, the white hill-country folk held plantation owners and African Americans in equal disregard: no class collaboration for them, but also no class solidarity across racial lines.[8] Cash himself was a liberal on issues of race and politics, and became one of only a handful of white journalists who called attention to incidents of lynching in this period. He made use of the interviews he did with diverse white folks in the South as research for his journalism to develop the analysis of white Southern attitudes that he develops in his 1941 book.

Cash was motivated to overturn the common culturalist and determinist characterizations of poor Southern whites as "shiftless or criminal," where these traits were taken to be "inherent in the germ plasm . . . handed on to their progeny, with the result that the whole body of them continually sank lower and lower in the social scale."[9] At the time of his writing, such views were dominant in mainstream histories of the South. Cash contested the idea of congenital inferiority, or what we might call today biological essentialism, by pointing to the success of the poor when given a chance. Impoverished indentured servants sent from Britain, what Cash called "convict servants," were the subject of particular scrutiny for their role in bringing down the "stock." Cash argued to the contrary that when "freed whites" (whites freed from the conditions of indenture) were able to gain some property, through avenues such as homestead laws, they were able to succeed, "to do what so many other men of his same general stamp were doing all about him: steadily to build up his capital and become a man of substance and respect."[10]

Hence, the white worker's racism and class allegiance with wealthy whites could not simply be explained by their stupidity, or capacity to be fooled, or acceptance of their socioeconomic station. The Southern historian Bertram Wyatt-Brown wrote an introduction to the fifty-year-anniversary issue of *The Mind of the South*, and explained that for Cash:

> Racism was much too powerful to permit the rise of a genuine insurgency against the problems of poverty and injustice. He identifies a kind of subordinate fraternalism (an elder brother's relation to a younger brother, as it were) that tied rich planter to distant poor cousin and provided a common bond. The former's condescension met the latter's abashed gratitude for the very gesture of notice. Rituals of uneven friendship, such as the election-day barbecue that the wealthy candidate hosted, made more palatable the established ranks of social order.[11]

The gentry had the cultural capital, money, and land; poorer whites were economically dependent and a bit starstruck. Thus, on this reading, the white poor are making a conscious transaction: to ally with the elites in order to be acknowledged as kinfolk even in a lesser status. They do not presume that they will or should be treated as full equals yet are happy "for the very gesture of notice."

Note that a key element of Cash's analysis involved the denigrated status of the white poor, such as the so-called white trailer trash who are continually and unapologetically derided today. Cash pointed out the hypocrisy of these determinist views of the poor, given that Southern elites "did not spring up to be aristocrats in a day."[12] Rather, they emerged mainly from farmer or laborer backgrounds but had the good luck to settle in the early days of the colonies when "unclaimed" lands were plentiful. True aristocrats could not have survived the harsh challenges of settling forests with hostile Indigenous neighbors who had the advantage of local knowledge. Cash's disregard for the injustice of the settlers toward Indigenous peoples is apparent in these pages, and yet his argument remains persuasive that the better explanations for the persistence of white poverty are specific historical and economic conditions. Poor white settlers who came later found a country legally and politically controlled by elites and were less able to garner sufficient property. Cash fills *The Mind of the South* with historical sketches of figures who rose to power straight out of the "coon-hunting populations of the backcountry," whether in Virginia, the Carolinas, or the Mississippi Delta.[13] Feudal patronage systems ruled subsequent social relations, producing the familiar ranked but fraternal solidarity still in place when Cash wrote.

Cash believed these rituals of uneven friendship between white yeoman and gentry testified "to the festering of the irritation and resentment which had existed in the depths of the common white even in the Old South," that is, a concern with their economic and social status and an effort to find some political means to change it.[14] Hence, he finds the alliance with the gentry as an expression of their class aspirations rather than a form of defeatism. This is an important shift since it creates the grounds for a conversation of the following sort: Given these aspirations, what is a more likely way to achieve them than trusting elites? Anti-Black racism can be an aid to maintaining friendly relations with the gentry, but more effective strategies to address class aspirations will require targeting racism.

The deterministic account of the white poor as constitutionally ignorant ignores available counterexplanations, yet persists into the present. A recent example is Charles Murray's 2012 book, *Coming Apart: The State of White America, 1960–2010*, that takes the "culture of poverty" thesis normally directed at Black and Latinx groups and applies it to poor whites to argue that their poverty is self-inflicted because they make poor life choices.[15] This is also the thesis of J. D. Vance's celebrated 2016 book, *Hillbilly Elegy: A Memoir of a Family and Culture in Crisis*.[16] As Elizabeth Catte astutely notes:

Conservatives believed that *Elegy* would make their intellectual plat-
forming about the moral failures of the poor colorblind in a way that
would retroactively vindicate them for viciously deploying the same
stereotypes against nonwhite people for decades.[17]

Attacking poor southern whites provides an alibi for racism, oddly enough.
By contrast, Cash's analysis uses history and psychology to the cross-class,
race-based alliance. While white yeomen could gain some economic benefits
from the jobs thrown their way by the planter class, he suggests they were
also flattered to be included at events with the county big shots, even as secondary players, easing their irritations and resentments. And he suggests a
further ingredient that will connect to Marx's analysis to be discussed next.
For Cash, culturalist explanations are tied to class and economic explanations: these elements hang together to produce motivations. Marx, as we'll
see, makes a similar point.

As noted earlier, the economy of the South has relied mainly on agriculture. Its light winters and longer growing season allow for longer crop
production (nearly twelve months in some areas) as well as better climates
for livestock. Thus, it has historically been a region dominated more by peasants than industrial workers. In a famous historical case study, Marx argued
that workers and peasants had divergent and often conflicting interests. In
The Eighteenth Brumaire of Louis Bonaparte (1978 [1852]), he argued that
the small farmers then typical in France became supportive of Bonaparte
and antagonistic to the radical working-class social movements because the
nature of their livelihood led to different political motivations. The peasants
were not interested in increasing the size of the state since it could then interfere with and regulate their practices; they favored disengagement, to be left
alone. Marx writes that:

> The small peasants form a vast mass, the members of which live
> in similar conditions, but without entering into manifold relations
> with one another. Their mode of production isolates them from one
> another, instead of bringing them into mutual intercourse. The isola-
> tion is increased by France's bad means of communication and by the
> poverty of the peasants. Their field of production, the small holding,
> admits of no division of labor in its cultivation, no application of
> science, and, therefore no multiplicity of development, no diversity
> of talents, no wealth of social relationships. Each individual peasant
> family is almost self-sufficient; it itself directly produces the major
> part of its consumption and thus acquires its means of life more
> through an exchange with nature than in intercourse with society.[18]

In Marx's view, the social position, experience, and mode of economic activity of the peasants diverged from, and in some cases pitted them against, the

interest of middle-class entrepreneurs, or the bourgeois. Entrepreneurs pursued economic developments that required social change, and this led them to support struggles that would unseat feudal power. Although working-class social movements also agitated against feudal power and for social change, their agenda also diverged: their agitation for state interventions in the form of worker protections or limits on the rate of exploitation pitted them against both bourgeois and peasants. The peasants had no material interest in enlarging the state's power to intervene in economic production.

Note that for Marx, the peasants' tendency toward conservatism is not based on their innate ignorance, lack of education, or a culture of stubbornness but on their manner of work which largely isolated them. Thus, workers and peasants have divergent political orientations because of differences in the nature of their work. A worker-peasant alliance would have to be built through political work of coalition and negotiation across their differences to find common ground, rather than taken for granted.

Marx is describing Europe in the nineteenth century, and in most of his writings he imagines it to be free from hatreds or competition based in ethnic identities. The economy that developed in the southern United States is distinguished from this in several important ways. The history of the "Right-to-Work" laws that disable unionization in every Southern state initially gained support not from libertarian individualism but the push to "protect" whites from being forced to integrate.[19] This means that fewer white workers in the South than elsewhere have an experience of collective cross-racial collaborations concerning the conditions of their work lives. The work of farmers and other agricultural workers were impacted by slavery as well as a century of legalized racial segregation in the labor market. More recently, small farms have been overtaken by large agribusinesses that industrialized agriculture and livestock production and operated quite differently from the isolated and self-sufficient villages and kinship groups Marx describes. Agribusinesses have proletarianized low-wage farm and ranch labor not only to pick crops but also to clear and till the land and move cattle. Wages are kept low by hiring more economically vulnerable immigrant workers, mostly Central Americans, and also African Americans.

Drawing from Cash and Marx, we have two causal elements on offer. Marx's analysis of peasant politics, based on both the experience and the interests of small farmers, holds that the economic interests of peasants can be more easily aligned with bourgeois interests than they can be aligned with workers' interests. Small land-holding farmers have little experience of collective political endeavors and may view the national government as a likely obstacle to their livelihood. Cash's analysis adds a focus on the psychology of a white lower class habituated to social subordination and ranking but desirous of making an alliance with landowners. Their economic vulnerability can make them grateful to be included, even in a lesser role. In slave-based economies, the nonslave poor, in this case white, might be strongly motivated to be allied with the planters rather than the slaves or those working in slave-like conditions in the Jim Crow South. The fact that indentured servitude operated throughout the US for two centuries before race-based chattel slavery became consolidated could have made these white poor feel grateful to elites for sparing them a horrific fate. It is not entirely clear that slavery would have been relegated to African peoples: the English Parliament debated the question of enslaving the Irish in 1659.[20] The white poor had reason to feel vulnerable.

Racial Tribalism

The 2016 presidential election in the United States yields further explanations for the existence of a cross-class alliance among whites. I should stress here that my point is to consider explanations, not justifications. The white lower-class vote for Trump was undoubtedly motivated in no small measure by the belief that, if elected, Trump would promote a nationalistic economic agenda—that he would, as he promised, be a bourgeois nationalist as opposed to a bourgeois internationalist. A nationalist bourgeoisie might bring more jobs to the landless class, just as the landed gentry promised jobs for the landless yeomanry. The contrast between Trump and Clinton on this point seemed clear: pro-global economic elites like Clinton showed little concern about the influence of transnational capital on declining wages and employment at home. Since the 1970s, both showed significant stagnation, despite increases in worker productivity (up 74 percent), as well as improved pay for the top 1 percent of wage earners (up 138 percent). There was no break in these trends during any Democratic presidential terms.[21] The Economic Policy Institute reports that these trends are the result of policy decisions; the voters were not wrong, therefore, to believe these decisions could be changed, and changed in their favor. In this case, the alliance was a straightforward exchange: votes for the nationalist candidate in return for a promise of better jobs. The fact that Trump was untrustworthy and his promises largely did not prevail is beside the point: no one in decades had run such an anti-global campaign; voters had reason to hope, even if those reasons were slim.

How should we set these motivations alongside racism? Besides his promises to redress the effect of globalism on the US economy, Trump's nationalist platform was a thinly concealed white nationalism: he campaigned on less-than-subtle promises to beat up on immigrants seeking to enter the U.S. from poor countries and curtail black activism against police violence. The unambiguous nature of his rhetoric demands analysis: either his supporters considered these issues too insignificant to alter their votes (meaning they would be comfortable in a racist state as long as they had decent-paying jobs), or they fully shared his antipathies. In either case, Trump voters are racists. Yet, this gives us no specific data on the Southern question, since, as stated earlier, Trump supporters were strong in every region of the nation outside of major cities.

A further interesting element that may yield more insight is revealed in a Rand study from early 2016, in which 86 percent of Trump supporters agreed with the statement "people like me don't have any say."[22] Compare this percentage to the percentage of agreement by other voters: only 7 percent of Clinton supporters and 8 percent of Bernie Sanders supporters agreed with this statement, and there was a negative correlation with Ted Cruz supporters. Of course, this is what pollsters call a feeling thermometer, that is, a perception that may or may not reflect political realities. In truth, this largely white constituency is far from powerless given how much of the political discourse is directed to them, with dog whistles in full force, and how important their votes are to winning both national and local elections. The idea that Trump "sees" these voters in a way that others do not may remind us of what W. J. Cash described as a desired closeness to glamour and power even in a secondary status. The motivating concern, then, is *their relation to power*, more so than the agenda that power pursues or enacts.

The complaint of Trump supporters that they have no "say" can be interpreted in multiple ways. On the one hand, it could indicate they are feeling abandoned by the pro-global elite and are looking for a sector of the elite class who will invite them in, as in the days Cash describes, even as a subordinate or symbolic partner. It may also indicate, however, that the white poor's satisfaction with their status in the social pecking order has deteriorated. This could be based on the real changes in their economic conditions, the real precariousness of the Walmart workforce, and their understanding that the current political regime is not managing the US economy with any concern for the well-being of the white masses of workers and poor. They have lost their special status as a favored class and are beset by low wages, poor health care, drug addictions, an economic draft, decreased mortality, and high suicide rates.

Although the Rand study surveyed a fallible self-perception, rather than dismissing the results outright I would suggest we consider this in the context of decreased unionization, one of the few avenues working people have for having a "say." The South has long had lower levels of unionization than the rest of the country—by about half. Yet it too has suffered precipitous declines in union levels over the last few decades.[23] Nationally, unionization has dropped from 20.1 percent in 1983 to 10.5 percent in 2018. In the South, the drop is even more dramatic: for example, between 1964 and 2014, Kentucky levels went from 25 percent to 11.1 percent; Tennessee went from 22.1 percent to 5.1 percent; and Arkansas fell from a high of 27.1 percent to 8.4 percent.

We must remember that unions play a much larger role in people's lives than a protection of the wage floor: good unions are participatory (and since the 1980s many unions with histories of corruption fought successfully to force out bad leadership and operate with more transparency and democracy). Contract negotiations cover economics as only part of a long list of issues that include job security, intradepartmental transfer opportunities, scheduling, staffing levels, work assignments, and a variety of benefits from health care to retirement plans. Before contract negotiations can begin, the workforce meets to discuss and vote on the demands that will take priority, in some cases choosing those issues that will lead to strike actions. In the best cases this is a deliberative project in which the differences in the workforce—including those based on race, class, gender, immigration status, sexuality, and trans issues, among others—must be worked through over multiple meetings, since these differences often impact priorities for different groups of workers. For example, there may be differences that break down over racial lines about the importance of in-house transfers, since workers of color are often hired into jobs in hospitals, for example, with lower skill sets and lower wages, hoping to be able to transfer to better positions. There are also differences over prioritizing language rights, domestic partner benefits, or allowing long vacation times so immigrant families can reconnect. In this way unions are opportunities to have, and to develop, one's voice in a meeting of peers with a common project. The demise of unions in this country is a severe retraction of such opportunities.

Agribusinesses have largely replaced the small farmer, both in the South and the Midwest, affecting both Black and white farmers and leading to a proletarianization of farm work. Yet the workers in this sector have very low rates of unionization. The white South has become more proletarianized just at the moment when the proletariat has lost its unions and its job security.

Marx's sociology of the peasant class may characterize lingering habits and patterns of political consciousness that continue to fuel some of the current strains of individualism and libertarianism, but the question is how long these can linger in the absence of land or jobs. Yeoman farmers—those who own their land—are increasingly rare as agribusinesses, predatory banks, and their lobbyists made it impossible for small farmers to survive economically. Some argue today that the demise of effective cross-race working-class solidarity, coupled with the increase in inequality, poverty, insecurity, and mortality, has motivated a renewed "racial tribalism" among whites.[24] A precarious work force needs group solidarity of some sort. In truth, white racial tribalism has long existed, so the reality may be instead that tribalism is all that some whites believe they have left to rely on as a strategy of survival. But the question is, what kind of survival can be advanced when white racism tears apart the possibility of a broader solidarity across class, across different sectors of a workplace, from the cleaning crew to the skilled trades? A labor market that has long segmented workers by race and gender provides fertile ground for the divisions that separate waged work. Hence, as Michael Dawson has argued:

disadvantaged whites, men and women, saw their class, racial, and gender interests as being identical for all practical purposes, given their submersion in an ideology of white supremacy that portrayed disadvantaged blacks as the worst threat to both their status privilege and their material interests.[25]

The point here is that whites at the lower end of the economy have not seen their class interests as separable from race. Their position in the pecking order within the working class—their job title and resultant wage levels— has long been tied to their race and their gender. These are the precise sorts of strategies Cash describes: to make an alliance with the planter class as a way to secure jobs. These jobs might be overseers, prison guards, or other types in which racism is directly enacted, but they may also be factory jobs, agricultural jobs, maintenance jobs, or the fast growing sector of security jobs. In this case, we might want to say that it is not simply "their submersion in an ideology of white supremacy" that is at play here, as Dawson puts it, but real material benefits that could spell family survival. I will return to this point in the conclusion; but first, let us consider a real-world example of just the sort of alliance Cash has described and see how it turned out.

The Instability of Racism

Rather than understanding racism as the singular determinative feature of white dispositions, or as the unique feature of the South, I want to suggest here a different approach. Racism should be understood as a recurrent national phenomenon that can rise and fall and rise again, but it must also be understood as jostling for position with other motivating forces, in particular, material interests, psychological forces, and aspects of the social imaginary. Consider the story of C. P. Ellis, whose biography was paradigmatic of the Southern working classes, even while it took an unexpected turn.[26] Having served as the Exalted Cyclops of the Durham, North Carolina, chapter of the Ku Klux Klan, Ellis came to change his understanding of race, class, and his own position in society during the tumultuous period of the civil rights struggles in the 1960s.[27]

Ellis was a poor man far from the middle class. As a child, the focal point of his consciousness was the same as it is today for so many low-income kids: the clothes he wore to school. As Ellis explains:

When I went to school, I never seemed to have adequate clothes to wear. I always left school with a sense of inferiority. The other kids had nice clothes, and I just had what Daddy could buy. I still got some inferiority feelin's now that I have to overcome once in awhile.[28]

Ellis's father worked in textile mills and died of brown lung at the age of forty-eight. This event forced Ellis to leave school in the eighth grade and begin a lifetime of scraping out an insubstantial living for his family. He never escaped poverty or the run-down mill houses in which he and his family lived, but through a fluke of good luck, Ellis was able in his twenties to buy into a gas station and escape mill work. However, despite working the station seven days a week, the income Ellis earned kept his family in poverty. He lay awake at night worrying that his kids would face the same ridicule he had when growing up, when he was jeered at for being the son of a "linthead"—a painful, ridiculing epithet used against mill workers.

Ellis's decision to join the Klan was motivated by watching the astounding progress of the civil rights protesters in his hometown of Durham. He took note of their collective action and expressed amazement and envy about the rate of their progress against the persistence of poverty that also applied to whites such as himself. He imagined the Klan as an avenue for collective group action that would mimic the NAACP.

The racial order of the world Ellis knew was turning upside down, and the Klan offered an explanation, blaming Northern Jewish communists who promoted miscegenation toward the aim of destroying, or replacing, the white (Gentile) race. The ultimate enemy, from the Klan leadership's view, was communism. By the early 1960s, a decade of McCarthyism and regular rants on the radio by Jesse Helms made this theory plausible for much of the white North Carolina population. "What the Russians are counting on," Helms fumed, "is an internal breakdown in this country."[29]

Importantly, Ellis's membership in the Klan gave him, for the first time in his life, a social position of respect. In his interview with Studs Terkel, Ellis described how moved he was by the pageantry of the swearing-in ceremony when hundreds of sheeted men saluted him, C. P. Ellis, the poor son of a mill worker: "After I had taken my oath, there was loud applause goin' through the buildin', musta been at least four hundred people. It was a thrilling moment for C. P. Ellis."[30] Beneath the sheets, his poor clothes were invisible.

Ellis had a knack for organizing and political strategizing and quickly rose to leadership. He wanted to make the Klan a public player in Durham politics, to advocate for the white poor in the inevitable changes that integration would bring about. He was also intoxicated by the fact that powerful men began to call him in the evenings and showed confidence in his capacities. He had a place in society now. Later, he surmised: "I can understand why people join extreme right-wing or left-wing groups. They're in the same boat I was. Shut out. Deep down inside, we want to be part of this great society. Nobody listens, so we join these groups."[31]

However, Ellis ultimately came to the view that poor whites such as himself were being used by the wealthy, and that the cause of the Klan was wrongheaded. In the course of his public activity in Durham, he discovered with his own eyes facts he had not known about the Black community. He began to realize that poor whites and poor Blacks had a lot of problems in common, and that wealthy whites were not going to help his children have a better life. The story of how Ellis's consciousness changed is worth studying; I will just give a brief overview.

In public spaces, white elites in Durham hid their Klan sympathies behind a veneer of neutrality. Yet they kept up a regular line of communication with Ellis, calling him at home and visiting his gas station. Ellis had even visited their homes, secretly, for strategy sessions. Yet one day he found himself snubbed on the street by a city councilman that he had met with many times. The man wouldn't even acknowledge Ellis's presence and turned abruptly to wade into traffic rather than rub elbows with the Klansman. That night in bed, Ellis replayed the moment over and over: though he understood the need for secrecy, this felt like the childhood snubs he and his father had experienced when they walked downtown in their poor clothes. Ellis began to realize that for town leaders like the councilman, he would never become an equal and never be treated as a person worthy of public respect.

Ellis also had an entirely new experience when he agreed to work in a multiracial committee on integration. Howard Fuller, an experienced community and political organizer, had been hired by the city of Durham to bring residents from both sides of the racial divide together to create a plan for school desegregation with the hope of ensuring, if possible, a nonviolent transition. Fuller, an African American, had to choose two principal leaders, and he shrewdly offered the positions to Ann Atwater, a well-known militant civil rights activist, and C. P. Ellis, the Grand Cyclops of the local Klan. This was a high-stakes gamble: neither Atwater nor Ellis was committed to nonviolence. But Fuller had observed them both at city council meetings, noting their organizing skills, and knew that each had legions of like-minded supporters that might be brought into the project.

Ellis hesitated before accepting Fuller's offer. His racism was visceral, and the idea of multiracial meetings with a woman he despised was difficult to contemplate. Atwater was from a poor background, unlike the middle-class Black people who often spoke for the movement, and yet she had a bold and uncompromising style of leadership that incensed Ellis. Durham in this period was no scene of peaceful deliberative democracy: nonviolent civil rights activists were being physically attacked, and some of the Black youth had started a campaign of firebombing strategically targeted sites to warn those who wanted to slow down the pace of change. Atwater was known to be involved in this. Meanwhile, the Klan was engaged in its own violence, and Ellis himself had recently narrowly escaped conviction for shooting and wounding a young Black teenager. He and Atwater had also had run-ins.

What drove Ellis to accept Fuller's proposal was not his organizational agenda to make the Klan more public but his personal agenda to make the newly desegregated schools safe and fair for his own four children. He knew that the middle- and upper-class whites in town would respond to enforced desegregation by simply pulling their kids out of the public schools and enrolling them in private schools. Ellis and other poorer whites had no such option: if their kids were going to get an education, it was going to be in the public schools.

In the course of the committee's meetings and open forums, Ellis learned a lot of things he had never known. He was driven to the area of town where the segregated Black schools were so that he would see firsthand their run-down conditions, and he was stunned to find out that their kids were treated as "troublemakers" before they had even opened their mouths in class, just as his kids were treated. He came to realize that the African American children in town were having as bad a time in the schools as his own kids—worse, in fact. He ruminated on these thoughts at night, until one afternoon he found himself alone with Atwater after a set of meetings, and uncharacteristically, he walked over to sit next to her. For the first time, he asked her about her kids, and they began to marvel at the similarity of their worries. They shared accounts of how hard it was to raise children without much money and how they had to try to counteract the shame their children felt each day at school. It turned out both had grown up on dirt roads. Ellis found himself talking adult to adult, unburdening a load of pain with someone who understood exactly.

From that day forward, Ellis changed his mind about the Klan. At first, with the zeal of a convert, he began to plot how he could bring his Klan colleagues around to his new understanding. Their response was to threaten his life. Soon jobless and bereft, he eventually found a position as a maintenance worker at Duke University and was elected to the position of union shop steward by a constituency that was majority African American. He remained close friends with Ann Atwater until the day he died in 2005.

Conclusion: Grounds for a Shared Agenda?

The power of social identities such as race needs to be understood in their constitutive relationality. Following theorists such as Frantz Fanon and Stuart Hall, we can see that the substantive content of racial identities is given by the policies and practices that organize labor markets by race, with subsequent hierarchies of pay and power, as well as by the collective actions undertaken in response to these policies and practices. Neither whiteness nor Blackness has meaningful content outside of these concrete historical contexts. Relationality also involves how we see each other and are seen, or snubbed, or accepted. Ellis's story provides support for the emphasis that both W. J. Cash and the Rand study put on the importance of respect and relational empowerment: not simply the ability to speak, but to be heard by those who count. Ellis lacked much formal education, but this did not keep him from understanding that the secret support he had from the town leaders could not be relied upon to help his personal circumstances. Being invited to the Sunday barbecue, as Cash describes the old racial patronage system, while wages fall and jobs dry up, provides little security. Ellis initially took his race as the means to establish a white, cross-class solidarity that would raise him in status until he became disillusioned with the limited success this strategy would provide for his children. His eventual transformation also provides support for the idea that an experience of democratic deliberation over shared concrete projects intended to benefit the group as a whole, as one finds in unions among other institutions, can motivate working through differences and disagreements and becoming open to learning new things.

There is no inevitability to the South's progress toward racial justice. However, we can say the same thing about the idea that it will forever remain a bulwark for reactionary white nationalism. As I hope to have shown, there are multiple dynamics and causal forces in play that may reaffirm or strain cross-class alliances of whites. The denigration and economic deterioration of the white Southern poor provides potential grounds for a shared justice agenda. The key question will be whether poor whites will continue to settle with being the lesser partner of elites—gratefully picking up favors from the gentry class—or whether a significant portion of them will aim for more.

Notes

1. Nancy MacLean, *Democracy in Chains: The Deep History of the Radical Right's Stealth Plan for America* (New York: Random House, 2017), 2–3.

2. Charles E. Noyes, "Economic Changes in the Southern States," in *Editorial Research Reports 1939*, Vol. 1 (Washington, DC: CQ Press, 1939), 89–106.

3. Michèle Le Doeuff, *The Philosophical Imaginary*, trans. Colin Gordon (Stanford, CA.: Stanford University Press, 1989), 3.

4. Le Doeuff, *The Philosophical Imaginary*, 3.

5. Ian Haney López, *Dog Whistle Politics: How Coded Racial Appeals Have Reinvented Racism and Wrecked the Middle Class* (New York: Oxford University Press, 2014).

6. Shannon Sullivan, *Good White People: The Problem with Middle-Class White Anti-Racism* (Albany: SUNY Press, 2014).

7. W. J. Cash, *The Mind of the South* (New York: Vintage Books, 1991).

8. Bertram Wyatt-Brown, introduction to *The Mind of the South*, by W. J. Cash (New York: Vintage Books, 1991), xi.

9. Cash, *The Mind of the South*, 6.

10. Cash, *The Mind of the South*, 7.

11. Wyatt-Brown, introduction to *The Mind of the South*, xx.

12. Cash, *The Mind of the South*, 5.

13. Cash, *The Mind of the South*, 15.

14. Cash, *The Mind of the South*, 162.

15. Charles Murray, *Coming Apart: The State of White America, 1960–2010* (New York: Crown Forum, 2012).

16. J. D. Vance, *Hillbilly Elegy: A Memoir of a Family and Culture in Crisis* (New York: Harper Books, 2016).

17. Elizabeth Catte, *What You Are Getting Wrong about Appalachia* (Cleveland: Belt Publishing, 2018), 61.

18. Marx, Karl, 1978, "The Eighteenth Brumaire of Louis Bonaparte" in *The Marx-Engels Reader*, 2nd ed., edited by Robert C. Tucker, p. 608.

19. Michael Pierce, "Vance Muse and the Racist Origins of Right-to-Work," *American Constitution Society Blog*, February 22, 2018, https://www.acslaw.org /acsblog/vance-muse-and-the-racist-origins-of-right-to-work/.

20. Michael J. Monahan, *The Creolizing Subject: Race, Reason, and the Politics of Purity* (New York: Fordham University Press, 2011), 69. Monahan suggests, rightly I think, that although the Irish were not considered black at this time, they were not considered (by the English) white either, so this debate does not settle the matter as to whether Europeans could countenance white people as slaves. But the English apparently did believe that the Irish were closer to themselves than Africans were, and so were concerned about a domino effect of brutalization coming too close for comfort.

21. Lawrence Mishal, Elise Gould, and Josh Bivens, "Wage Stagnation in Nine Charts" Jan. 6, 2015, https://www.epi.org/publication/charting-wage-stagnation/. Even the wages of young college graduates have been falling since 2000.

22. Michael Pollard and Joshua Mendelsohn, "Rand Kicks Off 2016 Presidential Election Panel Survey," *The Rand Blog*, January 27, 2016, https://www.rand .org/blog/2016/01/rand-kicks-off-2016-presidential-election-panel-survey.html.

23. Quoctrung Bui, "50 Years of Union Membership, in One Map," Feb. 23, 2015, https://www.npr.org/sections/money/2015/02/23/385843576/50-years-of -shrinking-union-membership-in-one-map. See also "News Release: Bureau of Labor Statistics" U.S. Department of Labor, Jan. 22, 2020, https://www.bls.gov /news.release/pdf/union2.pdf.

24. Jefferson Cowie, *Stayin' Alive: The 1970s and the Last Days of the Working Class* (New York: The New Press, 2010).

25. Michael C. Dawson, *Blacks in and out of the Left* (Cambridge, MA: Harvard University Press, 2013), 42.

26. I came across Ellis's story while researching my book *The Future of Whiteness* (Cambridge, UK: Polity Press, 2015). The remainder of this section is adapted from pages 196 to 203 of that book.

27. Osha Gray Davidson, *The Best of Enemies: Race and Redemption in the New South* (Chapel Hill: University of North Carolina Press, 1996); Studs Terkel, *American Dreams: Lost and Found* (New York: Pantheon Books, 1980); Studs Terkel, *Race: How Blacks and Whites Think and Feel about the American Obsession* (New York: The New Press, 1992).

28. Terkel, *American Dreams*, 198.

29. Quoted in Davidson, *The Best of Enemies*, 119.

30. Terkel, *Race*, 272.

31. Terkel, *Race*, 273.

Bibliography

Alcoff, Linda Martín. *The Future of Whiteness*. Cambridge, UK: Polity Press, 2015.

Cash, W. J. *The Mind of the South*. New York: Vintage Books, 1991.

Catte, Elizabeth. *What You Are Getting Wrong about Appalachia*. Cleveland: Belt Publishing, 2018.

Cowie, Jefferson. *Stayin' Alive: The 1970s and the Last Days of the Working Class*. New York: The New Press, 2010.

Davidson, Osha Gray. *The Best of Enemies: Race and Redemption in the New South*. Chapel Hill: University of North Carolina Press, 1996.

Haney López, Ian. *Dog Whistle Politics: How Coded Racial Appeals Have Reinvented Racism and Wrecked the Middle Class*. New York: Oxford University Press, 2014.

Le Doeuff, Michèle. *The Philosophical Imaginary*. Translated by Colin Gordon. Stanford, CA: Stanford University Press, 1989.

MacLean, Nancy. *Democracy in Chains: The Deep History of the Radical Right's Stealth Plan for America*. New York: Random House, 2017.

Marx, Karl. "The Eighteenth Brumaire of Louis Bonaparte." In *The Marx-Engels Reader*, 2nd ed., edited Robert C. Tucker, 594–617. New York: W. W. Norton and Company, 1978.

Monahan, Michael J. *The Creolizing Subject: Race, Reason, and the Politics of Purity*. New York: Fordham, 2011.

Murray, Charles. *Coming Apart: The State of White America, 1960–2010*. New York: Crown Forum, 2012.

Noyes, Charles E. "Economic Changes in the Southern States." In *Editorial Research Reports 1939*, Vol. 1, 89–106. Washington, DC: CQ Press, 1939.

Pierce, Michael. "Vance Muse and the Racist Origins of Right-to-Work." *American Constitution Society Blog*. February 22, 2018. https://www.acslaw.org/acsblog/vance-muse-and-the-racist-origins-of-right-to-work/.

Pollard, Michael, and Joshua Mendelsohn. "Rand Kicks Off 2016 Presidential Election Panel Survey." *The Rand Blog*. January 27, 2016. https://www.rand.org/blog/2016/01/rand-kicks-off-2016-presidential-election-panel-survey.html.

Sullivan, Shannon. *Good White People: The Problem with Middle-Class White Anti-Racism*. Albany: SUNY Press, 2014.

Terkel, Studs. *American Dreams: Lost and Found*. New York: Pantheon Books, 1980.

Terkel, Studs. *Race: How Blacks and Whites Think and Feel about the American Obsession*. New York: The New Press, 1992.

Vance, J. D. *Hillbilly Elegy: A Memoir of a Family and Culture in Crisis*. New York: Harper Books, 2016.

2

Southern Land

Indigeneity, Genocide, and Racialization in Whitened Lineages

Ladelle McWhorter

As a feminist and a philosopher trained in the work of Nietzsche and Foucault, I cannot disavow or ignore the forces that shaped my life and thought from its earliest beginnings in the southeast United States. Thinking is embodied, located, perspectival, pervaded, and constrained by the networks of power in which it occurs. For a white Southerner who grew up in the 1960s and 1970s, acknowledging those embodied and situated forces and attempting to think in alert awareness of their continuing force presents severe challenges. This chapter brings forward those challenges by first examining the idea that the essence of Southern identity is attachment to land and, along with it, the history of land theft and genocide that such attachments attempt to obscure. It then examines white Southern claims to Indigeneity in the context of global political movements of Indigenous peoples. Finally, it addresses these themes as formative of the flesh of white Southern philosophical thought.

Becoming Southern

I was thrown into the world (although I doubt my mother would have used that Heideggerian verb; from her perspective I imagine I was pushed, squeezed, thrust, or expelled into the world) sometime during the afternoon of January 7, 1960, in a room in Baugh Wiley Smith Hospital (so named because it was owned and operated by Drs. Baugh, Wiley, and Smith), a brick structure about three stories high, long since condemned, and likely by now dismantled. From the window of that room, my mother, her deliverers, and her visitors might have seen the Tennessee River, or at least the calm backwaters spreading behind a Tennessee Valley Authority dam.

Or even if they could not see the water itself, then perhaps they could see the Keller Bridge (so named because it was designed and engineered by a brother of the famous Helen Keller). Or perhaps they could not see even the bridge; I don't know. I only know that I could not see it, or see much of anything else, because that which would become "my" perspective had not yet gathered itself.

Most of that self-gathering occurred a couple of miles from that room in and around another brick structure, one story high, the house in which I was conceived and lived with two parents and various siblings and cats for the next eighteen years. In terms of geography, then, that becoming-perspective occurred in the Tennessee Valley of north Alabama, Morgan County, deep in the Heart of Dixie. In terms of history, it occurred, first of all, in the 1960s. My earliest datable memories, other than the birth of my sister in 1962, are not of family gatherings or vacations or holidays but of political events—the 1964 presidential race between Lyndon Johnson and Barry Goldwater, the 1965 police beatings of civil rights activists, and their march to the state capitol at Montgomery from Selma's Edmund Pettus Bridge. I recall a few facts from those events, but the facts are just a means of dating the feelings. The memories are heavy with feeling—unease, tension, apprehension, confusion, and the strange but acute attunements that such affects precipitate. These feelings and attunements far outlasted the duration of the events themselves.

I knew those events were connected, one way or another, to the harassing phone calls to our house after my older brother ran afoul of the John Birch Society, to visitors' tires slashed in our driveway, to the gun in my parents' bedroom that did not always remain there. I knew they were connected to the whispers of caution about what could not be mentioned in front of this or that relative or family acquaintance. When I recall those years, it seems to me that political conflict, racial tension, and the specter of communism pervaded everything, even the air we breathed. As my body grew toward adult proportions, it formed itself in and with the smoke and fumes of that time and place just as surely as with the pinto beans and the cornmeal it ingested. The perspective that gathered itself incorporated all of that. I am a product of that place and time. My perceptions began and arranged themselves in that atmosphere and my thoughts arose from there.

Like it or not, therefore—and for much of my life, I have not—nobody is more a Southerner than I am. But what does that mean, really? And, especially, what does that mean philosophically and in my own philosophical work? I reject the idea that philosophy is about the universal, the eternal, and the transcendental. Human thought does not transcend time and place but is always contingent upon them. How I see, how I feel, and of course how I think formed there and still is, in some ways, of that place and time. But what does that mean? How do I think *that*?

The Trouble with Land

Many Southern studies scholars have asserted, or just assumed, that Southern identity is tightly bound up with the land—that whatever it means to be
Southern has to do with attachment to the land and region itself. And there
are some good reasons for this. At times, the land seems to be as much a
character in Southern literature as any of the human beings that populate
it. Think of William Faulkner, Eudora Welty, James Dickey, Carson McCull-
ers, Tennessee Williams, or Flannery O'Connor. Even when the land does
not take on the tones of impersonal personhood, it often figures into plot-
lines as that which must be saved, regained, restored, and passed on, or as
that which is haunted with the ghosts of previous occupants. Southerners
are often depicted as taking especial pride in hereditary land ownership, the
more so the further back in time that it extends.

We hear this rhetoric of pride in hereditary land ownership today in efforts
to stop oil and fracked gas pipelines through the Blue Ridge Mountains and
Virginia's horse country—stories of great-great-grandparents working the
same land, of passing the land down as a sacred heritage to be preserved
intact from generation to generation. The rhetoric sometimes seems to imply
that it is this heritage, not mere property interests or even ecological concerns,
that is threatened by enormous energy companies backed by the powers of
governmental authority, intent on blasting away mountaintops and laying
pipes that will ruin the view, disrupt wildlife habitats, and inevitably leak
poison into soil and contaminate both surface water and groundwater. The
fight is not about corporate capitalists versus landed capitalists; it takes on
mythic proportions as the sacred versus the profane.[1]

The land looms large in music as well, even in contemporary country
music. Numerous songs exalt the land in one way or another—as heritage,
as home, as safety, and as the site of lovemaking and happy memories. Many
describe aspects of the land, wildlife, and sounds and smells of Southern
out-of-doors. Beauty in Southern art of all sorts is more often natural than
humanly contrived.

This love of the "outside" has its less peaceful bucolic tones, however. An
internet search of the phrase "Southern land" brings up a song of that title
by Taylor Ray Holbrook and Ryan Upchurch.[2] The lyrics describe a group
of "rowdy" male friends who drink beer, shoot deer, build bonfires, and ogle
women on a remote piece of property the singer says he inherited from his
father and expects to pass on to his children. This enjoyment of the land,
the song implies, is the very essence of good Southern living, despite the fact
that there are such groups of rowdy friends in every rural area in America,
north, south, east, and west, and that a majority of self-identified Southerners do not attend such parties.[3] There is a deeper message beneath the lyrics'
banality (not to mention the tune's monotony), however. It is that Southern

white men who own rural acreage can do whatever they want on their own property, and that is a freedom worth fighting for—a message so ubiquitous in Southern popular culture that it hardly needs reiteration. And yet, it is reiterated, over and over again.

As such songs demonstrate, we white Southerners do not need outsiders to caricature us; we are perfectly capable of doing it for ourselves. The song "Southern Land" is not intended as caricature, however; rather, it is bragga-docio. The right to lay claim to the land and the freedom it shelters and allows is definitive of a certain strain of Southern white manhood. There really are young white Southern men who behave as the lyrics describe and admire one another greatly for doing so. I know; I grew up with some and both dis-dained and feared them. The image they seek to project of themselves is one of hypermasculine, heterosexual power grounded in property rights and fire-arms. But there is another strain in the din of raucous self-aggrandizement, and it sounds through the very necessity of repetition. Incessant reiteration of this sort of land claim bespeaks insecurity rather than strength. What too many scholars suppose such performances indicate, namely, a characteristic Southern attachment to the land, must be placed into question. For, when attachment to land—a claim of right to land—is repeatedly insisted upon, it is not because it is strong but because it is weak. It may be threatened from without; powerful forces may be conspiring to take it away, as is the case in the Virginia pipeline fights. Or, those forces may be imagined projections of doubts that originate within.[4] While there are Southerners who are deeply attached to land, whether to owned land or just to land they consider their home, that attachment is deeply troubled.

For many centuries prior to my arrival, the land under Baugh Wiley Smith Hospital and my parents' house belonged to the Muscogee Creeks. Part of the Mississippian mound-building culture, the Creeks had an extensive network of towns and trade routes; they raised maize and squash, among other crops; and they worked copper. Despite their centuries and perhaps millennia in that place, however, and despite their achievements and alliances, as an entire peo-ple, they were pushed, squeezed, thrust, and expelled from their homeland in a fraudulent and violent series of white land grabs between 1825 and 1836.

White Americans had claimed the land as theirs ever since the region was annexed by the US government in 1804. They declared it part of the Alabama Territory in 1817 and part of the state of Alabama in 1819. But much of that land was unavailable for individual white ownership, agriculture, and industrial development until the Creeks were dispossessed, so the white gov-ernment and white citizenry set about terrorizing them. Many were killed, in both military and extramilitary actions, and most of the rest were "legally" exiled to so-called Indian Territory by 1836. No doubt there were some who did not leave, who preferred for whatever personal reasons to stay behind and managed to hide or to blend well enough phenotypically to pass as white or African American. My ancestors, at least the few I can identify (two great-great-grandparents out of a presumptive thirty-two), arrived in 1855 and lived on that ground for five generations before I was born. Before them, the Creeks had lived there for perhaps five hundred generations.

I was born and came to be, to live, to perceive, to think on stolen land.

All non-Indigenous Southern people, regardless of race, were born on stolen land. Neither we nor our parents did the stealing, but it was white Europeans and Americans who did, and not very long ago. In the first third of the nineteenth century, whites killed and exiled Indigenous people in Alabama, Georgia, and elsewhere in the South because they wanted to take land that was not theirs. A mere three decades later, in conflict with the federal government, whites who by that time "legally" "owned" land in the South insisted on their absolute right to it—and their right to do on it whatever they chose to do. Whether what they chose to do was merely to drink beer, shoot deer, build bonfires, and ogle women or to extract wealth by draining the nutrients from it through unsustainable agricultural methods and enslaving descendants of Africans and forcing them to work ever harder to make up for the soil's loss of productivity, they reiterated their right to it, their attachment to it, their destiny upon it. Union military campaigns were invasions of *white Southern* land, even if it had only been so for a decade or two and contingent upon violent expulsion of the original inhabitants and even if most of the people actually occupying it were not white. This reiterated identification with the land intensified *after* the war, *after* much of the land was forfeited.

Becoming Indigenous?

For a great many prominent white Southerners, the Confederacy's defeat meant impoverishment. Without enslaved labor and without the means to pay for wage labor, they could not extract enough from the by-then-depleted soil to maintain themselves in the manner to which they had become accustomed. They had no choice but to sell big tracts to speculators. Defeat was not merely defeat; it was also loss, and the loss—at least for those relative few who had been wealthy—was profound.

Somehow, in the aftermath of all of that loss of wealth and status, Southern studies scholar Gina Caison tells us, "Euro-American southerners . . . mediated their racial identities through Native ones in order to feel appropriately and justifiably connected to their adopted and bellum-defended homeland."[5] White Southerners "indigenized" themselves through passionate and sentimental narratives of attachment to the land and their supposed distinction, in that attachment, from other American whites. Some even "identified" with Indigenous people in their profound loss, yet another means of indigenization.[6]

These mournful and falsely nostalgic narratives do not erase Indigenous people—not completely, at least. Rather than forgetting the exiled peoples altogether, white Southerners came to understand themselves as Indigenous people's *inevitable and therefore rightful successors*. The Creeks had been there, but they were gone, as Darwinism dictated, and the whites had taken their place as their heirs, so to speak. Of course, this meant that Indigenous absence had to be total, despite the existence of flesh and blood Indigenous people still living in the South, even unto this day, and their relatives living in exile in so-called Indian Territory west of the Mississippi.[7] Those living people were and are expunged from the story, and the South's history has been made to consist of political conflict with the white North and racial conflict between the descendants of African slaves and the descendants of European slave owners and their white-trash, redneck thugs too poor to own anybody. Indigenous peoples allegedly belong to another, long past, epoch.

The South, Southern identity, and Southern attachment to land are all social constructions less than two centuries in the making. What is now "the South" is neither culturally nor climatologically nor topologically nor linguistically homogeneous. Nevertheless, most Americans would probably assent to the proposition that there is a place in the United States called "the South" that is distinct from other regions and that people there are "Southerners," meaning that they are somehow different from other Americans in their being "of" that place, bound up with and reflective of it. Can we say, then, that white Southerners have succeeded in "indigenizing"?

It depends, of course, on what the word *indigenous* means, and that turns out to be a hard and politically fraught question to answer. The *Oxford English Dictionary* defines *indigenous* simply as "born or produced in a land or region." This can be said of people, animals, plants, agricultural products, art and literature, or characteristics of some particular thing's operation or way of being.[8] (The first historical example that the OED cites comes from 1646.) If we take the word in that sense, then certainly I and the previous five generations of my identifiable ancestry are indigenous, if not to "the South" at least to a couple of northern counties in Alabama, as are thousands of other white and African American people. The word *indigenous* in that sense merely means *native*. But, of course, there is *native* and there is *Native*. In Alaska, there are Alaska Natives and native Alaskans, and they are not the same people. Alaska Natives are Indigenous peoples, whereas native Alaskans are white, Asian American, Latinx, and African American people born in Alaska. In many contexts these days, Alaska included, *Indigenous* refers to people across the globe who are descended from people who lived in a particular place prior to European colonization.

The definition is not settled, however. In 1986, United Nations Special Rapporteur José Martínez Cobo defined "indigenous communities, peoples and nations" as:

> those which, having a historical continuity with pre-invasion and pre-colonial societies that developed on their territories, consider themselves distinct from other sectors of society and are determined

to preserve, develop and transmit to future generations their ancestral territories, and their ethnic identity, as the basis of their continued existence as peoples, in accordance with their own cultural patterns, social institutions and legal systems.[9]

Cobo's definition is fairly specific and restrictive. Three years later, in 1989, the International Labour Organization offered a slightly less restrictive and avowedly provisional definition of Indigenous peoples in its International Indigenous and Tribal Peoples Convention 169, ratified by twenty-one countries, to wit: "Peoples in independent countries who are regarded as indigenous on account of their descent from the populations which inhabited the country, or a geographical region to which the country belongs, at the time of conquest or colonization."[10] Neither definition, however, found its way into the United Nations Declaration on the Rights of Indigenous Peoples, adopted in 2007.[11] The UN's Working Group on Indigenous Peoples, which drafted the declaration, left the definition open so that groups could self-identify as they chose.[12] This openness reflects the situation on the ground. There is disagreement over whether we can say that there are Indigenous peoples in places where European colonization either did not take place at all or was never fully established, even if those peoples have occupied their territory for dozens of generations—peoples in parts of Africa and Asia, for example. There is disagreement, furthermore, over whether any European peoples in Europe should be considered indigenous or Indigenous. And some people who seem to qualify as indigenous/Indigenous under the most stringent of definitions object to being so labeled, such as the Aymara speakers in Bolivia.[13]

Some activists and scholars argue that Indigeneity is a political, not an ontological, category. Andrew Canessa, for example, says that Indigeneity is best understood "as a contemporary social relation articulated in terms of the past."[14] It does not name some fundamental characteristic common to the peoples who claim it. Its meaning resides not in what it refers to but in what it does, namely, serving to unify a disparate collection of living people in distinction to another disparate collection of living people by calling up both groups' long-deceased ancestry in order to assert various property, civil, economic, and sovereignty rights in the present day. Somewhat paradoxically, Indigeneity connotes locality while taking shape primarily upon an international stage. As Courtney Jung puts it, "Notwithstanding the claims of indigenous people to ancient ethnic heritages, spiritual connections to specific territorial regions, and cultural practices that rely on community and kinship, indigenous identity is both new and global."[15] In fact, its political power resides in its ability to ally very different groups of people across the world, people who in fact have no ancestral, religious, or historical connections to each other but who do have common political interests formed in response to European colonization and law, liberal individualism, and the forces of contemporary global capitalism. What else, after all, could possibly bind together the Māori, Zapotec, Houma, Inuit, and Gaddi peoples?

Indigenous peoples, taken together, are the most diverse human group imaginable. Aileen Moreton-Robinson points out that prior to the arrival of English settlers in 1788, Australia was already multicultural, with an estimated five hundred different languages spoken on the continent.[16] The construction of Indigenous Australians as a single race was an effect of—one might with very good reason even say a constituent practice of—European colonization. This practice had been developed in the previous century in British North America, where it proved extremely effective as a means to consolidate colonial power. There the Algonquin, Iroquois, and Seminole peoples became one "tawny" and then one "red" race when a multiethnic band of European settlers deemed it necessary to unite themselves across their own linguistic, cultural, and economic differences into a single people. They called themselves "white," over and against the equally multiethnic people they kidnapped from Africa and compressed into a single race they called "Negro" or "Black."[17] Examining this colonizing strategy, Moreton-Robinson asserts that, simply, racialization "is the process by which whiteness operates possessively to define and construct itself as the pinnacle of its own racial hierarchy."[18] To racialize peoples as black, brown, tawny, red, or yellow is to colonize them, to categorize them according to terms convenient for colonizers and colonizing processes. Resisting now-institutionalized colonizing strategies must involve resisting racialization. To claim Indigeneity as a subject position, as an identity with absolutely no essence, is to resist the racial identities that colonizers have imposed. It is to assert a difference that is pure difference.

Applying this insight to the Southern context, we can make the following observation: in order to fit the Cherokees, Creeks, Choctaws, Seminoles, and other original inhabitants of the land into "white" world history and property law, white Southerners needed to homogenize them into a single primitive race already caught up in a natural process of giving way to their white superiors. It was hard to homogenize them as long as it was necessary to negotiate with their various leaders in their varied presence. Not only did whites want those peoples' land; they also wanted to be able to tell themselves a good story about why the land should belong to whites and not to "Indians." Both needs—to take the land and to claim Indigenous peoples had no title to it in the first place—dictated removal of Indigenous people by killing or exile. In other words, in the South, effective racialization required genocide.

Racialization is, then, a colonizing strategy. Present-day Indigeneity can be seen as a means of resisting that strategy. The twenty-first-century self-Indigenization occurring now on a global as well as local stage is a strategic alignment of peoples and forces in opposition to global capitalism. Indigeneity is not a racial category, even though those who claim it as a racial identity for political purposes are mostly victims of racism. Indigenous identity is,

rather, "a political achievement," as Jung terms it in her discussion of Indigenous activism in Chiapas, Mexico. She writes, "The link between identity
and culture is deeply contingent, dependent on history and politics. It is a
resource that allows millions of the world's poorest and most dispossessed
to challenge the terms of their exclusion."[19] Indigeneity is a category of
antiracialization that seeks political transformation in this post-colonizing,
racialized world.

Once we place Indigeneity in its historical and political context, it is clear
that neither white nor Black Southerners can ever actually "indigenize"
ourselves—especially if we hold onto our racial identities. Our relation to the
land will never be comparable to that of the Creeks or the Chickasaws, no
matter how many generations of our families owned and will own Southern
land. Our status as members of a white or Black race stands as a mark of that
incomparability. To be raced is to have been assimilated to the processes of
colonization, to have been in part generated within those processes, whereas
to be Indigenous is to resist them. Anyway, very few of us actually hold a title
to land that was owned by any of our ancestors for more than a couple of
generations. In fact, most of us own no land at all or at most a mortgaged
house lot. We are immigrants—forced arrivals, as in the case of Africans, or
voluntary settlers, as in the case of most Europeans[20]—even if we are not
ourselves thieves.

So, then, is our cultural identity as Southerners nothing more than a racist delusion? Is the South itself nothing more than a fantasy born of greed,
rapine, and the emasculating humiliation of military defeat? One thing is
sure: If the South is a mere fantasy, it is not merely a Southern fantasy. It is an
American fantasy. More than one white academic has told me over the years
that although they will fly through Charlotte or Atlanta and maybe even
attend a conference in some other major Southern city, they would be afraid
to drive a car through the South—too many rowdy beer drinkers with deer
rifles, too many fat sheriffs suspicious of out-of-state tags, too many vigilante
Christians out for fresh souls. The South is a place of virulent racism, abject
poverty, willful ignorance, violence always happening or just about to happen, and rampant disrespect for the rule of law. It is this South, the hated,
ridiculed, and feared South, that I saw on television day after day through my
early years. It is this South that I have seen on the faces of educated people
upon learning where I am from. It is this South that informed the reception
my younger sister received upon her arrival at Harvard Law School in the
1980s. Her fellow law students (as well, most likely, as some of her professors) assumed that she was an ignorant racist bumpkin whose likelihood of
success was nil, and they made sure she knew they knew it.

All Southerners of my generation are intimately familiar with both of
these Souths and a few others as well. We live them—and not as mere fantasy
or delusion. They are the material conditions of our becoming and of our
perspectives on the world. So, I have to say that the South is not an illusion,

even though it is an historical construction generated in part through a series of fantasies of various sorts. The South will not be dispensed with so easily. It is a set of forces that those of us who are "of" it must reckon with.

Perspective and Knowledge, Finitude and Power

For over seventy years, feminist thinkers have critiqued and rejected the ideas that truth is apolitical and that knowledge can only be had by way of detached observation. All observation occurs from an embodied perspective, they have insisted, which means it comes from some particular place and bears the marks of that place upon it. All observers, all thinkers, all knowers are placed, situated, and their placement and situation inform their perceiving and thinking and knowing. This inevitability ought not to be denied but avowed and even affirmed. What we know is always contingent upon who—which involves where and when—we are.

Feminist thinkers raised this issue against the background of generations of masculinist dismissal of women's claims. As Simone de Beauvoir observes in *The Second Sex*, men have frequently undermined women's testimony and beliefs by explicitly tying them to their womanhood. "You only think that because you are a woman," she quotes some of her own male interlocutors as saying.[21] Beauvoir reports wanting to respond, "And you think the contrary because you are a man."[22] But she does not, and her colleagues and critics seem unaware that they too have bodies and hormones and histories upon which their claims and beliefs are equally contingent. Arguing, logically and persuasively, that all knowledge is situated and dependent upon an embodied perspective has enabled feminists to counter such overtly sexist dismissals.

Feminists have not only insisted that all knowledge is situated and perspectival, but they have invented methods of inquiry based on that fact. Examining women's embodied experience, sorting through the differences and commonalities across our lives, and developing theories to account for them was standard practice in and through the Second Wave. Meditations on personal experiences fill the pages of anthologies from that time: *Sisterhood Is Powerful*, *The Black Woman*, *This Bridge Called My Back*. Cherríe Moraga and Gloria Anzaldúa, editors of *Bridge*, call their work and that of their contributors "theory in the flesh."[23]

This fleshly, situated starting point made it inevitable that all feminists, and white feminists especially (who otherwise might not), would have to confront the issue of race and racism. White feminists were not *women* and what they examined was not *women's* experience, Black, Chicana, Indigenous, and Asian American feminists repeatedly pointed out to them; they were *white* women and their experience and perspectives were as much formed by their race as by their sex, age, religious background, citizenship, and socioeconomic status. In the 1980s and 1990s it was not unusual for a feminist author to begin her (or occasionally his) essay or book with a string of demographic qualifiers: "Speaking as a . . . I . . ." Self-location became de rigueur.

I learned this lesson of self-location in my intellectual youth from feminist scholars, and it was refined and reinforced by my philosophical training in Martin Heidegger's analytic of Dasein and the genealogical work of Michel Foucault. An individual's pursuit of knowledge is thoroughly conditioned by experiences, Heidegger taught me, first and foremost by experiences of frustration and desire; only when something unexpected and undesirable happens in our pursuit of something do we stand back and consider what things are and how things work. The questions that we ask and pursue are always conditioned by our desires and the situations in which we find ourselves. Foucault's writing made it very clear to me, moreover, that knowledge is not only conditioned by desire but is produced under constraints of historical networks of power and always bound up with the regimes that generate it and give it its significance. There is no knowing that transcends time and place.

Knowledge is also multiple—Foucault speaks of knowledges—and one way of knowing can be turned against another. Foucault's own genealogical practice necessarily operated within the twentieth-century European regime of truth (or, as he puts it in his later work, regime of veridiction) that governed French scholarly production in his lifetime, but he found that he could dig out of various archives buried or discredited knowledges that challenged dominant assumptions and conclusions drawn from them. By placing previously unquestionable premises, concepts, and narratives into question, Foucault was able to depict the various forces and interests that shaped and maintained them. He brought to light the violence and injustices that often accompanied their producers' good intentions and revealed the accidents and unreason embedded within their rationalities. As a consequence, his work tends to undermine those knowledges' claim to transcendent truth and, in turn, their power to regulate what and how we might think and feel.

My training and the kind of work I do make me acutely aware that I think and know out of my own history, as well as the histories that created the conditions for my personal history. The thinking that I do is made possible by the experiences that I have had, which are the experiences of a white woman born in Alabama in 1960 and raised and educated there. Despite the facts that "the South" is a relatively recent phenomenon and that it was fabricated under shameful circumstances, it is where I was formed. I am a Southerner. I cannot *not* be that any more than I cannot *not* be an American or *not* be white. And I cannot control what those things mean. Nevertheless, both my feminist and my philosophical integrity require that I avow those things in their contingency as well as in their power.

There are two familiar ways for white people to do that. One is to take pride in the racism, violence, and genocide. That way, however, runs directly counter to my nature, formed as it was in the midst of a nonviolent Christian struggle inspired by the vision of a beloved nonhomogeneous community.

The other is to take on guilt for the racism, violence, and genocide. That way, however, also runs counter to my nature, formed as it was in the midst of a liberal Christianity that emphasized individual ownership of actions and individual attention to the salvation of one's own soul. For all the mistakes I have made and all the layers of racism I have yet to peel away from the institutionalized practices I engage in, I do not feel guilty for racism or genocide. On the contrary, I feel angry, and in anger I find another way to avow my formation in racism, violence, and genocide.

I feel angry, of course, for the injustices and violence inflicted on Indigenous people and African Americans, for all they suffered and lost. But the anger of this alternative way to avow the history that bears me is more: there is also what anti-Black racism did to Southern white children, most especially those of the working class. Systematic anti-Black racism cost white people a lot, and most of the cost was borne not by the elites who received so much material benefit from it but by the working class and poor, and especially by their children. Maintaining that system kept our parents' wages and our families' standard of living low. Beginning in the late 1950s, it precipitated elite and government disinvestment in public schools and public transit systems. It required that lies fill our textbooks and our school and public libraries. It deprived us of the pleasures of neighborliness and the joys of friendship with African American and Indigenous peers. We were made witness to acts of violence at tender ages. And we learned, without anyone having to teach us, that the world we lived in was built upon such violence and that that violence would be turned against absolutely anyone who questioned, let alone broke, any number of unwritten rules. I am not personally guilty. But I am personally angry about what I was required to sacrifice in order for the Bull Connors, the George Wallaces, and all the less well known official bullies of that particular "Southern way of life" to maintain their masculinity and exercise their sadism in the service of the executives and stockholders of US Steel, Tennessee Coal, Iron, and Railroad Company, Chemstrand, Wolverine Industries, and every other giant corporate and petty local player in the Southern economy of the second half of the twentieth century. Just as racialization was a tool for colonization, racism is a tool for extracting profits and propping up little white egos.

I know all this, I believe all this, and I feel all this as a white Southerner, as one thoroughly formed and informed by it. I think from out of it. As a feminist, I affirm that I speak from out of it. I cannot do otherwise. But as a philosopher?

Philosophy of the South?

When I hear the phrases "philosophy of the South" or "Southern philosophy," I think of John C. Calhoun. On the US Senate floor in 1837, Calhoun, who was then a senator from South Carolina, declared that only the most naive of statesmen could fail to see that exploitation and poverty are necessary components of every great civilization. Great scientific, artistic, technological, and political achievements are only possible if there is a leisure class able to dedicate itself to those pursuits while a vast underclass labors in poverty. And, since poverty and exploitation naturally breed resentment among members of the class condemned to it, that vast underclass must be carefully contained and strictly disciplined. Slavery is the best institution for maintaining the necessary surveillance and tight control over the laboring class. Calhoun stated it thusly:

> I hold then that there never has yet existed a wealthy and civilized society in which one portion of the community did not in point of fact live on the labor of the other. . . . The devices are almost innumerable, from the brute force and gross superstition of ancient times to the subtle and artful fiscal contrivances of the modern. . . . It is useless to disguise the fact. There is and always has been in an advanced stage of wealth and civilization a conflict between labor and capital. The condition of society in the South exempts us from the disorders and dangers resulting from this conflict.[24]

This was John C. Calhoun's political philosophy, and it was undoubtedly a product of "the South"—hence, Southern philosophy.

In addition to his South Carolinian heritage, Calhoun located himself in the lineage of ancient Rome and Greece. There, enslaved people did the work necessary for individual and collective physical survival, while slaveholders created a beautiful way of life filled with pursuit and appreciation of the finer things. They designed beautiful art and architecture to endure through the ages, made discoveries, and thought the great thoughts and gave the great speeches, all because they were freed from the daily drudgery of getting a living by the enslaved men, women, and children who toiled in the kitchens, baths, and fields. Pursuit of truth and beauty is predicated upon mass exploitation and suppression. I can almost see Calhoun turning to us to ask, "Is it not?"

"No!" we democrats want to shout. But the question echoes down the decades: "*Does* it not?"

I am formed out of and still within such turmoil, such conflict of values and truths, such clashes of claims and lineages of ideas and meaning, that I cannot dismiss that question. In fact, it seems to me, to insist on a unitary truth, a highest value, a single right way is, inherently, to suppress and exploit and reduce and deny the myriad forces and dimensions of lives as they happen on whatever ground in whatever land, ever.

Less than fifty years after Calhoun made his speech on the Senate floor, Friedrich Nietzsche published these words:

The will to truth which will still tempt us to many a venture, that famous truthfulness of which all philosophers so far have spoken with respect—what questions has this will to truth not laid before us! What strange, wicked, questionable questions! . . . Is it any wonder that we should finally become suspicious, lose patience, and turn away impatiently? That we should finally learn from this Sphinx to ask questions, too? *Who* is it really that puts questions to us here? *What* in us really wants "truth"?

Indeed we came to a long halt at the question about the cause of this will—until we finally came to a complete stop before a still more basic question. We asked about the *value* of this will. Suppose we want truth: *why not rather* untruth? and uncertainty? even ignorance?[25]

Calhoun stands, facing me, that smile on his lips as he repeats, "Does it not?" What if Calhoun is right? If you want Truth and Beauty and the Good, do you not have to accept and even affirm and perpetuate exploitation, oppression, unspeakable cruelty, devastating loss and suffering? That is the price, and of course we will pay it because Truth is of the highest value. Is it not?

All those forces, swirling and ricocheting and refusing to yield clarity and precision—all those forces that shape me in my perspectival gathering on stolen, bloody ground—bring me to turn around to Calhoun, that Sphinx, and answer not with a declaration but with another question, Nietzsche's question, a question that Calhoun never dared ask and never imagined anyone could ask: What is the value of your values? What is the value of your civilization? Why not rather untruth?

I have no Southern philosophy to counter Calhoun. I have only my awareness of the multiplicities of Southern lineages and heritages and legacies that form me, an awareness Calhoun himself in his spectacular self-assurance clearly lacked. If I want to be faithful to what I am in my particular and local ongoing becoming, I must think and speak not of truth but of that contingency, that absence of any certainty, and that awareness of difference, conflict, accident, and unreason that accompany all my good reasons and best intentions and commitments. In and through my Southern locality, I know that I own no land and stand on no ground. My living and thinking occur in a whirlwind over an abyss.

Notes

1. I hasten to add that I am allied with those big landowners in these fights against both the Mountain Valley and the Atlantic Coast pipelines, not to protect their property rights but to protect the environment and the poor landowners who will lose every asset they have if the pipelines go through. I support Friends of Buckingham County, in particular, who are in what for them could be a fight to the death to prevent a compressor station in one of Virginia's oldest free African American settlements and currently home to an African American population

that Dominion Energy's assessment documents grossly undercount. Compressor stations are exactly what they sound like; they move product through pipelines by force, increasing pressure at strategic points along a long pipeline so that it will continue to flow. As a result, these stations are subject to explosions that are fatal for all living things for miles around. They are also very, very loud. Ground zero for a station proposed in Buckingham County includes two historic African American churches and many homes. Dominion seems to think the risk to these people is worth the profit they expect to make. If we have to invoke the myth of sacred white Southern land to save the residents of Buckingham County, we will do that. I wish that we lived in a world where protecting an African American community from annihilation was a good enough reason not to build a pipeline, but we do not.

2. Taylor Ray Holbrook and Ryan Upchurch, "Southern Land," by Austin Jenckes, Ryan Miller, Jared Sciullo, Taylor Ray Holbrook, and Ryan Upchurch, released May 2016, Phivestarr Productions.

3. I have no source to cite for this claim, but here is my evidence. First, many Southerners do not drink for religious reasons. Second, many Southerners live in urban areas where house lots are small and deer hunting is prohibited. Add to those some number of rural, beer-drinking, deer-shooting men and women who just don't like rowdy parties, and I am sure that the total will exceed 50 percent of the population.

4. Aileen Moreton-Robinson makes a similar point in the context of discussing Australian Prime Minister John Howard's rhetoric regarding Indigenous rights and immigration in the late 1990s. Aileen Moreton-Robinson, *The White Possessive: Property, Power, and Indigenous Sovereignty* (Minneapolis: University of Minnesota Press, 2015), 140–44.

5. Gina Caison, *Red States: Indigeneity, Settler Colonialism, and Southern Studies* (Athens: University of Georgia Press, 2018), 19.

6. Caison suggests that some Southerners even imagined that the Confederacy's loss was divine punishment for the sin of banishing Indigenous people. See *Red States*, 110.

7. Caison, *Red States*, 136, 218.

8. *Oxford English Dictionary* entry for "indigenous."

9. Quoted in Jan Hoffman French, "The Power of Definition: Brazil's Contribution to Universal Concepts of Indigeneity," *Indiana Journal of Global Studies* 18, no. 1 (2011): 246.

10. Quoted in Andrew Canessa, "Who Is Indigenous? Self-Identification, Indigeneity, and Claims to Justice in Contemporary Bolivia," *Urban Anthropology and Studies of Cultural Systems and World Economic Development, and Politics in Contemporary Bolivia* 36, no. 3 (2007): 203.

11. At that time, 144 countries signed the declaration. Only four countries refused to sign: the United States, New Zealand, Canada, and Australia, which by some counts are collectively home to nearly half of the Indigenous peoples in the world. Australia finally signed in 2009, and the other three countries signed in 2010, all insisting that the document is not legally binding upon them and will have no effect on the laws and policies governing their Indigenous populations. For analysis of the oppositional rhetoric, see Moreton-Robinson, *The White Possessive*, chapter 12.

50 Ladelle McWhorter

12. For some description of the process by which the declaration was developed over many years, see J. Kēhaulani Kauanui's interview with Tonya Gonella Frishner in J. Kēhaulani Kauanui, ed., *Speaking of Indigenous Politics: Conversations with Activists, Scholars, and Tribal Leaders* (Minneapolis: University of Minnesota Press, 2018), 123–31.

13. Canessa, "Who Is Indigenous?," 209.

14. Canessa, "Who Is Indigenous?," 217.

15. Courtney Jung, *The Moral Force of Indigenous Politics: Critical Liberalism and the Zapatistas* (Cambridge: Cambridge University Press, 2008), 11.

16. Moreton-Robinson, *The White Possessive*, 11.

17. For a genealogical account of some of this process, see Ladelle McWhorter, *Racism and Sexual Oppression in Anglo-America: A Genealogy* (Bloomington: Indiana University Press, 2009), chapters 2 and 3.

18. Moreton-Robinson, *The White Possessive*, xx.

19. Jung, *The Moral Force of Indigenous Politics*, 11.

20. Jodi A. Byrd, *The Transit of Empire: Indigenous Critiques of Colonialism* (Minneapolis: University of Minnesota Press, 2011).

21. Simone de Beauvoir, *The Second Sex*, trans. Constance Borde and Sheila Malovany-Chevallier (New York: Vintage Books, 2011), 5.

22. Beauvoir, *The Second Sex*, 5.

23. Cherríe Moraga and Gloria Anzaldúa, *This Bridge Called My Back: Writings of Radical Women of Color*, 4th ed. (Albany: SUNY Press, 2015), 19.

24. Quoted in Irving H. Bartlett, *John C. Calhoun: A Biography* (New York: W. W. Norton, 1993), 227.

25. Friedrich Nietzsche, *Beyond Good and Evil: Prelude to a Philosophy of the Future*, trans. Walter Kaufmann (New York: Vintage Books, 1966), 9.

Bibliography

Bartlett, Irving H. *John C. Calhoun: A Biography*. New York: W. W. Norton, 1993.

Beauvoir, Simone de. *The Second Sex*. Translated by Constance Borde and Sheila Malovany-Chevallier. New York: Vintage Books, 2011.

Byrd, Jodi A. *The Transit of Empire: Indigenous Critiques of Colonialism*. Minneapolis: University of Minnesota Press, 2011.

Caison, Gina. *Red States: Indigeneity, Settler Colonialism, and Southern Studies*. Athens: University of Georgia Press, 2018.

Canessa, Andrew. "Who Is Indigenous? Self-Identification, Indigeneity, and Claims to Justice in Contemporary Bolivia." *Urban Anthropology and Studies of Cultural Systems and World Economic Development. Power, Indigeneity, Economic Development, and Politics in Contemporary Bolivia* 36, no. 3 (2007): 195–237.

French, Jan Hoffman. "The Power of Definition: Brazil's Contribution to Universal Concepts of Indigeneity." *Indiana Journal of Global Studies* 18, no. 1 (2011): 241–61.

Holbrook, Taylor Ray, and Ryan Upchurch. "Southern Land." By Austin Jenckes, Ryan Miller, Jared Sciullo, Taylor Ray Holbrook, and Ryan Upchurch. Released May 2016. Produced by Phivestarr Productions.

Jung, Courtney. *The Moral Force of Indigenous Politics: Critical Liberalism and the Zapatistas*. Cambridge: Cambridge University Press, 2008.

Kauanui, J. Kēhaulani, ed. *Speaking of Indigenous Politics: Conversations with Activists, Scholars, and Tribal Leaders*. Minneapolis: University of Minnesota Press, 2018.

McWhorter, Ladelle. *Racism and Sexual Oppression in Anglo-America: A Genealogy*. Bloomington: Indiana University Press, 2009.

Moraga, Cherríe, and Gloria Anzaldúa, eds. *This Bridge Called My Back: Writings of Radical Women of Color*. 4th ed. Albany: SUNY Press, 2015.

Moreton-Robinson, Aileen. *The White Possessive: Property, Power, and Indigenous Sovereignty*. Minneapolis: University of Minnesota Press, 2015.

Nietzsche, Friedrich. *Beyond Good and Evil: Prelude to a Philosophy of the Future*. Translated by Walter Kaufmann. New York: Vintage Books, 1966.

3

✦

Between Socrates and Grandma

On Being a Black Southern Philosopher

Arnold L. Farr

"Democracy is hard to love."[1] This is the first sentence of chapter 1 in Iris Young's book *Inclusion and Democracy*. Young goes on to explain that while most of us believe in democracy as an ideal, the actual development of a democratic society requires a lot of work, the kind of work that most of us avoid. For the purposes of this chapter, I want to begin with the claim that critical self-reflection is hard to love. I make this claim as one who has had to struggle with the demand to engage in critical reflection and critical self-reflection while my ability to do so was doubted on the basis of my race and geographical origin. That is, the discipline of philosophy harbors a contradiction that undermines its very demands. While philosophy demands critical self-reflection, it has also insisted that this reflection be carried out by a disembodied subject who reflects from nowhere in particular. An example of this attempt to reflect as a disembodied subject is the Rawlsian veil of ignorance. The philosopher is asked to shed any identity markers as he or she reflects on principles of justice so that his or her identity will not produce a biased outcome. However, somewhat contradictorily, in academic settings some of us are quite often reminded of our identity in ways that question our ability to critically reflect. I nonetheless affirm that if philosophy is to provide us with any information about the human condition, the philosopher must take notice of place, forms of embodiment, and situation. We all live under the gaze of the other, and the nature of that gaze has an impact on how we experience life and provides the raw material for self-reflection.

My survival and success in America and especially in American institutions of higher learning has been based on my ability to accept a certain degree of discomfort as a way of life. I have had to negotiate the tension between always belonging and not belonging at the same time. The field of philosophy has traditionally been a white male space dedicated to the concerns of white male intellectuals who for the most part come from a place of privilege. Their place of relative social comfort allows them to raise the type of questions that can only come from a place of relative comfort. However, since these questions and their answers are presented as universal, other types of questions are excluded from philosophical discourse. The Black Southerner who enters the field of philosophy must be willing to bracket the kinds of questions that arise out of the way in which he or she is forced to engage the world and accept the principles, questions, and methods proposed by comfortable white male philosophers.

And yet, the Black Southern philosopher carries a text that does not lend itself to the kind of analysis that white male philosophers are used to. Since this text is not familiar to white male philosophers, it may be rejected by them altogether. But if the Black Southern philosopher abandons this text, he or she runs risk of denying his or her humanity and connection to others. That text is "Grandma's metaphysics." In this chapter, I will examine the tension between the form of wisdom that develops in Southern dark spaces (the Black community) and that form of wisdom that is championed in the academy. While Socrates is portrayed as an icon of wisdom in the academy, I argue there was just as much wisdom in Southern spaces. One form of wisdom develops from a place of relative comfort. Although Socrates was killed because of his teachings, he was quite old and had the opportunity to escape death. For him death came at the end of a long life. His wisdom is of a very different nature from that form of wisdom that develops in a social context where one is dead at birth. Not teachings but skin is the mark of death from the moment of birth for Black people. The beginning of wisdom in the Black world is learning how to navigate life in such a way that the death sentence one received at birth is not carried out. The struggle of the Black Southern philosopher is learning how to play by the rules of traditional philosophy while still recognizing that side of life that most philosophers never have to deal with.

Body, Geography, and the Examined Life

In Plato's *Apology* Socrates states that "the unexamined life is not worth living for man."[2] In the *Charmides* he admonishes us to "know thyself."[3] It is unfortunate that the self that is to be known after modern philosophy is a disembodied self and the life to be examined is a life so general that it ignores human life as it is lived altogether. For me, to know thyself is to know how one is situated in the world and what that situatedness means in terms of one's ability to be self-determining and to have the necessary resources for self-development. Descartes's cogito, ergo sum, Kant's transcendental subject, Fichte's striving I, Hegel's Geist, and John Rawls's subject under the veil of ignorance all signify a form of subjectivity that is basically the same for all individuals. To examine life is also to investigate the ways in which the subjectivity or selfhood of certain individuals and groups experiences erasure by certain forms of social organization, as well as how individuals and groups respond to such forms of social organization.

Karl Marx argued in *The German Ideology* that "it is not consciousness that determines life, but life that determines consciousness."[4] That is, we encounter the world as beings with material needs and we find ourselves from the beginning embedded in certain material relations. My focus here is not on material needs, conditions, or relations but rather on how forms of materiality as well as geography produce certain material relations and thereby forms of consciousness or ways of thinking. Academic philosophy often attempts to uproot philosophy from forms of materiality. The philosophical subject is asked to reflect as a disembodied subject and from no place in particular. In his critique of the Cartesian subject regarding race, Charles Mills writes:

> Contrast this *sum* with a different kind, that of Ralph Ellison's classic novel of the black experience, *Invisible Man*. What are the problems that this individual faces? Is the problem global doubt? Not at all; such a doubt would never be possible, because the whole point of subordinate black experience, or the general experience of oppressed groups, is that the subordinated are in no position to doubt the existence of the world and other people, especially that of their oppressors. It could be said that only those most solidly attached to the world have the luxury of doubting its reality, whereas those whose attachment is more precarious, whose existence is dependent on the goodwill or ill temper of others, are those compelled to recognize that it exists. The first is a function of power, the second of subjection. If your daily existence is largely defined by oppression, by *forced* intercourse with the world, it is not going to occur to you that doubt about your oppressor's existence could in any way be a serious pressing philosophical problem; this idea will simply seem frivolous, a perk of social privilege.[5]

One of the luxuries that white philosophers and white people in general share is the luxury of not having their humanity questioned simply on the basis of race. White skin signifies the presence of a self or soul, while black skin signifies the opposite in a racist environment. Further, the philosopher never works in a vacuum. The world in which the philosopher works is a world that is already filled with various attitudes and prejudices that shape the environment wherein thought happens. The luxury or lack of luxury that one has is a part of the environment where philosophical thought occurs. As such, to examine one's life and to know one's self is to examine this environment and the effect that it has on all involved.

At some point the Black philosopher is forced to address the problem of racism. She does not have the luxury of worrying about the existence of other minds. Her questions are: How is it that some minds are such that they oppress others? How can this oppression be overcome? How do I establish my subjectivity and human value in a world that constantly puts my humanity under erasure? It is not my task to answer these questions here since I only use them rhetorically. My point is that members of oppressed groups are forced to engage the world differently than those who are not oppressed. The experience of the Black Southerner is that of always trying to navigate a world that is hostile to those of us with dark skin. In my case, I have had to navigate a world that is hostile to my Blackness and also hostile to my Southernness.

My entrance into the field of philosophy was marked by two distinct but related worries. The first was my Blackness. The second was being a Southerner. Both were sources of self-doubt. Both worries were rooted in two different perceptions of intelligence. First, there is the old view that Blacks are intellectually inferior to whites. Philosophy as an almost entirely white discipline seems to perpetuate that idea, especially since the discipline is greatly shaped by the experience and questions of white male philosophers. Second, there is the prejudice against Southerners or the perception of people from the US South as lacking intelligence. Hence, the Black philosopher is subject to the racialized gaze that questions his very humanity as well as being subject to the gaze of Northern whites who question his intellectual ability on the basis of geographical origin.

Although my entrance into the field of philosophy was clouded by moments of self-doubt because of stereotypes of Black people and Southerners, the self-doubt often gave way to confidence and a sense of calling. As I reflect on my career, it seems to me that the confidence and sense of calling had its origin in the very sources that produced self-doubt. That is, being a Black Southerner was the source of my self-doubt and my sense of calling. In other words, there was something in being Southern and Black that laid the foundation for challenging the sources of my self-doubt. A brief detour through the Frederick Douglass story will disclose the nature of the source of my confidence as a Black person and Southerner.

Frederick Douglass, Grandma, and the Struggle for Human Dignity

In his autobiography and in his book *My Bondage and My Freedom*, Frederick Douglass mentions that his mother died when he was young. Although he did not know her very well, he still remembered her visits at night. The central figure in Douglass's formative years was his grandmother. In chapter 1 of *My Bondage*, Douglass talks about being raised by his grandmother and grandfather.[6] Although Douglass's fight with the slave breaker Mr. Covey represented a turning point in his life with respect to his sense of freedom, it was his experience with his grandmother that really prepared him for his future struggle. In his youth, he had a sense of dignity instilled in him that made his future demand for freedom possible.

In *My Bondage*, Douglass talks in detail about the place where he was raised. He does this because for him knowledge of place is important for understanding the author. Douglass's experiences in a particular place with particular people helped shape the way in which he would engage the world around him. In his childhood Douglass received a form of recognition from his grandparents that would ignite his future struggle for recognition and freedom. Unlike Hegel's belief that the self emerges in the struggle between master and slave, for Douglass a sense of self emerged in his early childhood that made his struggle against Mr. Covey and the system of slavery possible. Cynthia Willett contrasts the two views as follows:

> In this regard, it is significant that while the *Phenomenology* locates the emergence of the self in the kind of contest that often character-izes adolescent rituals of manhood, Douglass's autobiographies point toward what may be a more originary happening of the self. In the opening chapters of *My Bondage*, Douglass writes that it is his early childhood experience, not the struggle with the slave breaker, that provided for him "the veriest freedom" (*BF*, 32). And while Douglass writes little about his early childhood, what he does write is quite telling. Especially interesting is his focus on "the strong and spir-ited hands" of the grandmother who raises him (*BF*, 32). Douglass describes these hands in terms that are almost magical: "Superstition had it, that if Grandmamma Betty but touches them [seedling pota-toes, but also the children that she reared?] at planting they will be sure to grow and flourish" (*BF*, 29). The nurturing caresses that he must have received from his grandmother are acknowledged explic-itly from his mistress, Sophia (*BF*, 91).[7]

Douglass's story is of great importance here because it gives us an account of the emergence of selfhood that poses a real challenge to typical philosophical accounts of the emergence of selfhood. It is not possible to address the many philosophical accounts of the emergence of selfhood here. I can say that the one thing that most of them have in common is a disembodied view of the self that emerges. However, Hegel's theory of the emergence of the self is one of the most advanced and useful in the history of philosophy. His theory of recognition is a more accurate portrayal of the human experience as well as human needs. Embedded in Douglass's story is also an account of the struggle for recognition, but it is one that is still more accurate than the Hegelian account.

Before I examine Douglass's account of the emergence of the self as com-pared with Hegel's account, let me say a bit more about Willett's use of the Douglass narrative. In her book *Maternal Ethics and Other Slave Moralities*,

Willett challenges traditional philosophical theories of ethics and morality. One of the problems with traditional moral and ethical theories is that they are the products of white males who have eliminated from philosophy the experience of women and children. Hence, their theories are based on a view of the self that is disembodied and void of important emotional attachments. For Willett, no adequate ethical or moral theory is possible without consideration of forms of embodiment and emotional attachments. The development of moral and ethical consciousness is always "located."

Both Hegel and Douglass believed that the self emerges through a struggle for recognition. However, Hegel's account seems to suggest that the struggle for selfhood between two individuals occurs between two fully formed selves. This is because Hegel has no room in his theory for women and children. The fight between Douglass and the slave breaker Mr. Covey does resemble the type of struggle that Hegel describes in the Master-Slave section of *The Phenomenology of Spirit*; however, Douglass's writings suggest that a sense of self existed prior to the fight with Mr. Covey. In fact, his resolve to fight may very well have been the result of a sense of self that developed much earlier in his life. As Willett points out, although Douglass did not say a lot about his childhood, what was said is very important. The first few pages of the first chapter of *My Bondage* make it clear that a positive sense of self emerged during Douglass's childhood. His grandparents, and his grandmother especially, were largely responsible for his positive early childhood experiences.

It is clear that Douglass greatly admired his grandmother and that he felt loved by her. What is interesting about Douglass's story is that in early childhood he did not know that he was born into slavery. The other children raised by his grandmother were all her grandchildren who were left with her as her daughters were sold into slavery on distant plantations. Douglass writes about the beauty and tranquility of his grandmother's small cabin. He did not know as a small child that, not only was the cabin not Grandmother Betty's property, she was not her own property. She was a slave who in her old age was released from her usual duties on the plantation to raise her grandchildren whose mothers had been sold. Douglass eventually became aware that something was not right as he heard his grandmother talk about "Old Master" with a tone of fear in her voice.[9] Douglass states that as a small child the only authority that he knew of over him and the other children was Grandmother Betty.[9] He eventually learned that this was not the case. Once Douglass and the other children reached a certain age, it was Grandmother Betty's duty to deliver them to Old Master where they would then assume their role as slaves.

Before his fight for freedom and his fight with Mr. Covey, Douglass had already had a taste of freedom subjectively. That is, although his objective situation was slavery, he did not yet know it. In the context of living with his grandparents, he developed a sense of self that was then sent out to be erased by the objective reality of slavery. We might follow object relations theorists here and say that Douglass began his life in a holding community where he received recognition without having to fight for it. The term "holding community" is an extension of what object relations theorists call a "holding environment" or what Jessica Benjamin calls a "supportive social context."[10] It is when Douglass was delivered to a system of misrecognition (slavery) that he would have to fight for recognition and freedom. It seems to me that Douglass developed a form of double consciousness that made the fight for freedom possible, as the two contradictory sides of consciousness could not be reconciled. There is his consciousness of himself as loved, valued, and worthy of recognition. This consciousness developed in the context of the holding community provided by his grandparents and others who lived in close proximity to them. The other side of consciousness was produced within the dehumanizing context of slavery.

Douglass's story is important for me here because of what it contributes to the understanding of the emergence of the self and a liberated consciousness at two levels. Both levels reflect my own experience to some degree. At the first level, there is the problem of racism. At the second level, there is the experience of the Southerner who leaves his or her holding community in the South to go out into a society where Southerners are considered less intelligent than those who are not from the American South. In this chapter I've moved back and forth between these two problems. The Black person in America and the American Southerner are both victims of stereotypes that denigrate their humanity. The point in discussing Douglass's story is to bring to light the power of one's holding community in shaping an attitude of resistance.

Grandma Metaphysics and the Black Southern Epistemic Community

Holding communities, including community members who play a role in shaping one's consciousness and sense of self, are also epistemic communities.[11] As epistemic communities, holding communities are responsible for educating its members. This education need not be formal at all. In fact, the educators themselves may have no or very little formal education. However, because of their situation in life, they have been forced into a type of intercourse with life that has produced great wisdom and even cunning. Survival requires knowing how the world works.

Black grandmothers in the American South occupy a unique place in the family and the community. The song "Grandma's Hands" by Bill Withers expresses the same sentiments about his grandmother that we see expressed by Douglass. Although grandfathers play an important leadership and mentoring role, grandmothers seem to be the family glue that holds everyone together. I have titled this chapter "Between Socrates and Grandma: On Being a Southern Black Philosopher" because I wanted to juxtapose two distinct forms of wisdom and influence in my philosophical life. Of course, Socrates for me represents the entire official philosophical enterprise. He is an iconic figure who represents the quest for wisdom and knowledge. But he is not the only wise philosopher who has shaped my thinking and my life. My many grandmothers were, too. My grandmothers provided unconditional love and a form of wisdom that was rooted in their knowledge of dangerous forces in this world as well as a strong faith in a God who would help them overcome. Survival in this world was made possible for them by an unshakable faith in God. Hence, the term "grandma metaphysics" refers to the religious faith of my grandmothers which was necessary for their practical engagement with a world that insisted on dehumanizing them and everyone whom they loved.

It may seem very odd to locate Socrates and one's grandmother(s) as the bookends of one's quest for knowledge. This is especially strange since neither of my grandmothers received higher than an eighth-grade education. Both were forced to quit school and work in the fields, one in the seventh grade and the other in the eighth. I also had the privilege of knowing two of my great-grandmothers. Both were a part of my life until I became a teenager, around which time they both passed away. They were both former sharecroppers and had no formal education. My paternal great-grandmother was taught to read and write by my paternal grandmother's youngest sister. These four "uneducated" women were among my first educators. It is from them that I learned how to survive in a society that was built on denying the humanity of people like my grandmothers and me. All four grandmothers were very strong women with unshakable religious beliefs. My paternal great-grandmother was actually one of my first best friends. I recall spending hours drinking black coffee (I was twelve at the time) with her and talking or watching television (which was new to her).

My four grandmothers were my holding community as well as my epistemic community. Unlike Douglass, I was not separated from my parents. However, my brothers and I, as well as several cousins, practically lived with my grandparents during most of the day as our parents worked full-time. When I was born, my parents lived in my grandparents' house for a short time. Their first house was next door to my great-grandmother's house, which was next door to the home of my grandparents. The street that we all lived on was like one big community or extended family. Most of the old people were former sharecroppers or the children of sharecroppers. There are four things that guided me in my youth that were provided by my grandmothers and other members of my holding community: education, community, self-respect, and religion—the last of which I will call "Grandma's metaphysics."

Although centered in religion, Grandma's metaphysics also stressed education. While my grandmothers and many members of my community had little to no formal education, they instilled in me the importance of education. It was simply accepted that I would go to college. They understood that education would present me with more opportunities than they had and that it would also provide me with the necessary tools to overcome the kind of adversity that they faced as Black Southerners. We were very small children when my paternal grandmother made us learn the ABCs and at least attempt reading. We also had to memorize the phone numbers of several relatives so that if we were ever lost or in trouble, we could call someone. When we would complain about our teachers, my grandmother would say, "that teacher has her education, you have to get yours." In addition to stressing the importance of education, there was also a form of worldly wisdom imparted to us by my grandmothers and holding community. This was no doubt the result of their having to struggle with poverty and racism. We learned from them that the society in which we lived contained resources that we needed to live a fulfilled life as well as destructive forces which were to be avoided if possible.

Religion was always at the center of family life when I was a child. My paternal grandfather was one of several ministers in my family. The Southern part of the United States is often referred to as the Bible Belt. Outside of the US South, this term often has negative connotations. Southerners are viewed as stupid, backwards, superstitious, and so on. It is quite unfortunate that many people view religion in the South as being the reactionary, hateful form that we have seen from many Trump supporters. Since Christianity was the form of religion that I grew up with, I will only discuss the form I am familiar with. While it is true that Christianity can be used to produce and support hate, it should not be reduced to that. Christianity can also be liberating and community building. Although I became an atheist in later adult life and am an agnostic now, I am not concerned here with the truth value of Christianity. My concern is strictly with its social, emancipatory, political, and existential functions.

These four concerns were also the concerns of white Christians during the time of the first Great Awakening in America. On one hand, the Christian message could be used to trick Black slaves into being more docile. On the other hand, it could be used by the slaves as a resource for the demand for freedom. C. Eric Lincoln writes: "But the main objection to the spiritual enlightenment of the Blacks derived from the fear that a slave who became a Christian might somehow claim freedom on that account."[12] Although many whites used Christianity for the purpose of slave management, many slaves eventually created a slave subculture where a more emancipatory interpretation of Christianity developed. This Black Christian subculture still lives in the South and has played a major role in shaping the Black psyche in the American South. It was as a member of this subculture that my own quest for social justice was born and nourished.

As an agnostic today, I would not want to undo my childhood religious experience. My present agnosticism is the result of religious skepticism which is a purely theoretical development. However, what is more important is the role that the Church community played in my development. The Church became an extended holding community which helped me develop the kind of confidence that I would need later in life, especially as I would encounter racism and bigotry toward the South. The Black Church was a safe place where one could freely express one's self and know that one was respected and loved. It was there that people gathered after dealing with the harsh reality of racism and economic exploitation to provide each other with recognition and assurance of their human value. The Church provided hope in what sometimes seemed to be hopeless situations. James Cone describes his childhood church experience as follows:

> I was born in Arkansas, a lynching state. During my childhood, white supremacy ruled supreme. White people were virtually free to do anything to blacks with impunity. The violent crosses of the Ku Klux Klan were a familiar reality, and white racists preached a dehumanizing segregated gospel in the name of Jesus' cross every Sunday. And yet in rural black churches I heard a different message, as preachers proclaimed the message of the suffering Jesus and the salvation accomplished in his death on the cross. I noticed how the passion and energy of the preacher increased whenever he talked about the cross, and the congregation responded with outbursts of "Amen" and "Hallelujah" that equaled the intensity of the sermon oration. People shouted, clapped their hands, and stomped their feet, as if a powerful, living reality of God's Spirit had transformed them from nobodies in white society to somebodies in the black church. This black religious experience, with all its tragedy and hope, was the reality in which I was born and raised. Its paradoxes and incongruities have shaped everything I have said and done. If I have anything to say to the Christian community in America and around the world, it is rooted in the tragic and hopeful reality that sustains and empowers black people to resist the forces that seem designed to destroy every ounce of dignity in their souls and bodies.[13]

Although things had improved a bit by the time I was born, and the Ku Klux Klan and their crosses were not as present, racism and economic struggle were still very much a part of the world that I grew up in.[14] After one's humanity had been put under erasure all week, Sunday morning was a time to have one's humanity reinstated, at least for a short while.

The reality described by Cone above was very real for my grandparents and, to some degree, my parents. My parents went to segregated schools and therefore grew up feeling the full effect of Jim Crow laws. In the midst of the experience of dehumanization the Black Church brought people together in the spirit of love and affirmation. Christian teachings provided meaning in a meaningless situation. It gave people hope and enabled them to endure the hardship of everyday life as Black and poor. My experience and connection to the Black Church and my original holding community is not theological but rather existential and political. Even today I am moved by the songs that we used to sing and I still sing them. Cone is relevant again here:

> However, the black experience as a source of theology is more than the so-called "church experience," more than singing, praying, and preaching about Jesus, God, and the Holy Spirit. The other side of the black experience should not be rigidly defined as "secular," if by that term one means the classical Western distinction between secular and sacred, for it is not antireligious or even nonreligious. This side of the black experience is secular only to the extent that it is earthy and seldom uses God or Christianity as the chief symbols of its hopes and dreams. It is sacred because it is created out of the same historical community as the church experience and thus represents the people's attempt to shape life and to live it according to their dreams and aspirations. Included in these black expressions are animal tales, tales of folk figures, slave seculars, blues, and accounts of personal experiences.[15]

Cone's point in the above quote is that although the Black experience does give birth to a particular form of theology, it is also the source of other non-church forms of expression that are still rooted in the Black experience. The blues is a good example. I believe that not only the Black experience gives birth to unique forms of expression as one tries to give shape to one's life but also the Southern experience. I will say more about that in a later section.

Let me now expound more on what I mean by "Grandma's metaphysics." The term came to me almost fifteen years ago. In a conversation with Cornel West, I was struggling to explain what seemed to be some form of religious attachment that I felt even though I was and am an agnostic. While I rejected abstract religious teachings, I realized that the religious teachings imparted to me by my grandmothers and other members of my holding community were deeply rooted in concrete experience and the struggle for survival. They developed a way of looking at and interpreting the world that made life not only bearable but also even joyful. Again, I am not concerned with the truth value of religious claims. The focus here is on their existential and social meaning. The historical truth of the exodus experience is less important than how belief in the exodus experience helps one survive. How does such belief guide one's orientation in life? I realized that although I no longer held a propositional belief in many Christian stories, they still provided a certain political and social orientation. Hence, my grandmothers, who were among my first teachers, and my original holding community were not eclipsed by Socrates and the Western philosophical tradition. In fact, as I will argue in the last section of this chapter, it was my grandmothers and my Black Southern holding community that determined not only the value of philosophy for me but also how to approach philosophy. But first, I need to address a few mis-conceptions of the American South.

The South as Scapegoat

Although it was in the South that I first encountered American racism and had to learn to navigate my life in terms of negative interpretations of Blackness, it was also there that my self-doubt was transformed into self-confidence. In the above section, I focused on the transition from self-doubt to self-confidence within the context of racism and the bonds that were created in the Black family and the Black community. Here I want to focus on the South in general, because the South in general has been the target of disrespect from other regions of the nation. Southerners are typically viewed as less intelligent than persons from other regions of the country, and white Southerners are also taken to be more racist.

The US South is a complicated and multifaceted place. Even with its racist history and continued forms of racism, it is still a place that tends toward some form of civil community. Whites and Blacks both take some degree of pride in simple, good old country living. The US South is also the victim of certain narratives that are reductionistic and fail to capture the complexities of the region. The South is often degraded by whites from other regions of the country as they seek a sense of purity over and against Southern whites. This desired purity is achieved at two levels by othering Southern whites. First, Northern whites overemphasize the racism in the South so that the racism in the North becomes less visible to them. Secondly, the othering of Southern whites creates in Northern whites a sense of pure white identity. As Shannon Sullivan has argued:

> The division between white trash and proper white people also is slip-pery, revealing how white trash operate as whiteness's abject. White trash are opposed to the proper, white subject, but their opposition is troublesome because it isn't clear, sharp or absolute. Like people of color and black people in particular, white trash are excluded from whiteness proper. But the othering of people of color and of white trash tends to happen in different ways. White trash lie uncomfort-ably closer to proper white people, threatening the dissolution of hegemonic forms of whiteness from within. Because of their white-ness, white trash threaten the coherence and identity of the proper, white subject in a related but different way than people of color gen-erally do.[16]

Although race is the primary issue addressed by Sullivan here, I want to take her analysis of the othering of whites by whites to address an attitude that goes beyond race. As one who has lived in the South and the North, I have witnessed this othering first hand. My encounter with white intellectuals and academics in the North disclosed to me a two-edged attitude to people from the South that helped whites in the North maintain their white purity. Race became a tool such that even when it was not spoken of it was still present.

In August of 1996, I assumed my first academic post at a university in Philadelphia, Pennsylvania. I remember meeting a colleague from another department. He asked me where I was raised. When I said South Carolina, he looked at me as if to pity me and then asked, "What was it like down there?" It was clear to me that he was talking about racism in the South. The tone of his voice indicated to me that he was creating a distance between himself and the "white racists" in the South. His question to me was a means of othering the white Southerner. Invisible to him were the very visible forms of racism and segregation in Philadelphia.

In 2008 I accepted a job offer from the University of Kentucky. In the summer of 2008, my children and I vacationed at a progressive camp in New Hampshire. We have visited this place every summer since 2000. Most of the guests are progressive or liberal whites from Boston, New York, New Jersey, and Philadelphia. When my friends got the news that I was moving to Kentucky, they all wondered, "Why would he move down there?" I found myself having to defend my move to a bunch of white people who were looking at me as if I had lost my mind. My last visit to this camp was the summer of 2018. Ten years after my move to Kentucky, people were still looking at me with deep concern in their eyes as they asked, "So, how are things in Kentucky?" The degree to which these progressives and liberals expressed their disdain for the South was astonishing. This disdain for the South originates in a narrative wherein white Southerners are demonized so that white liberals and progressives in the North can give themselves more credit than they deserve. That is, by locating racism in the South, Northern whites do not have to recognize the subtle forms of racism in their own backyard. The South becomes a scapegoat that allows Northern whites to feel good about themselves.

When I lived in Philadelphia, I found that neighborhoods were as segregated as they are in the South. Middle-class white neighborhoods were cleared after a snowfall much quicker and more thoroughly than Black neighborhoods. Schools in white suburbs were much better funded than schools in Black neighborhoods.[17] Blacks in the North are still subject to police brutality and racial profiling as much as or perhaps more than in the South. Somehow all of this goes unnoticed by my white liberal and progressive friends. Much of the violence done to Blacks in the North takes place in the isolated ghettos of the North where whites dare to tread. As James Cone explains:

> No one can understand the full meaning of Malcolm X's nightmare
> without first gaining an awareness of what black's lives were like in

the urban ghettos of the North prior to and during Malcolm's life. The great migration of blacks from the rural South to the urban North, which began before the First World War and continued through the 1950s, marked a significant change in the context and texture of their lives. The contrast between what blacks expected to find in the "promised land" of the North and what they actually found there was so great that frustration and despair ensued, destroying much of their self-esteem and dignity.[18]

Cone continues to talk in more detail about the lack of freedom and the ghetto experience of Blacks in the North. On another occasion he writes: "However, when King took his nonviolent movement to Chicago and failed at almost every point, because he and Black preachers failed to analyze the complexity and depth of northern racism, it began to dawn upon many radical Black preachers that King's approach had serious limitations."[19] Cone's point is that the North is no less racist than the South. In the North there was and is a subtle, quiet racism that operates beneath the surface but became very visible when King attempted to integrate certain neighborhoods in Chicago.

There are two things that are worth noticing with regards to scapegoating the South. First, the Northerners to whom I refer here live in a bubble of protection which then creates a certain form of ignorance about the South and even their own cities. Second, their narrative of the South is overly simplistic and fails to adequately represent the South. Regarding the first, many Northern liberals live in neighborhoods with people just like them. They live in a bubble of liberal or progressive, well-intentioned white people who are perhaps truly antiracist, but they maintain a safe distance from the real daily struggles of Black people in their own cities. They tend to be acquainted with a few Black people who live in their neighborhood and belong to some of the same social groups. The camp that I discussed is populated by white people from very similar neighborhoods in Boston, New York, New Jersey, and Philadelphia. The small number of Black people who attend this camp are people like me: a handful of highly educated and professional Blacks who basically work and live in completely white spaces.

Interestingly, it is in Kentucky where I experienced more activism than I did in the North. For poor white people in the South, more is at stake than for middle-class liberals in the North. In Kentucky people are fighting against lingering racism, but people of different races have also come together to fight against mountaintop removal, poverty, and diseases such as black lung disease caused by working in the coal mines, among other things.

The second problem deals with the overly simplistic narrative about the South. While it is true that the South is greatly racialized and that its history is tainted with the blood of slaves and brutalized Black people, it is also true that the South has always been engaged in a struggle with its own demons. The South cannot be completely defined by racism. Many white abolitionists and participants in the civil rights movement were white Southerners. In many areas of the South, there are bonds of solidarity between Blacks and whites. One of the positive results of integration was that, once whites and Blacks could go to school together, face-to-face interaction began to dissolve the negative stereotypes by which white people defined Black people. Although racism and some stereotypes remain, it is still the case that relationships between Blacks and whites have improved.

The Wisdom of Socrates Meets the Wisdom of Grandma: Healthy Southern Skepticism and Philosophy from Below

Finally, let me address how being a Southerner and Black has impacted my own approach to philosophy. I can only speak for myself here. My Southern upbringing has produced in me a form of skepticism that goes hand in hand with a form of self-confidence. Central to that and my philosophical orientation has been Grandma's metaphysics. From the beginning, philosophy for me was a tool to be used in the struggle for freedom and self-respect.

I took my first philosophy class as a sophomore in college. My decision to major in philosophy was the result of a feeling of liberation that fell upon me as I studied and engaged in classroom discussion. The new form of critical reflection that I was now engaged in put a wedge between me and my original holding community to the extent that I became dissatisfied with the religious teachings of my holding community. I was not yet mature enough to understand the existential, social, and political resources that had been given to me by some of those teachings. At that time the objective truth value of religious belief was more important. Hence, my first form of skepticism was skepticism about religious belief.

When I went to graduate school, self-doubt about my Southernness developed. Although I was in Kentucky, many people whom I met were from other regions of the country. My first job was in Philadelphia, which only exacerbated the problem. However, philosophy was to be an equalizer that would prove my intelligence in spite of being Southern. To prove myself worthy of the mantle of philosopher, I found myself moving farther away from my roots. Submerging myself deeper into the Western philosophical tradition allowed me to redefine myself beyond my Blackness and Southernness. However, the Western philosophical tradition and the academic world in which I lived seemed to ignore the ultimate concerns of my original holding community. In fact, as I discovered the racism of which some of our most cherished philosophers were guilty, I couldn't help but think about my grandmothers. To discover that Immanuel Kant (on whom I wrote half my dissertation) would not consider my grandmothers fully human was more than I could stand. I found myself needing to return to the teachings of my holding community. I flipped the script so that it would not be Kant or any other white male philosopher who determined the value of my grandmothers; my grand-mothers would determine the worthiness of Western philosophy.

To know thyself is to get to the root of who one is and how one became so. The wisdom of Socrates is a wisdom developed in response to curiosity. Such wisdom is a luxury. The wisdom of Grandma is a wisdom developed in response to the need to survive. Such wisdom is a necessity. In the subtitle to this section I use the term "philosophy from below." When I apply this term to the South and to Black people, I do not literally mean that Black people and Southerners are below anyone. I simply mean that if philosophy is really going to address the human condition, it must come down to where people live, move, and have their being. It cannot dwell in ivory towers. Prior to now, the Southern experience has not often been a topic of philosophical inquiry; nevertheless, it is a part of the human condition that philosophers make claims about. The human experience is not an experience in general. It always occurs at a specific time and place among particular human indi-viduals and communities. Being Black and Southern need not be viewed as a liability but instead can be appreciated as a rich resource to be used in advancing philosophical discourse.

Notes

1. Iris Marion Young, *Inclusion and Democracy* (New York: Oxford Univer-sity Press, 2002), 16.

2. Plato, *Apology*, in *Five Dialogues: Euthyphro, Apology, Crito, Meno, Pha-edo*, trans. G. M. A. Grube (Indianapolis, IN.: Hackett Publishing Company, 1981), 41.

3. Plato, *Charmides*, in *Plato: Collected Dialogues Including the Letters*, ed. Edith Hamilton and Huntington Cairns (Princeton, NJ: Princeton University Press, 1963), 110.

4. Karl Marx, *The German Ideology* (Amherst, NY: Prometheus Books, 1998), 42.

5. Charles Mills, *Blackness Visible: Essays on Philosophy and Race* (Ithaca, NY: Cornell University Press, 1998), 8.

6. Frederick Douglass, *My Bondage and My Freedom* (New York: Penguin Books, 2003), 30–31.

7. Cynthia Willett, *Maternal Ethics and Other Slave Moralities* (New York: Routledge, 1995), 170.

8. Frederick Douglass, *My Bondage*, 33.

9. Frederick Douglass, *My Bondage*, 32–33.

10. See Jessica Benjamin, *The Bonds of Love: Psychoanalysis, Feminism, and the Problem of Domination* (New York: Pantheon Books, 1988), 22. D. W. Win-nicott describes the holding phase as follows: "During the holding phase other processes are initiated; the most important is the dawn of intelligence and the beginning of a mind as something distinct from the psyche. From this follows the whole story of the secondary processes and of symbolic functioning, and of the organization of a personal psychic content, which forms a basis for dreaming and for living relationships." See D. W. Winnicott, "The Theory of Parent-Infant

Relationships," in *Essential Papers on Object Relations,* ed. Peter Buckley (New York: New York University Press, 1986), 241.

11. I have borrowed the term "epistemic community" from Charles Mills and Lorraine Code. In his critique of the Cartesian knower, Mills points out that knowledge is social and the idea of the "autonomous knower" needs to be replaced by the idea of a "community of knowers." Mills goes on to cite Code: "To a much greater extent than the examples commonly taken to illustrate epistemological points might lead one to believe, people are dependent, at a fundamental level, upon other people . . . for what they, often rightly, claim to know. . . . Far from being autonomous in the senses discussed above, knowledge is an interpersonal product that requires communal standards of affirmation, correction, and denial for its very existence. So a study of the workings of epistemic community is as important a focus of epistemological inquiry as is an analysis of perception- and memory-based knowledge claims." See Charles Mills, *Blackness Visible*, 33.

12. C. Eric Lincoln, *Race, Religion, and the Continuing American Dilemma* (New York: Hill and Wang, 1999), 43.

13. James H. Cone, *The Cross and the Lynching Tree* (Maryknoll, NY: Orbis Books, 2015), xv.

14. Economic struggle was also a daily reality for most white people. There were moments when Blacks and whites could find some solidarity regarding economic struggle.

15. James H. Cone, *God of the Oppressed* (New York: Seabury Press, 1975), 23.

16. Shannon Sullivan, *Good White People: The Problem with Middle-Class White Anti-Racism* (Albany: SUNY Press, 2014), 32.

17. For an informative analysis of inequalities in the funding of education, see Jonathan Kozol, *Savage Inequalities: Children in America's Schools* (New York: Harper Perennial, 1992).

18. James Cone, *Martin and Malcolm and America: A Dream or a Nightmare* (Maryknoll, NY: Orbis Books, 1992), 89–90.

19. James Cone, *For My People: Black Theology and the Black Church* (Maryknoll, NY: Orbis Books, 1990), 56.

Bibliography

Benjamin, Jessica. *The Bonds of Love: Psychoanalysis, Feminism, and the Problem of Domination.* New York: Pantheon Books, 1988.

Cone, James H. *The Cross and the Lynching Tree.* Maryknoll, NY: Orbis Books, 2015.

Cone, James H. *For My People: Black Theology and the Black Church.* Maryknoll, NY: Orbis Books, 1990.

Cone, James H. *God of the Oppressed.* New York: Seabury Press, 1975.

Cone, James H. *Malcolm and Martin: A Dream or a Nightmare.* Maryknoll, NY: Orbis Books, 1992.

Douglass, Frederick. *My Bondage and My Freedom.* New York: Penguin Books, 2003.

Kozol, Jonathan. *Savage Inequalities: Children in America's Schools.* New York: Harper Perennial, 1992.

Lincoln, C. Eric. *Race, Religion, and the Continuing American Dilemma.* New York: Hill and Wang, 1999.

Marx, Karl. *The German Ideology*. New York: Prometheus Books, 1998.

Mills, Charles. *Blackness Visible: Essays on Philosophy and Race*. Ithaca, NY: Cornell University Press, 1998.

Plato. *Charmides*. In *Plato: Collected Dialogues Including the Letters*, edited by Edith Hamilton and Huntington Cairns. Princeton: Princeton University Press, 1963.

Plato. *Apology*. In *Plato: Five Dialogues*, translated by G. M. A. Grube. Indianapolis, IN: Hackett Publishing Company, 1981.

Sullivan, Shannon. *Good White People: The Problem with Middle-Class White Anti-Racism*. Albany: SUNY Press, 2014.

Willett, Cynthia. *Maternal Ethics and Other Slave Moralities*. New York: Routledge, 1995.

Winnicott, D. W. "The Theory of Parent-Infant Relationships." In *Essential Papers on Object Relations*, edited by Peter Buckley. New York: New York University Press, 1986.

Young, Iris Marion. *Inclusion and Democracy*. New York: Oxford University Press, 2002.

Part II

Southern Borders

4

✦

Are You a Yankee?

Purity, Identity, and "the Southern"

Michael J. Monahan

In the early 1990s I spent a summer in the town of my birth, living with my grandparents and working as a tree trimmer to save up money for school. The town in question lies just north of the Ohio River, due west of Louisville, Kentucky, in Harrison County, Indiana. One morning early in the summer, as I was driving one of our crew members to our work site, he turned to me, gave me a long steady look, and asked, "Are you a *Yankee*?" Now, for those not familiar with this portion of the "Midwest" of the United States, there is a relatively clear division between the north and south of Illinois, Indiana, and Ohio. This division is in part topographical, with the northern parts being quite flat and the southern parts very hilly. That division is complemented by a further, and equally pronounced, cultural division. South of Springfield or Indianapolis or Columbus, there are readily apparent changes in accent and cuisine, for instance, such that one may find that one is not simply in the southern part of one of these states, but that one is in *The South*. Indeed, many people in this area self-identify as Southerners. This fact may well raise an eyebrow or two in Mobile or Memphis, but it explains why this coworker pegged me as an interloper on my natal soil.

The purpose of this autobiographical vignette is to raise questions about Southernness. If my coworker and I could be from the same place, yet he be a Southerner and I a Yankee, what does it mean to be Southern? If, as is the case, the natives of my current home, Memphis, Tennessee, would chuckle (and perhaps offer a consoling "bless your heart") to hear my coworker refer to any part of Indiana as "the South," what could the term be picking out? To complicate things further, folks from Mississippi seem not at all convinced that Tennessee is *really* Southern, so there appears to operate a core-periphery distinction even *within* the South in the US context. One way to resolve the issue might be through appeal to the US Civil War of the 1860s, such that "the South" simply refers to those states and territories that were part of the Confederate States of America (with the rest of the country being either "the North" or "the West"), but this is unsatisfying for reasons I will develop below. Further, the particular role that "the South" plays in the larger imaginary in the United States and beyond shares important features with the concept of the "Global South," which I will argue indicates that at least part of Southernness as a concept has to do more with relations of power than geography: center to margin, dominant to subordinate, *political* North to *political* South. Working my way from a more global set of questions back to the particularity of the US context, my argument in this chapter will be that a key feature of the concept of the South (and the North) is a dialectical relation organized around a hierarchical normative structure situating the North and the Northern in a position of superiority *as such*. Ultimately, it is a dialectic predicated upon pretentions to *purity*; Northern and Southern, as well as the North and the South, are maintained in their relation through mutual acts of exclusion and purification.

Geography, Coloniality, and Metaphor: North and South as Global

The term "Global South" has come relatively recently to replace categorization schemas that relied either on political divisions or relations to poverty. Prior to the collapse of the Soviet Union, common parlance divided the globe into first, second, and third "worlds" based upon each country's status as a global superpower or ally (first world), satellite nation of a superpower (second world), or nation who was either not a significant "player" in the Cold War at all or served as a proxy and venue for that larger struggle (third world). This categorization scheme persisted for a while after 1990 but was gradually replaced by a division into "developed" and "developing," where the former term referred to industrialized and wealthy nation states and the latter to impoverished nations. Increasingly, the terminology of development has been replaced with the distinction between the Global North and the Global South. Thus, what was once the "third world" became the "developing world" and is now most commonly known as the "Global South." The idea, in theory, is that this is a more empowering term (for those in the South) because it is less hierarchical than the first-third world terminology, and less evolutionary or teleological than the developed-developing world schema.[1] There is an academic journal called *The Global South*, centers at universities dedicated to the study of the Global South, and the term is widely used in NGO circles. By far, "the Global North-South" has become the favored terminology by which to refer to the principal division of the globe—the haves and the have-nots or the powerful and the disempowered.

One question that quite clearly emerges from this shift in our lexicon, however, has to do with the association of the South with the *negative* end of this binary relation. What is it about poverty, marginalization, disempower-ment, and lack of "development" that suggests "South?" Put differently, why does it seem so "natural" to associate the powerless with the South and the powerful with the North that it would strike most of us as simply "off" to do otherwise? Imagine if, in an effort to subvert the dominant paradigm of normative geographical orientation, there had been an attempt to call the dominant countries "the Global South" and the impoverished countries "the Global North." It seems hard to credit that there would be much uptake of this nomenclature, and so the effort would have stalled. This is because, I am suggesting, "the South" is obviously the "backwards" part of the equation once we are committed to this terminology.

Perhaps this problematic can be avoided if the term is not meant in the normative sense at all but is simply a descriptive accounting of the global distribution of resources. Insofar as the bulk of the world's impoverished nation-states lies south of the thirtieth parallel north,[2] then clearly the poorer part of the world is the southern part. Even within Europe, the northern countries (Denmark and Germany, for instance) tend to be richer than the southern countries (like Spain and Greece). Of course, like any such effort to impose a binary categorical framework, there are some notable excep-tions (such as Australia and New Zealand), but overall this seems plausible, and insofar as it eschews a teleological concept of development, perhaps it is indeed a more "empowering" terminology. Furthermore, the northern part of the globe is, after all, the "here" from which those NGOs, think tanks, and research centers offer their analyses and implement their policies, so it seems only natural that they refer to the object of these studies and interventions as "the South." I submit, however, that this is not a satisfactory explanation, and that it obscures some very important features of this discursive shift.

Let me begin by making an appeal to another form of geographic termi-nology often used to subcategorize the globe. The familiar concept of "the West" is still very much in use and serves a very similar function to "the North." The two are even largely coextensive, with the clearest exceptions being China, Japan, and South Korea, all of which are part of the Global North but not part of the West. Unlike the North-South divide, however, the East-West divide has been subjected to sustained and rigorous critical scrutiny by scholars stretching back decades. Edward Said's articulation of "Orientalism," for example, points out how "the East" is very much a kind of discursive creation of "the West," which in this very act of describing (inscrib-ing) "the Orient" was constituting itself *as* "Western."[3]

Walter Mignolo's work emphasizes how the historical shift of the center *around* which the Western world came to *orient* its notions of East and West shifted over time from Jerusalem to Europe (or, in the case of the Anglophone world, to Greenwich, England, in particular). He explores this shift to show how the principal function of the division has always been to establish this *normative* center as such, rather than to observe simple descriptive divisions in the world.[4] The general account advanced by these scholars, and carried forward by many others in the decades since they began their work, is one in which "the West," as represented in the first instance by Christendom, then by Europe, came to establish itself *as such* in and through the act of articulating the "Oriental" or "Eastern" other, whose exclusion articulated the boundaries of these newly constituted collectives. In other words, Europe becomes Europe (as opposed to just a collection of sovereign states sharing more or less contiguous territory) by describing and contrasting itself with what is *not* Europe. This process, during the colonial era and into the early years of the twentieth century, expanded to include what would become the United States, Canada, Australia, and New Zealand as the Indigenous peoples of those continents were subjected to genocide and displacement by colonizers from "the West" and their descendants, who most decidedly continued to think of themselves as Westerners in precisely this sense even if they did not necessarily continue to think of themselves as "European."[5]

There is a similar operation at work in the "Global South" terminology. The "Global North" constitutes itself as such in and through its juridical and discursive evocation of the "Global South."[6] The turn to a strictly geographical nomenclature in this instance has the appearance of being natural, neutral, and purely descriptive—it is merely a geographic fact, or at least a general geographic trend, after all. However, the apparent naturalness belies a deep-seated historical contingency and normativity in the very drawing of the distinction, even in geographical terms. As in the case with "the West," the division is not about a line being drawn as if from outside or beyond the relation being identified but rather about the generation of the *center*—the "where" *from which* the perspective that draws the distinction originates. The West is west of somewhere, as is the East, and as must be the North and the South. The use of apparently descriptive terminology effectively obscures this normative centering and the histories and ongoing political relations that inform and legitimate it. It is not simply the case that, for example, those conducting research on global poverty or "development" studies working in and supported by institutions located in wealthy and powerful nation-states happen to find themselves north of the thirtieth parallel and thus coin the term "Global South" in their efforts to diagnose the failures of their objects of study. There are, rather, long histories of colonial depredation, resource extraction, environmental pillaging, political manipulation, and cultural destruction that generate the very distinction that "North-South" is meant to capture. Europe came over time to designate itself as the "here" from which the future course of humanity would be set, leading to shifts in cartography that began to orient maps with the North at the "top," and turned its gaze to "the South" as it sought resources to exploit and lands to settle. This is, I argue, a significant part of the answer to the question of why the "North-South" terminology found such easy and "natural" uptake. The apparently "descriptive" appeal to simple geographical terminology, in other words, hides the ways in which those in the Global North are beneficiaries of centuries-long projects of the impoverishment of the Global South, which projects are, in various ways, ongoing and all too often in the guise of "aid."[7]

The underlying concern here is that the North-South divide perpetuates long-standing colonial practices and relations that are obscured behind allegedly neutral, descriptive, and geographical nomenclature. It is no accident, in other words, that the Global North is largely comprised of colonial powers and their settler-state progeny (the United States and Australia being two obvious examples), while the Global South is made up primarily of those who suffered exploitation and colonialism in various forms. Descending as it does from colonialism and the distinctions between developing and developed and first and third world, the North-South divide maintains the Global North as the standard against which the Global South must be measured and, inevitably, found wanting. As Sylvia Wynter puts the point with respect to the intimate connection between colonial projects and the enlightenment conceptions of the human being, those from what became "the Global South" were not viewed as exhibiting different ways of being human "but rather [came to be understood] as the Lack of what they [European colonizers] themselves were; as such, as the 'vile Race' Other to *their* 'true' humanness, the evil nature as opposed to their 'good natures.' "[8] The Global North has thus implicitly endorsed itself as the standard against which human development and achievement must be measured even as it has come to eschew the explicit use of the term "development" in its academic lexicon.

This distinction between those who are fully realized and those who are in progress and in some way lacking is represented in part in the historical division between the "modern" and the "traditional." Modern societies are future oriented and characterized by a developmental trajectory while traditional societies are stuck in the past and locked in a stasis of obedience to a tradition that rules out any kind of change or development, according to this view. The modern, as Lewis Gordon argues, is understood as belonging to the future, such that those who are modern are justified in displacing those who, through their *lack* of this future orientation, have become, in effect, the deadweight of human development.[9] The terminology of "developing" and "developed" worlds is clearly predicated upon precisely this distinction and was rightly rejected for the way in which it carried forward this colonial distinction. However, as Caroline Levander and Walter Mignolo argue, "In a nutshell, the 'Global South' (like democracy, development, and many other concepts) is now the place of struggles between, on the one hand, the rhetoric of modernity and modernization together with the logic of coloniality and domination, and, on the other, the struggle for independent thought and decolonial freedom."[10] Thus, the claim here is that the North-South divide is ultimately yet another iteration of the modern-traditional dichotomy, which in turn is constitutively linked to colonial worldviews in which the colonizers, as the representatives of modernity and thus the future of the species, have an imperative to lead or direct those who are "premodern" into the project of modernity where such a move is possible, and to displace them utterly when it is not.[11]

As a consequence, it is important to question, with Sinah Kloß, whether the terminology of the "Global South" is no more than a "fashionable buzzword that legitimizes new research" in institutions (mostly in the Global North) whose organizational structure and guiding *ethos* is increasingly modeled after multinational corporations as institutions of education and research globally fall to the predations of neoliberal logics.[12] The North can in this way satisfy itself that its goals and methods are pure by studying the Global South as a site of *failure* or *lack*. To be sure, poverty, political instability, environmental devastation, disease, and malnutrition are all very real problems that demand serious study. The idea here is not that these should be ignored or normalized. Rather, what Kloß and others are pointing out is the problem of seeing these very real problems as problems *of* the Global South rather than as problems resulting in large part from the historical and continuing projects of resource extraction, exploitation, and domination on the part of the Global North. What the analyses of Levander, Mignolo, and Wynter point out are that these projects were also projects wherein Europe, the first world, the developed world, and the Global North all constituted themselves *as such*, and that this process of self-constitution is predicated upon a denigrated and dominated *Other*.

Wynter offers a compelling way to understand the historical development of this binary relation between center and periphery that serves as the model for the contemporary discourse of North-South. Her basic story, put very briefly, is something like this: The project of European modernity emerged out of the medieval period and came to articulate itself *as European* in part through appeals in the first instance to *Orientalism*—to a heathen, backwards, and decadent other in contrast to their own progressive Christianity. The primary division was thus between Christendom and the Pagan-Heathen. The colonial enterprises of the emerging modern European nation-states allowed for a rearticulation of this fundamental distinction in terms of *rationality*. The Christian thus became the "*rational Man*,"[13] the bearer of civilization, progress, and the light of reason to the benighted, *dark* corners of the earth and the irrational "savages" who populated them. In time, scientific development, and especially developments in evolutionary biology, linked this telos of progress and rationality to one's inherent biological makeup in the form of *race*, such that the rational gifts of colonizing Europe were innate, and that the displacement and exploitation of colonized non-Europeans was simply a feature of natural selection and, in this way, a legitimate expression of the telos of European *Man*.[14] Wynter's ultimate point is that the European self-concept as *rational Man* took itself to be the norm for humanity as such, and shored up this sense of self in and through practices of the exclusion and marginalization of the debased, irrational "human Other to *Man*" understood by these Europeans first and foremost through the relation of *lack*. In short, European modernity and its settler-colonial descendants understood themselves as the fullness of the human as *rational Man* over and against those human Others to *Man* that were constitutively deficient.

This historical narrative is deeply bound up with what I have called elsewhere "the politics of purity." In short, the politics of purity refers to practices and methods that have a kind of conceptual *purity* as their ultimate aim.[15] In this instance, the purity in question is bound up in a particular view of rationality and the conception of the human to which it is so intimately connected. It is a "politics" of purity because that ideal of purity demands an ongoing political intervention for its maintenance. Thus, if the essential or defining feature of humanity is *reason*, understood first and foremost as the capacity to put oneself and one's larger environment to good use (in a vaguely Lockean sense), and the European-cum-"white" is the purest or highest manifestation of reason (and thus of civilization, progress, and modernity), then the European (and their later settler-colonial descendants) is the *purest* manifestation of the human as such. Given this understanding of reason, in fact, one best demonstrates one's rationality through the control or domination of one's environment. Thus, rational individuals control their instincts, drives, and "natural" inclinations *internally*, and control those nonrational or less rational elements that surround them *externally*. This includes not only the world of objects but the world of less rational humans. To fail to be in control is to fail to be fully rational, and so those who are rational face the imperative to assume control or risk being controlled by the more rational. In this way, we can see that the colonial logic of domination is a manifestation of the politics of purity. The colonizers encounter others who they interpret to be part of, rather than in control of, their environment, and thus demonstrating a corrupted or impure rational capacity. If those colonizers should fail in their turn to assume control—to dominate—then their own rationality, too, must be called into question. Thus, as I have argued elsewhere, they face in effect an *imperative* to colonize as a means to demonstrate and maintain their status as the purest manifestation of reason and thus humanity.[16]

However, purity in these cases is only ever mythological. Engagement with reality always tends toward ambiguity and what I describe as processes of "creolization." Scratch the surface of any alleged purity and one will find a disavowed or hidden mixture. This is why the politics of purity demands an ongoing practice on the part of those who hold purity dear. The only way to maintain the idea that a given nation-state, for example, is a single, discrete, and "pure" entity is through a misreading of its history and the porous, ambiguous, and often *mixed* status of its present. The same is true with notions of North and South. The idea of the "Global South" is clearly the inheritor of the status of Wynter's "human Other to *Man*." Those who fail to measure up to the standards of rationality, expressed increasingly in terms

of economic development and "success" measured in terms of material productivity, in effect emerge as the raw material through which those who take
themselves to be the purest manifestation of reason can demonstrate that
purity. The control they assume can be more or less direct, through World
Bank or International Monetary Fund austerity measures, for instance, or it
can be indirect, through reducing the less rational to the status of objects for
study and theorization on the part of the more rational. The North defines
itself (or, for those more phenomenologically inclined, *constitutes itself*) as
the pure and normative center against which all of humanity must measure
itself (and be found lacking). The geographical and descriptive pretensions
are simply an effort to obscure this underlying commitment to establishing
and maintaining the myth of Northern purity.

This idea can be further seen in the way in which the global rhetoric of
North-South often ignores or disavows impoverished and disempowered
communities *within* the Global North. It is not as if the nation-states of the
Global North are utopic polities of perfect prosperity and equality. Indeed,
the rise of conservative or authoritarian populism throughout much of the
Global North in the present moment can be understood in large part as a
reactionary response to the crisis those nation-states face as a result of the
increasingly restive "Southern" *within*. As I have already mentioned, one
can see this at the continental level with respect to Northern and Southern
Europe, but also within Northern European nation-states such as, most notably, France and Germany. This presence of a South within the North has led
some scholars to pursue critical work in "Global South Studies" focusing
on "the South" within the United States and at the same time leading US
scholars in "Southern studies" to move in a direction more sensitive to transnational linkages.[17] This chapter is a contribution to this literature in a sense,
though approaching it as part of a philosophical project focused upon what I
will argue are very deep *conceptual* linkages between the two.

As we can already see, the problematic with which I opened regarding
the exact boundaries and contours of "the South" within the United States
is in some ways recapitulated in the context of the Global South. I have
argued that the North-South terminology presently in favor is a legacy of the
enlightenment-colonial ways of demarcating the modern from the traditional
and the civilized from the savage. Europeans of the sixteenth and seventeenth
centuries came to understand themselves *as European*, and as the normative
center of the ongoing historical *development* of humanity, by designating a
periphery that was at once anthropological (in the sense of philosophical
anthropology) and geographical. Absent the Orientalized other, there would
be no "West," and this mutually constituting relationship is carried on in its
basic structure in the North-South relation. The North *requires* the South
as the underdeveloped, backwards opposite to its own sense of self as the
highest and purest manifestation of humanity as a historical (in the Hegelian
sense) achievement.

There Is Always a South within the North

Let us return our focus from the global to the national, and take up again the questions raised by my opening anecdote. What can all of this tell us about what makes the US South "the South," and what makes a Southerner "a Southerner" and a Northerner "a Yankee"? To be sure, any Southerner is likely to resist the idea that their being is in some sense reducible to a negative relation with the North, or in some way a product of the Northern imaginary. And well they should. The idea that the South is a distinct region in its own right goes back to the original thirteen colonies. The southern colonies of English North America were economically directed more toward plantation models of production than their northern neighbors, including notably the reliance on vast numbers of enslaved laborers and the development of large-scale cash crop production. Most northern colonies, and later states, though not all of them, certainly permitted the ownership of human beings, but the plantation-based economic model of the Southern states set the course for their development along a markedly different trajectory from the North. Indeed, this use of large numbers of enslaved laborers on large plantations devoted to cash crops makes the case that the US South has more than a little kinship with the Caribbean.[18] This, paired with particularities in terms of European colonization and immigration, resulted in the development of cultural norms and practices that certainly have regional specificities but are nonetheless in some way distinctively "Southern."

It is, however, the US Civil War of 1861 to 1865 that, in the present, seems to most define "the South" in the larger US imaginary. One straightforward move would be to define the South as those states which were once part of the Confederate States of America (CSA). Might this not provide a relatively descriptive and objective way to determine what the South is? I do not think so. First, there were areas where Confederate sympathies were dominant (including the practice of slavery), but Union control was maintained by fiat or force, such as Maryland, Kentucky, and Missouri. Simply ruling those places out because they were not part of the CSA seems unsatisfactory. Second, as already discussed, the divide between the North and the South predates the Civil War considerably. Patterns of immigration, agricultural development, and religious practice developed along divergent trajectories beginning in the colonial era—it meant something to be a Southerner well before the war for US independence from England, let alone the Civil War nearly a century later. The third problem with simply saying that the South is coextensive with the CSA has to do with the Southernness of the enslaved and their descendants, who were, in significant ways, *in* but not *of* the CSA. Simply reducing the question of Southernness to an historical relation with the US Civil War is therefore unsatisfactory.

The South can be understood in the US context to be in part a matter of a certain historical relation to plantation economies and, above all, to enslaved labor, but the function of the term today, and the role it plays in the ways in which "Southerner" functions as an identity, cannot be captured simply through this appeal to the plantation and the slave. This is because of the way in which the ongoing *interpretation* of Southernness plays out a sort of dialectical relationship with Northernness which, though frequently (if not always) appealing to that history, transcends it in myriad ways. This does not mean that the positive content of Southernness is illusory or even parasitic upon Northernness but rather that such positive content was and continues to be developed in and out of that relation (as is any positive content of Northernness).

Food culture, music, religious life, and patterns of speech can all be traced back to the salient differences of the colonial era, including climate, patterns of European migration, interactions with Indigenous populations, and, of course, the presence of enslaved Africans and their descendants. The point of the prior discussion was not that "the South" is in the end nothing more than a fabrication but rather that these original differences become relevant, entrenched, and even exaggerated through the now centuries-long effort on the part of both Northerners and Southerners to draw attention to and make meaning out of those differences. Furthermore, just as the Global North comes to understand itself as the locus of rationality and progress (development), the Northern United States maintains its self-concept in a similar fashion in part by contrasting itself to the "backwards" and underdeveloped South. In the Northern imaginary, the South exists either as bucolic but hopelessly antiquated and stagnant, or as irredeemably steeped in and the source of all our political ills; it is racist, xenophobic, patriarchal, religiously intolerant, and authoritarian. Indeed, the racism, inequality, environmental degradation, and injustices of Northern states can be effectively ignored or disavowed because these ills are all in fact *constitutive* of the South.[19] If *we* could only sort out the mess that is the Southern states, we could redeem *our* country. It is no accident that Southern studies, as an academic field, has virtually no representation in the Northern United States[20]—Northerners already know all they need to know about the South, so what is there to study?

The South, at the same time, cultivates its own self-concept in which a relationship to the North plays a significant role. This is in part a matter of simple contrast. There is the specificity of cuisine, of course, and of the larger culture, including music and language in particular, along with a valorization of politeness (which by no means always equates with friendliness), all of which is surely bound up in stereotypes but not reducible to them. It was, for instance, impossible to get a decent biscuit in Milwaukee, and addressing people with a title and their first name (i.e., Mr. Mike, Ms. Sally) is most definitely a Southern norm quite peculiar to the Northern ear. The sense of Southern identity transcends racial distinction, often more so than many Southerners themselves recognize. There are certainly differences across race, as there are across regions, but in many cases these differences are a result of disavowal of shared root practices mixed with an often explicit Jim Crow program of segregating cultural expressions along with the people who participate in them. Southern culinary folkways, to return to a favorite example, are, of course, varied, but more similar across racial lines than dissimilar. Music, likewise, is often more creolized than people realize, especially historically, and what segregation there is results from efforts on the part of white Jim Crow producers and marketers of music to exorcise the Blackness from blues and gospel (yielding country).[21] Significantly, the differences across the races grow less distinct when one focuses on impoverished communities. It is a deep truth that poor whites often have as much if not more in common with poor Blacks than wealthy whites culturally speaking, but systematic racism often obscures this fact. Indeed, understood in this way, we can see how the great migrations of African Americans in the early twentieth century to the Northern industrial cities was also a migration of *Southerners* to those cities, a fact which is often overlooked in discussions of this important historical moment.

By no means should this suggest that race is marginal or unimportant in understanding North-South relations in the United States. As already mentioned, the North, in centering itself, tends to reduce racism to an essentially Southern problem, disavowing its own profound racism.[22] As for the Southern self-concept, it must, in effect, be understood as having two modes: one is profoundly segregated; the second mode is this larger set of Southern cultural norms that often transcends race, even if this is often ignored or disavowed. This is only part of the picture, however. There is a strong thread of specifically white Southern identity that is bound up with a sense of Northern domination and resentment of and resistance to that domination. This sense of a Northern boot always upon one's neck is a thread woven deeply into the specifically white Southern fabric, and is no doubt bound up intimately with the "lost cause" revisionist history of the Civil War.[23] The preponderance of public monuments to the Confederacy is, without doubt, a celebration of white supremacy, but it is also a constant reminder to white Southerners that "we" fought the good fight, and may have lost, but one day the Northern yoke shall be thrown off for good. This is the aspect of Southern identity that led my white coworker to call me out as a Yankee. In this way he tied me to a larger narrative of Northern interlopers paternalistically meddling in (and often profiting from) white Southern affairs.

Interestingly, this latter view can even go so far as to portray the South as a "colony" of the North. There is a sense in which, as Jon Smith points out, the US South was a site for at least three kinds of colonialism.[24] There was, first, the original settler colonialism that included the genocide and displacement of Indigenous people, the enslavement and transport of millions of Africans, and the imposition of a Black-white binary. Second, the predominantly Southern white view of the Civil War and Reconstruction as Northern aggression and domination. Third was, ironically, the Jim Crow assertion of white domination as a response to Reconstruction, which generated a kind of internal colonization and which, in turn, links the civil rights movement of the 1950s and 1960s to global decolonial struggle. While the second sense is problematic to put it mildly, the original colonization and the imposition of Jim Crow both draw important attention to the way in which the South has always been, since the sixteenth-century Spanish colonization of Florida, a site of anticolonial resistance. Indigenous resistance, maronnage, slave rebellions, labor struggles, and the struggle for civil rights all exemplify a resistance to the plantocracy, to enslavement, racism, and economic exploitation (sometimes all at once). Thus, when Levander and Mignolo claim that the Global South is a site for "the struggle for independent thought and decolonial freedom," these histories (and current times) of resistance in the South make a clear case for the link between the US South and the Global South. Nevertheless, as Smith points out, "Politically, because of the United States' winner-take-all electoral system, the US South may be said to run the world."[25] Smith's view is that the domination of the US political system by white Southerners places this sense of the US South as part of the Global South in an ambiguous position. Of course, given the ongoing realities of racial jerrymandering and black disenfranchisement (both formal and informal), it is the *white* South about which Smith is clearly speaking.

It is also worth noting that there is yet a justifiable resentment of the North on the part of nonwhite Southerners, as well. The roots of this resentment extend back to at least the antebellum federal support of slavery (including especially the Fugitive Slave Act) and the forced displacement of Indigenous peoples, but focus in particular on the abandoned promises of reconstruction, the later aiding and abetting of Jim Crow, and the indifference to and foot-dragging with respect to the struggle for civil rights. The North, in this nonwhite Southern perspective, has much to answer for (quite probably as much as the white South), and looms as an often malevolent and occasionally indifferent outside force. Quite correctly, nonwhite Southerners observe that the rupture of the US Civil War was, as Anthony Marx argued, largely healed by building white solidarity across the North-South divide at the expense of African Americans in particular.[26] Thus, Southern whites and nonwhites alike view the North as a dominating force, though for quite different reasons.

This is why it is so crucial to recognize the politics of purity at work here. The North and the South each make sense of themselves through practices and rituals of purification. The North purifies itself morally by locating all racism and backwardness in the South, for example, thus insulating itself from a painful encounter with its own profound problems. The white South, likewise, sees its problems as a result of Northern meddling and domination rather than facing its own failings. The Black South can see the ways in which the larger US polity purifies itself by at best abandoning any commitment to the well-being of Blacks and at worst actively pursuing Black poverty and death. Above all, there is an effort to define and distinguish each from the other. The parallels to the discussion of the Global North-South divide are striking. The Northern United States functions as the modern and progressive center in relation to the impoverished and backwards Southern periphery. This center-periphery relation takes on a clear racial dimension, insofar as any "backwardness" of and in the South is linked inextricably to its *Blackness* by whites on both sides of the North-South divide. For its part, the US South shares certain features with the Global South, but as part of the United States, many of these similarities fall apart. However, as I discussed earlier, there is always a South *within* the North, and these categories are never as pure as they pretend. This is certainly true in the US context. The Northern states have deep pockets of poverty (not coincidentally linked in many cases to those historical moments of Southern migration mentioned above—a very literal South within the North) that have grown increasingly worse in the last decades, while the Southern states remain as stratified as ever by race and class; wealthy Southern whites sit comfortably in the Global North despite their Southern mannerisms, while poor folks remain at the "underdeveloped" periphery.

The upshot of all this is the idea that there are, in the end, many different ways to be Southern. Not just in the sense that "Southernness" varies from Lexington to Richmond, from Savannah to Houston, or even from Jackson, Mississippi, to Jackson, Tennessee. There certainly are real differences (though also real similarities), but what I mean instead is that one can, in what is basically an existential sense, be Southern, or relate to one's Southernness, in fundamentally different ways. There are ways to reify it, either through appeals to an idealized (and often "whitewashed") history, the positing of some innate Southern nature or essence, or by seeing the historical conflict between North and South as a defining and absolute characteristic. This way of being Southern will tend toward practices and narratives of purity, seeking both to make clear distinctions between North and South and to preserve the authentic or pure Southern character (and this latter practice will inevitably have a racialized character). This will work in a similar way, and in tandem with, similar accounts of the North and Northernness. There are alternatives, however, as I will briefly suggest in the remainder of this chapter.

Conclusion: Sites of Struggle

The relation between North and South is far more complicated, both globally and in the context of the United States, than the simple binary terminology would suggest. There is a history that at once explains and conditions the real cultural distinctions between the regions but also reveals a profound level of mutual influence, cultural "borrowing," and creolization. The idea that there is a true and pure North or South that must be defended, or brought to rise again, has only ever been a fiction developed to serve the interests of those who derive some material or psychological benefit from that appeal to a mythical purity. Again, to say that its *purity* is mythical is not to say that the very notion of Southernness is mythical, only that it is often ambiguous, changing, and never pure.

As I see it, there are two crucial lessons here. The first is that we all must attend to the ways in which the South within the North (and vice versa) belies the ideal of purity. As we saw in the discussion of the Global North, this appeal to purity serves to support an ideal of Northern modernity and development that undermines or obviates any serious engagement not only with those failures of justice *within* the North but also with the role that the North plays in the historical and ongoing *impoverishment* of the South (including, of course, the South within). In the context of the United States, this disavowal of the South within the North both misrepresents the history of and debt to the roles that Southerners played in the intellectual and cultural life of the North (as my earlier mention of the great migrations of the early twentieth century shows quite clearly) and facilitates the myth that racism and injustice are only ever Southern problems.

Second is the lesson that, when one looks beyond the white myth of Southern pure identity, one finds that the South has always been, and continues to be, a site of struggle and contestation against the forces of racism, colonialism, and exploitation. This is certainly true of Black Southern life, but there have been white, Indigenous, and Latinx Southern struggles as well. This aspect of Southern life and Southern identity needs to be brought to the foreground in our thinking about the complex relations between North and South both in the US context, globally, and our thinking about what it means to be Southern.

In the end, I still am not sure what the proper response to my coworker should have been, or should be if I were asked the same question now. That is, I would argue, because the very phrasing of the question invites a binary yes-or-no response, which is never adequate to these sorts of situations. I both am and am not "a Yankee" in a variety of different ways. And as for my coworker, his "Southernness" had as much to do with his virulent racism and commitment to a mythologized and white-supremacist Southern identity politics as it did with his place of birth, accent, or taste in cuisine. The latter factors would make *him* "a Yankee" in Memphis or Birmingham. The point here is that these claims can only be answered in this binary yes-or-no way when one has an a priori commitment to the purity of these categories (such that they do not allow for a "both" or "and" response). By undertaking this exploration of the complexity of how these larger categories of North and South function, I hope to have opened a space for that "both" or "and" response with respect to these categories, and to have raised some awareness both of their pernicious function and the ways in which they can point to vital and often overlooked sources and resources for critical resistance.

Notes

1. Andrea Wolvers et al., introduction to *Concepts of the Global South: Voices from around the World*, ed. Andrea Wolvers et al. (Cologne, Germany: Global South Studies Center, 2015), 1.

2. Jonathan Rigg, "The Global South," in *Concepts of the Global South: Voices from around the World*, ed. Andrea Wolvers et al. (Cologne, Germany: Global South Studies Center, 2015), 6–7.

3. Edward W. Said, *Orientalism* (New York: Vintage Books, 1979), 49–73.

4. Walter D. Mignolo, *The Idea of Latin America* (Malden, MA.: Blackwell Publishing, 2005). See especially chapter 1.

5. There are occasional exceptions, as in the example of the contemporary white nationalist group "Identity Europa," who make explicit appeal to the ongoing connection to Europe and Europeanness in their efforts to justify white superiority as the progenitors and rightful inheritors of "Western Civilization."

6. Roberto M. Dainotto, "Does Europe Have a South? An Essay on Borders," *The Global South* 5, no. 1 (2011): 39.

7. None of this is to imply that it is the intention of scholars who work in Global South or Development Studies to reify or legitimize these pernicious divides (often quite the contrary), nor to erase or ignore these histories of colonial and "postcolonial" domination. My point here is about the larger symbolic function of this terminology, not the individual motivations of scholars who employ these terms. Indeed, until a new and hopefully more felicitous term gains traction, it is rather hard to avoid making use of this terminology (I confess that my own authorial hands are not clean in this regard).

8. Sylvia Wynter, "On How We Mistook the Map for the Territory, and Re-Imprisoned Ourselves in Our Unbearable Wrongness of Being, of *Désêtre*: Black Studies Toward the Human Project," in *Not Only the Master's Tools: African-American Studies in Theory and Practice*, ed. Lewis R. Gordon and Jane Anna Gordon (Boulder, CO: Paradigm Publishers, 2006), 125.

9. Lewis R. Gordon, "Thinking Through Some Themes of Race and More," *Res Philosophica* 95, no. 2 (2018): 335.

10. Caroline Levander and Walter Mignolo, "Introduction: The Global South and World Dis/Order," *The Global South* 5, no. 1 (2011): 4.

11. For a more developed version of this account of modernity and coloniality, see Michael J. Monahan, "The Politics of Purity: Colonialism, Reason, and Modernity," in *The Creolizing Subject: Race, Reason, and the Politics of Purity* (New York: Fordham University Press, 2011).

12. Sinah Theres Kloß, "The Global South as Subversive Practice: Challenges and Potentials of a Heuristic Concept," *The Global South* 11, no. 2 (2017): 5.

13. Sylvia Wynter, "1492: A New World View," in *Race, Discourse, and the Origin of the Americas: A New World View*, ed. Vera Lawrence Hyatt and Rex Nettleford (Washington, DC: Smithsonian Institution Press), 13–14. This brief account uses Wynter's own terminology, which uses the masculine terminology quite deliberately.

14. Sylvia Wynter, "Unsettling the Coloniality of Being/Power/Truth/Freedom: Towards the Human, after Man, Its Overrepresentation—An Argument," *The New Continental Review* 3, no. 3 (2003): 324.

15. Monahan, *The Creolizing Subject*, 83–186.

16. Monahan, *The Creolizing Subject*, 161.

17. Annette Trefzer et al., "Introduction: The Global South and/in the Global North: Interdisciplinary Investigations," *The Global South* 8, no. 2 (2014): 1–15; Sharon Monteith, "Southern Like US?," *The Global South* 1, no. 1&2 (2007): 66–74; Jon Smith, "The U.S. South and the Future of the Postcolonial," *The Global South* 1, no. 1&2 (2007): 153–58.

18. Immanuel Wallerstein supports this contention, referring to the Southern United States as part of the "extended Caribbean." Immanuel Wallerstein, *Modern World System II: Mercantilism and the Consolidation of the European World Economy, 1600–1750* (New York: Academic, 1980), 67.

19. A clear example of this phenomenon at a key moment in its historical development can be found in Karl Hagstrom Miller's extraordinary discussion of the late-nineteenth-century links between the efforts of scholars in the then-emerging field of Folklore, the growing commercialization of music, and the mythologization of a pastoral "South." Karl Hagstrom Miller, *Segregating Sound: Inventing Folk and Pop Music in the Age of Jim Crow* (Durham, NC: Duke University Press, 2010), 85–120.

20. Monteith, "Southern like US?," 68.

21. Again, see Miller's *Segregating Sound* for a detailed and enlightening discussion of this history.

22. See Shannon Sullivan, *Good White People: The Problem with Middle-Class White Anti-Racism* (Albany: State University of New York Press, 2014) for a thorough discussion of this phenomenon.

23. For an in-depth discussion of the "lost cause" narrative, see Gary W. Gallagher and Alan T. Nolan, eds., *The Myth of the Lost Cause and Civil War History* (Bloomington: Indiana University Press, 2010).

24. Smith, "The U.S. South and the Future of the Postcolonial," 154–55.

25. Smith, "The U.S. South and the Future of the Postcolonial," 155.

26. Anthony W. Marx, *Making Race and Nation: A Comparison of South Africa, The United States, and Brazil* (New York: Cambridge University Press, 1998), 120–57.

Bibliography

Dainotto, Roberto M. "Does Europe Have a South? An Essay on Borders." *The Global South* 5, no. 1 (2011): 37–50.

Gordon, Lewis R. "Thinking Through Some Themes of Race and More." *Res Philosophica* 95, no. 2 (2018): 331–45.

Kloß, Sinah Theres. "The Global South as Subversive Practice: Challenges and Potentials of a Heuristic Concept." *The Global South* 11, no. 2 (2017): 1–17.

Levander, Caroline, and Walter Mignolo. "Introduction: The Global South and World Dis/Order." *The Global South* 5, no. 1 (2011): 1–11.

Marx, Anthony W. *Making Race and Nation: A Comparison of South Africa, The United States, and Brazil*. New York: Cambridge University Press, 1998.

Mignolo, Walter D. *The Idea of Latin America*. Malden, MA: Blackwell Publishing, 2005.

Miller, Karl Hagstrom. *Segregating Sound: Inventing Folk and Pop Music in the Age of Jim Crow*. Durham, NC: Duke University Press, 2010.

Monahan, Michael J. *The Creolizing Subject: Race, Reason, and the Politics of Purity*. New York: Fordham University Press, 2011.

Monteith, Sharon. "Southern Like US?" *The Global South* 1, no. 1&2 (2007): 66–74.

Puri, Hardeep S. "Special Report: Rise of the Global South and Its Impact on South-South Cooperation." Washington, DC: World Bank Institute. October 2010. Accessed September 7, 2018. https://openknowledge.worldbank.org /bitstream/handle/10986/6076/deor_12_2_7.pdf.

Said, Edward W. *Orientalism*. New York: Vintage Books, 1979.

Smith, Jon. "The U.S. South and the Future of the Postcolonial." *The Global South* 1, no. 1&2 (2007): 153–58.

Trefzer, Annette, Jeffrey T. Jackson, Kathryn McKee, and Kristen Dellinger. "Introduction: The Global South and/in the Global North: Interdisciplinary Investigations." *The Global South* 8, no. 2 (2014): 1–15.

Wallerstein, Immanuel. *Modern World System II: Mercantilism and the Consolidation of the European World Economy, 1600–1750*. New York: Academic Prints, Inc, 1980.

Wolvers, Andrea, Oliver Tappe, Tijo Salverda, and Tobias Schwarz, eds. *Concepts of the Global South: Voices from Around the World*. Cologne, Germany: Global South Studies Center, 2015.

Wynter, Sylvia. "1492: A New World View." In *Race, Discourse, and the Origin of the Americas: A New World View*, edited by Vera Lawrence Hyatt and Rex Nettleford, 5–57. Washington, DC: Smithsonian Institution Press, 1995.

Wynter, Sylvia. "On How We Mistook the Map for the Territory, and Re-Imprisoned Ourselves in Our Unbearable Wrongness of Being, of *Désêtre*: Black Studies Toward the Human Project." In *Not Only the Master's Tools: African-American Studies in Theory and Practice*, edited by Lewis R. Gordon and Jane Anna Gordon, 107–69. Boulder, CO: Paradigm Publishers, 2006.

Wynter, Sylvia. "Unsettling the Coloniality of Being/Power/Truth/Freedom: Towards the Human, after Man, Its Overrepresentation—An Argument." *CR: The New Continental Review* 3, no. 3 (2003): 257–337.

5

✦

Affective Economies from the Global South to the US South

Global Care Chains and Southern Sympathy Fatigue

Shiloh Whitney

Renowned sociologist Arlie Hochschild's work on "global care chains" tracks the phenomenon in which women from the Global South migrate thousands of miles for years at a time to serve as nannies and domestic workers in wealthier countries.[1] When Vicky Diaz[2] moved from her home in the Philippines to Los Angeles to care for Tommy, the two-year-old son of an affluent white family in Beverly Hills, she joined this migration pattern, one of the largest in human history.[3] Some scholars in the social sciences refer to this as a second colonization, one that mines affective resources from the Global South just as copper, gold, or zinc have been mined.[4] Many migrant women care workers have children of their own, and the work of caring for them is often passed down to still poorer women in their home countries. Not only care work, but a care deficit is passed down the global chain from North to South. The painful alienation from her own five children—some very young—that Diaz undergoes serves perversely to fuel an affective investment in the white American child she is paid to care for in Beverly Hills. "In my absence from my children," Diaz says, "the most I could do with my situation is give all my love to [Tommy]."[5] As a kind of affective labor, this work is not only the production of care for others but also the cultivation of Diaz's own disposition and persona in the service of that care. She is obliged to metabolize her own sense of loneliness and dislocation as fuel for the care she invests in her young charge in Beverly Hills.

Even where work passed down to Global Southerners involves, for instance, cleaning rather than care work, scholars in the social sciences increasingly treat it as a kind of affective or emotional labor, emphasizing that the nature of the work and the unique kinds of exploitation to which it is vulnerable cannot be fully understood without attending to its affective dimension.[6] Even service work done remotely over the phone or online that is outsourced to workers in the Global South is also increasingly understood in terms of affective labor. Kalindi Vora's study of Indian call center workers, for instance, positions this outsourced, long-distance customer service work as affective labor.[7] Call center agents, Vora writes, produce "attention, concern, and human communication" for distant customers at great affective cost to themselves and their own communities, "resulting in a net flow of affective resources to consuming nations at the expense of producing nations like India."[8]

Whence this affective cost? Since they usually must work while it is daytime in North America, the job requires long hours at night on the phone with distant customers, even as the agents miss daily life and events that are important in their local affective milieu and grow increasingly isolated from their local communities. Thus, even though Indian call center agents do not migrate spatially to countries in the Global North, their temporal dislocation produces an affective alienation from their locality in the Global South. There is also a dislocation of persona. The laboring process of Indian call center agents involves not only the production and manipulation of affects but the cultivation of a whole persona that matches the cultural and racial categories local to North American customers.[9] Call center agents are trained in a specific North American English dialect and accent, adopt a North American alias, and are instructed in the quotidian habits of North Americans. This dislocation of persona and the temporal dislocation of call center agents compound each other: even as they fall out of step temporally with the events of their local kin and communities, they spend long hours on the phone in character as their North American persona.[10] Like the Filipina nanny, the Indian call center worker must not only produce care and concerned attention for customers in the Global North; she must also cultivate a disposition and persona in the service of that work, metabolizing her own loneliness and isolation as fuel for the affective resources she invests in her customers from the Global North.

Vora joins an emerging tendency in social science research to invoke post-Marxist political philosophers Michael Hardt and Antonio Negri's notion of "biopolitical production" to frame the broader issues at stake in globalized affective labor. Hardt and Negri propose that global political economy is being reorganized such that the paradigm of work is shifting away from the production of material commodities and toward the production of information and subjectivities.[11] Seen in this framework, affective labor is not only the production of affects for others to consume but also the production of a profitable persona or marketable type of subjectivity in oneself. Hardt and Negri's "biopolitical" account of this shift situates it within an expansion of capitalism globally into the regulation of populations, and an increasing subsumption of life to labor that blurs distinctions between life and work.

If there is an emerging biopolitical regime of global political economy in which affective resources are flowing from the Global South to the Global

North, then what circulations of affect in the Global North support the coloniality of this global division of labor? If affective labor involves, not only the management of feeling to produce affects in others, but the production of a persona or form of subjectivity in oneself, what forms of subjectivity are being produced in this global political economy, not only in Global Southerners who migrate but also in Global Northerners who do not?

In her most recent project *Strangers in Their Own Land: Anger and Mourning on the American Right*, the sociologist Arlie Hochschild travels to the US South, to the red state of Louisiana, to understand the emotional landscape of the Tea Partier-cum-Trump supporter. A key feature of the emotional "deep story" she finds in this ethnography is "sympathy fatigue": "Liberals want us to feel sympathy for blacks, women, the poor, and of course I do up to a point," one interviewee tells Hochschild; yet he worries that this is too high a demand on his sympathy.[12] Says another interviewee at a Trump rally in Baton Rouge: "People think we're not good people if we don't feel sorry for blacks and immigrants and Syrian refugees. But I am a good person and I *don't* feel sorry for them."[13] Another interviewee shares her disgust with "liberal media" whose tone solicits compassion for "a sick African child" or a "bedraggled Indian."[14] Hochschild sums up this affective orientation: "You're a compassionate person. But now you've been asked to extend your sympathy to all the people who have cut in front of you . . . you have to close the borders to human sympathy."[15]

Thus, at the same time as we see a flow of affective resources from the Global South to the Global North under regimes of migration and dislocation, we also see an accumulation of "sympathy fatigue" in the Global North—a sympathy fatigue directed at the Global South ("immigrants and refugees"), and toward marginalized populations in general ("blacks, women, the poor"). Even as exhausting affective demands are produced in the Global North and passed down to workers from the Global South, white people in the US South claim sympathy fatigue as the reason they must "close the borders of human sympathy."[16] While Global Southerners are obliged to migrate or dislocate across the border between Global North and South at great affective cost, Global Northerners are shoring up our side of the border from within. A critical framework capable of addressing this connection must bring into view a *global affective economy*. We often speak of global political economy, but can we articulate a *global economy of affects* between these scenes, one that connects the production of a demand for affective labor from the Global South to the production of sympathy fatigue in the US South and Global North?

In this chapter, I propose that theorizing affects as *affective economies* can give us a framework to understand these scenes alongside each other and to formulate critical concerns about them in relation to each other. I develop a concept of affective economies using the work of philosophers Sara Ahmed and Kate Manne, and I use it to try and understand the "sympathy fatigue"

Hochschild finds in the US South as a site of production for the Northern side of a global affective economy. By showing how the demand for sympathy can be produced in affective economies of misogyny and coloniality, I argue that we must understand sympathy as an affective economy in order to develop a robust critique of its social and political function. Using this framework, I show how the affective economies of sympathy produce not only affects but also forms of subjectivity and affective agencies: they produces individuals' and collectives' capacities to affect and be affected by each other.[17] They also function as a *moral* economy, producing the affective weight of moral sentiment about who is deserving of sympathy and who is not; who ought to do the work of producing sympathy and who is entitled to be a beneficiary of that labor. Affective economies, then, are capable of producing uniquely affective forms of privilege and oppression: affective injustices.

The affective economy of sympathy fatigue, I show, is a symptom of a larger affective provincialism in which migration or border-crossing itself gets figured as line-cutting, cheating: giving up your place in line by trying to jump the queue, and positioning yourself as undeserving of sympathy and moral regard. And while I analyze this as a form of subjectivity and a set of affective agencies circulating in the Global North, I situate that in Hochschild's ethnography, analyzing its production in the US South, and amplifying Hochschild's provocative suggestion that there may be a uniquely (US) Southern provincialism being adopted as an attitude toward the Global South, or toward marginalized populations in general, and exported to the Global North.

Sympathy Fatigue in the Global North

As she travels through the American South, Hochschild describes meeting Madonna Massey, a charming white evangelical woman who sings in her church and praises Rush Limbaugh's takedown of "femi-nazis."[18] Massey shares her disgust with "liberal media," locating a lack of objectivity in a "*tone of voice*" that demands her compassion for the globally underprivileged. "Take Christiane Amanpour," Massey says. "She'll be kneeling by a sick African child, or a bedraggled Indian, looking into the camera. . . . She's using that child to say, '*Do* something, America.' But that child's problems aren't our fault."[19] Massey is incensed at the demand on her sympathy that she finds in Amanpour's tone. Hochschild glosses Massey's irritation: "I don't want to be told I'm a bad person if I don't feel sorry for that child."[20]

The term "sympathy fatigue" positions its subject as passive: overused and exhausted, beset and put-upon. But a more active element is conspicuous in Hochschild's descriptions of her interviewees. Their "sympathy fatigue" is a posture of refusal, a "feeling guard" against liberal demands to sympathize with the marginalized and against the moral weight those demands carry.

"That's *PC*," Massey protests against Amanpour's broadcast; "That's what liberals want listeners like me to feel."[21]

This refusal of sympathy takes the form of a moral outrage, claiming itself as righteous indignation against liberal feeling rules.[22] Recall the interviewee at the Trump rally: "People think we're not good people if we don't feel sorry for blacks and immigrants and Syrian refugees. But I am a good person and I *don't* feel sorry for them."[23] Thus the posture of "sympathy fatigue" is one that maintains that "blacks and immigrants and Syrian refugees" don't deserve sympathy; that they are cheaters or "line-cutters" usurping white folks' higher place in the socioeconomic queue,[24] such that in fact the liberal demand to feel sympathy for them displaces sympathy from its more deserving objects: white Global Northerners. This image of the line and marginalized people as line-cutters is what Hochschild calls the "emotional deep story" of the sympathy fatigue she finds in her subjects: they see themselves as patiently waiting in line for the American dream while people behind them ("immigrants and refugees" or "blacks, women, and the poor") jump the queue.

So "sympathy fatigue" is not a passing or superficial state Hochschild's interviewees find themselves in. It is shorthand for a certain kind of identification, a whole subject position, an orientation toward the world and others. This persona is that of otherwise sympathetic people who merely withhold their sympathy from populations who deserve a lower place in line for the American Dream but are cutting ahead. Hochschild's interviewees are not merely depleted in their sympathy reserves. They are actively building walls, patrolling the borders. They are not out of sympathy; they are stockpiling it. They must withstand immense pressure from "liberals" to reserve their sympathy for more deserving objects: their own people in the front of the queue—or at least people who know their place in line and stay there. The narrative of this attitude as "sympathy fatigue" allows Hochschild's interviewees to inhabit resentment of the marginalized as a heroic exhaustion and a moral indignation at cheaters.

Hochschild herself does not take this sort of critical stance toward her subjects. She is rigorous about the integrity of her account's goals as ethnography: she aims to empathize, not to critique. When she proposes her diagnosis of "sympathy fatigue" described through the metaphor of waiting in line for the American dream and marginalized people as line-cutters, she checks with some of her subjects to see if they approve (they do).[25] My own vantage point is critical, and from here the metaphor of waiting in line and of white folks perceiving marginalized people as line-cutters and ourselves as having been waiting in line the longest still looks apt.[26] But it is apt precisely insofar as the metaphor is a direct translation of the white entitlement that is the contemporary inheritance of white supremacy and coloniality. The image of the line figures racial hierarchy as a simple seniority, while occluding the history of white supremacy and settler colonialism that queued it up. If the "line" in the metaphor is US history, white descendants of settlers will always be first in line insofar as our settler colonialist ancestors' arrival in the Americas is the measure of the line's beginning. So, if white folks in the US South consider themselves and those who look like them to have been in that line longest, this is just an expression of our proximity to the privileges produced by colonial racism. The assumption that white Americans are first in line for the American Dream, that we are most deserving of whatever benefits and privileges are on offer, is just the uncritical contemporary inheritance of our ancestors' colonial racism. And if the line is the one queued up by the genocide of Native Americans and the transatlantic slave trade, then we should not accept it uncritically: we should reject the assumption that holding one's place in that line confers moral authority.

Hochschild's study was published in 2016, and the framing assumption of her study is that the US South is a privileged site for the cultivation of this "emotional deep story" of sympathy fatigue toward Global Southerners and other marginalized populations, as well as toward the liberal feeling rules that demand that sympathy. But Hochschild also suggests that this "emotional deep story" is being exported from the US South to conservatives in the North.[27] And indeed, the rhetoric of sympathy fatigue has grown even more widely recognizable since 2016. Examples have become too numerous to name, but I will point to one variation on the theme: in the summer of 2018, the Trump administration's "zero tolerance" border policy authorized the routine separation of migrant children from their families at the border.[28] It was common for outrage at the staggering cruelty of this policy from progressives in the States to be met with a response that echoes Hochschild's interviewees: we should worry about "our own" first rather than worrying about "illegals." Again, the "sympathy fatigue" exemplified here is not only the active withholding of sympathy rather than passive depletion; it is also the *redirection* of sympathy according to places in a queue of who is more deserving. In building walls around Global Northerners' sympathy, "sympathy fatigue" is a surface symptom of a whole affective economy: one which marks white people from the Global North as "in bounds," the deserving recipients of sympathy; and marks marginalized people—and liberal demands for sympathy on their behalf—as objects of morally deserved resentment. It produces the urgency of demands that the flow of sympathy from the Global North to the Global South in the "liberal sympathy sieve" must be reversed; that our proper places in line must be restored; that a sympathy wall must be built.

Affects as Circulation in Affective Economies

The philosopher Sara Ahmed theorizes affects as economies.[29] She introduces the model of affects as economies as an alternative to models that participate in a false dichotomy of positioning affects as either outside-in or inside-out phenomena.[30] Instead we must understand affects as fundamentally circulatory. She elaborates her view using the classic dilemma from the psychological literature of the child afraid of the bear: Does the child run because the bear is scary, or because she is afraid? Ahmed refuses what she terms the "Dumb View"[31] of emotions that reduces them to behavioral functions or automatic, prefixed mechanisms: "It is not that the bear *is* fearsome, 'on its own' . . . it is fearsome *to* someone."[32] Fear is not "outside-in," Ahmed argues, insofar as it involves intentionality: an embodied orientation to some object, making sense of a situation to some subject position.

But, Ahmed insists, neither are affects best understood as "inside-out," a constitution of meaning donated to the situation from the interiority of the subject, as if their affective force is mere projection. Ahmed's positioning of affective intentionality within the social and historical circulation of affective economies allows her to insist that, while the child's fear of the bear has intentionality, this orientation need not be understood as authored by the child in the immediacy of her situation. Just as fear is not outside-in, it is also not "inside-out": "We have an image of the bear as an animal to be feared, as an image that is shaped by cultural histories and memories."[33] The fearsomeness of bears—their capacity to affect bodies like mine with fear and the capacity of my body to be fearfully affected by them—is an affective agency that is produced not only in the immediacy of my encounter with the bear, but also within a material and sociohistorical circulation of affect I inhabit. In this way, the bodily immediacy of the fear reaction need not be "a sign of lack of mediation."[34] It is mediated by an affective economy whose scope encompasses millennia of interspecies history.

Ahmed thus denies that affects are purely private or sovereign: affects, like money, are a currency realized in circulation instead of being owned utterly by the individuals who undergo them. One of the reasons Ahmed chooses the model of economies is to capture the way that affect, like capital, is actually produced in circulation.[35] It is by being circulated that exchange value is realized and capital can accumulate. Similarly, objects can only accumulate affective charge by circulating. And it is in these circulations that affective force can materialize into the orientation and affect-ability of a given individual or group. Instead of our affects being states that belong to us, we are constituted (as both individuals and groups) in the circulation of affect. We are constituted in the sense that the meaning and force of our influences on each other—our capacities to affect and be affected, what I call our *affective agencies*—are formed and accumulated in the circulation of affects as affective economies.

Ahmed uses her notion of affective economies to analyze the cultivation of anti-immigrant political will in the UK (for instance, immigrants are circulated discursively as "swarms overflowing our borders"). Similarly, we can build an account of sympathy fatigue in the United States through this framework of affective economies. If the sympathy fatigue Madonna Massey shows in Hochschild's interview is the product of an affective economy, then her indignation at the broadcast featuring Amanpour and the "sick African child" or "bedraggled Indian"[36] is not merely outside-in (as if sympathy fatigue is a meaning contained within Global Southerners in themselves— they just *are* exhausting, as a feature or property they contain) or inside-out (as if sympathy fatigue is merely an idiosyncratic meaning Massey donates to these phenomena; it just happens to be how Massey feels about them). Instead, just as bears are circulated as objects of fear for humans, Global Southerners are circulated as objects of sympathy fatigue for Global North- erners. Just as the circulation of the bear as object of fear for humans has a history, so too does the circulation of Global Southerners as objects of too much sympathy, figures of those who have been given more sympathy than they deserve, and whose circulation as objects of sympathy is appropriately resented. Positioning sympathy fatigue as an affective economy in Ahmed's sense requires us to consider the history of colonial racism through which these affects accumulate their force.

In the affective economy of sympathy fatigue, the fact that Global South- erners are sometimes circulated as figures of a call for sympathy is itself an appropriate object of indignation. For the white US Southerners in Hochschild's ethnography, liberal appeals for aid on behalf of "blacks and immigrants and Syrian refugees"[37] is something that should not be merely politely declined. It is *offensive*: Madonna Massey is indignant at even the sub- tle appeal for compassion in Christiane Amanpour's *tone*. Why? Not merely because she criticizes Amanpour's individual investment of her sympathies. Instead, the mere fact of Amanpour's sympathy is seen as itself constituting a demand or pressure on Massey's sympathies, and on the sympathies of all of Amanpour's listeners—an illegitimate pressure that may appropriately be met with indignation. That active element of sympathy fatigue—building borders around sympathy, redirecting its flow—is implicitly positioned as something that Massey cannot accomplish alone.

Thus, in understanding Hochschild's sympathy fatigue through Ahmed, we can discern a tacit recognition among Hochschild's subjects that sym- pathy is produced in an affective economy: if Amanpour's tone is offensive to Massey, it must be because she recognizes it as having affective force, as *moving*. What angers Massey is the *circulation* of the sick African child as an object of sympathy, of attention and concern, a call to take responsi- bility. Massey is angered that Amanpour is circulating Global Southerners as objects of sympathy, and that this circulation could accumulate affec- tive force in Global Northerners. Massey is banking on the production of affect in circulation. What angers her is an affective economy that con- stitutes the Global North and Global South, and their capacities to affect and be affected through a circulation of sympathy that flows from North to South.

The Colonial History of Affective Economies of Sympathy

We might think that a decolonial or social justice–oriented critique of this sympathy fatigue would be on Amanpour's side: it would simply recommend sympathy for Global Southerners rather than sympathy fatigue. But we should remember that colonial conquest and occupation has historically been figured as a compassionate project. In her 2010 book *The Promise of Happiness*, Ahmed analyzes an episode in the history of these affective economies of colonizing sympathy.[38] James Mill (father of John Stuart Mill, the philosopher whose formalization of utilitarianism as an ethical theory is a germinal text in normative ethics) made a hedonistic utilitarian argument for the British imperial conquest of India relying on colonial racism's distinction between primitive and civilized cultures. Colonial conquest, he argued, amounted to giving the gift of (European, specifically, British) civilization to "primitive" Indigenous people.[39] While it might cause some immediate suffering, he reasoned, colonization would bring the Indigenous Indian people immeasurable happiness downstream, since it would displace their "primitive" religion and legal system, among others, with "civilized" (British) versions of these things.

In this affective economy of colonial racism, colonization was figured as a sacrifice for the British, a "white man's burden": colonial conquest would be expensive, and so involve suffering for the British people, but this investment of resources and compassion would ultimately net greater overall happiness than if the Indian people were allowed to remain victims of their uncivilized culture and religion.[40] Circulating the Indian people as objects of colonial racist sympathy functioned to motivate and justify colonization. One of Ahmed's interests in tracing this historical discourse is the way it can be used to understand contemporary discourses of migration in the UK in which happiness is figured as what migrants owe: if British civilization is the gift of happiness, then migrants who receive it should be made happy by it.[41] If they are not, then they are figured as undeserving of the gift.

Two inferences can be drawn from this that are especially relevant to contextualizing the "sympathy fatigue" Hochschild finds in the contemporary American South within global affective economies. First, colonial racist affective economies have long circulated people from the Global South as objects of sympathy and concern.[42] If Ahmed is right that affective force gathers across a history, then the affective force that now gathers around the figure of the Global Southerner for someone like Madonna Massey should perhaps be understood in the context of the history of producing (colonizing) sympathy in colonial affective economies. The current circulation of Global Southerners as objects of sympathy *fatigue* may gain some of its affective force from that colonial history of circulating them as objects of (colonizing) *sympathy*. Perhaps it is precisely insofar as they have been invested with colonizing sympathy in the past (and have not been made happy by this gift of colonizing sympathy, and thus undeserving of it) that they are now in circulation as figures who have already been given more sympathy than they deserve, and whose continued circulation as objects of sympathy is appropriately resented.

Second, decolonizing the affective economy of sympathy fatigue will not be successful if its only strategy is recirculating Global Southerners as objects of sympathy. In this colonial history of affective economies of sympathy, the sympathy that has been historically extended is a colonizing sympathy: a paternalistic sympathy grounded in colonial racist attitudes that figured Global Southerners as victims of their "primitive" (read: nonwhite, non-European) race and culture. This sympathy granted only the most restricted affective agency to Global Southerners: they could move the colonizer to pity them (and thus colonize them). But beyond that, this colonizing sympathy did not grant weight and force to affects produced in affective economies local to the colonized. Indeed, it functioned to discredit them: James Mill argues that the Indigenous people of India are like children, easily impressed and in need of the guidance of more "civilized" rulers.[43] Colonizing sympathy figured the colonized as people who needed to be taught to feel differently—to be made happy by the right things, more civilized (read: British) things. Colonizing sympathy did the work of affective domination, rendering Indigenous affects unmoving to colonizers, taking them out of circulation, and rendering colonizers insensitive to them.

Thus reversing the flow of sympathy so that it runs from Global North to Global South can also be a feature of colonizing affective economies. Whether sympathy is produced or not cannot function as the criterion of decolonial critique. We must look at the whole affective economy, including the affective agencies it produces in us. Imagining and cultivating a decolonial affective ecology will require a critical framework that attends not only to whether sympathy for the marginalized is produced but also to the just cultivation of affective agencies.

Misogyny as an Affective Economy of Sympathy

In the philosopher Kate Manne's study of misogyny, she analyzes a "gendered economy" of "emotional and social labor" in which "excessive sympathy" flows to men and away from women—even, and perhaps especially, in situations where men perpetrate egregious violence against women.[44] Manne coins the term "himpathy" for this "inappropriate and disproportionate sympathy powerful men often enjoy in cases of sexual assault, intimate partner violence, homicide and other misogynistic behavior."[45] Similarly, when a man is not "given his due"—the set of moral goods and services to which masculinity entitles him and which women owe him—then he may be "deemed entitled to *prevent*" women from competing with him for it; and "to the extent to which she tries to or successfully beats the boys 'at their own game' . . . she may be held to have cheated, or to have stolen something from him"—she may be figured as a line-cutter.[46]

In what sense is Manne describing misogyny as an "economy" here? Several times in the book she refers to it as a "moral economy," but I want to foreground the way it functions as an affective economy—and I think this adds a distinctive contribution to the critical framework of affective economies that I have so far been developing through Ahmed. First, it describes a (usually implicit) system for the production and consumption of affective benefits, sympathy in particular. Second, it describes a (usually implicit) class system in which the affective labor of producing this sympathy is assigned by gender. And third, it describes the way in which affective economies, especially of sympathy, produce *moral* sentiment: affective forces with the moral weight of just deserts, of what is *owed* to whom, and who is *deserving*, not only of which labors in the affective economy but also of which products.

What sort of benefit is sympathy? All other things being equal, no doubt sympathy is a nice a thing to have; but in Manne's analysis it becomes much more than that. Sympathy of the sort Manne describes is an affective orientation toward someone in which they become the focus of your attention and concern.[47] A gendered affective economy in which sympathy flows to men and away from women is not only one in which men enjoy a nice feeling that women are tasked with producing for them. It is an affective economy in which *men's feelings carry more weight than women's* precisely insofar as women are positioned as emotional laborers who owe the work of feeding egos and tending emotional wounds, while men are figured as deserving beneficiaries of that labor.[48] A uniquely affective kind of privilege is produced as an effect of the production of sympathy in this misogynistic affective economy.

Popular discussions about gender and emotional labor often proceed as if the problem is just one of distribution: women are doing more than their share of the emotional work. But seen as an affective economy, the problem is one of the kinds of subjects and affective agencies being produced: men are produced as people whose feelings must be taken more seriously, and their feelings are indeed made weightier in the circulation of the affective economy. Men are circulated as those who are owed attention and concern—and women as those who owe it. The injustice here is not only distributive: it is a uniquely affective modality of domination and exploitation, marginalization, and even violence.[49] Manne tends to cash out the results of her arguments in terms of epistemic injustice, but I think it is interesting to consider the ways in which there is a uniquely affective injustice operating here.[50]

The sympathy produced in this misogynistic affective economy differs markedly from the colonizing sympathy of the imperialist utilitarians. Global Southerners were not circulated as objects of sympathy in the sense that they were deserving of British emotional labor, the feeding of their egos and the tending of their emotional wounds. The sympathy produced in those early

colonial affective economies did not enable the affective agency of the colonized (their capacities to affect the colonizer, or the capacities of the colonizer
to be affected by the colonized) except in one tetanized joint: the colonizer
could be moved to pity by the colonized, who were circulated as pitiable and
deserving of sympathy in virtue of their "primitiveness." Thus, in this affective economy, sympathy took the form of colonization.

A crucial inference to draw from this is that not all sympathy is the same:
it is only in analyzing the *affective economy* producing that sympathy and
the kinds of affective agencies it produces that we can see the full dimensions
of its social and political function and develop a robust critique of it. In the
misogynist affective economy Manne describes, the production of sympathy
is a site of exploitative labor for the sympathetic. In the imperialist utilitarian affective economy Ahmed describes, the production of *sympathy* was a
technique of colonial racism. In the affective economy of *sympathy fatigue*
Hochschild describes, the refusal of sympathy is a means for producing a
border around who is deserving, a border that inherits its contours from
colonial racism.

My reading of Manne's gendered economy as an affective one is not a
dismissal of her own description of it as a *moral* economy. The sense of entitlement on which the economy operates is indeed a moral one: a sense of what
one deserves, and what another does not deserve. Misogyny is the affective
economy in which men *deserve* sympathy, especially women's sympathy, and
women do not deserve the same, such that if we compete with men for attention and concern then we are cheaters, thieves—line-cutters. Accordingly, the
morality of this economy can be understood as a third way in which it is
an *affective* economy: the economy of misogyny has as its currency a *moral
sentiment*, a sentiment of justice or just deserts. Men deserve sympathy, and
women owe it to them in the form of emotional labor that cultivates affective agencies for men that are refused to women. If the affective economy of
sympathy fatigue Hochschild tracks is a moral economy in this sense, it is one
that is producing moralizing affective agencies: moral sentiment concerning
who is deserving and who is not.

White Feminism as an Affective Economy of Sympathy Fatigue

How does the affective economy of Global Northerners' sympathy fatigue
function to produce protection for the locality of their affective investments?
What are the ways that Global Northerners are implicated in the affective
economies that produce sympathy fatigue and affective provincialism? Could
they be implicated even when they are not the red state, Tea-Partier-cum-
Trump voters Hochschild interviewed, even when they live in the liberal
Northeast, and are horrified by Madonna Massey's delight at Limbaugh's
mocking of "femi-nazis"? In particular, I am interested in how this production

is accomplished through the affective labor of affluent white women in the Global North, sometimes under the banner of feminism.

The day after Melania Trump returned from visiting migrant children separated from their families wearing a jacket announcing "I REALLY DON'T CARE, DO U?," I saw an Il Makiage cosmetics ad in the New York subway. "WHO WANTS TO BE LOW MAINTENANCE ANYWAY?" the ad sneers:

> And since when is owning a single, lightly tinted chapstick a good thing? To whomever started this no fuss trend, with all due respect, we'd cry for you, but our mascara is too damn expensive. Which is why we will be bold and unapologetic, as we champion the spirit of all the confident, successful women who are equal parts swagger and substance. The kind of women who know exactly what they're worth, and demand to be treated accordingly.[51]

The feminist manifesto here is the imperative to measure one's worth in terms of one's self-worth. Self-worth is in turn measured by how much women are willing to invest in their makeup and how boldly uncaring they are for women who don't care enough about themselves to spend thirty dollars on a lipstick. We are fierce, we care about ourselves, and we know this because we buy expensive mascara. The affective economy exemplified here is one in which our tears are precious, and we won't waste them. We know this because our mascara is expensive, and we won't waste it. Crying about those poor, besotted, "basic" women who stick to tinted chapstick diminishes us—and, the ad hints, diminishes the feminist cause. It is a waste of both our measures of self-worth (tears and mascara), a waste of sympathy better spent on ourselves. Because we are women who invest in ourselves—and because we are boldly uncaring of women who do not—we prove ourselves worthy of this investment. Only people who buy luxury mascara are worth our tears, because only people who invest in themselves are worth the mascara our tears will cost us.

This translates the affective economy of sympathy as moral sentiment into literal economic terms. You are worth sympathy in the moral sense that you deserve it insofar as you invest in self-care, and investing in self-care is literally investing in expensive products such as cosmetics.[52] This fusion of the affective and capitalist economies is triangulated through feminism. The infusion of feminist moral authority in this affective economy is at the same time a subsumption of feminism to consumerism and the expression of privilege. The feminism it offers is the sort commonly called "white feminism." This is a feminism that celebrates forms of privilege that bourgeois white men have enjoyed and seeks to expand these benefits to white women without critiquing the way this move reinvests in fundamental structures of domination and oppression.

This translation of the affective economy of sympathy as moral desert into literal economic terms is also crucial to the "emotional deep story" of the

Tea-Partier-cum-Trump-supporter, as Hochschild sees it. One interviewee describes sympathy fatigue as draining in a monetary sense: "Your money is running through a liberal sympathy sieve you don't control or agree with."[53] Here the affective economy in which sympathy is running out is directly correlated to the money economy in which labor and resources are at stake. Christiane Amanpour's tear-jerking tone about the sick African child is offensive to Massey insofar as it threatens to move her to waste not only tears but also the money she may have spent on mascara—not to mention tax dollars on foreign aid.

But there is another triangulation here, which is the triangulation of the affective economies of coloniality and misogyny through a demand for a very particular sort of (privileged, white) feminist affective labor from affluent Global Northern women. The ad locates both feminist agency and the production of one's subjectivity in the realm of affective or emotional labor—specifically, women's affective labor. However, this is not the labor of producing sympathy for others to consume that we find in Manne's analysis of misogyny or in the coloniality of affective labor. Rather, the ad calls upon women to do the feminist affective labor of producing sympathy for oneself—a task which is not so subtly figured as a corollary of the labor of withholding sympathy from others who are less well off, who are not "successful" and "confident." Their very marginality and poverty mark them as unworthy. The fact that they need aid is proof that they don't deserve it, just as the self-investment of the Il Makiage woman is proof she does deserve it.

The injunction to self-care thus has a violent edge: it contains an injunction to police the boundary between worthy and disposable lives. We are enjoined to self-care, which is measured not only in how much we invest in ourselves but also in how proudly we refuse to care about unworthy others. Feminism equals self-care equals building borders around one's sympathy, borders that constitute a form of class that marks the nonwealthy or nonsuccessful or nonprivileged as blameworthy and disposable, undeserving of attention and concern. We are authorized to treat the poor and marginalized as disposable, unworthy, and this is figured as a form of feminist agency.

Misogyny, Kate Manne explains, is an economy of moral goods and services, an emotional or affective economy in which women are positioned as givers and men as takers. But there is an affective economy in play in the Il Makiage ad which, while it intersects with the misogynistic one, is not directly or primarily in its service. Indeed, it offers a kind of superficial rebellion against misogyny (don't give your care to others; give it to yourself!). Yet this rebellion is in the service of white supremacy and coloniality (prove that you care for yourself and are worthy of care by policing the boundary between those who deserve care and those who are unworthy of it). The way in which affluent, privileged women are employed in this feminist affective economy as producers and givers of care (to ourselves, the worthy) also authorizes us as a kind of police. We are charged with policing the borders of care, defending against nonprivileged drains on our care as exploiters, undeserving, worthy of only contemptuously dry eyes.

Producing racial and colonial borders around sympathy has long been an affective labor of privileged white women. Consider, for instance, the white Southern woman shown in Raoul Peck's *I Am Not Your Negro* as she speaks out against integration: "God forgives murder and he forgives adultery," she says, "but he is very angry and he actually curses all who do integrate."[54] While women's anger has a history of being poorly received,[55] privileged women's anger in service of the supremacy of our race or class is often an exception, sometimes afforded conspicuous uptake. This triangulation of racism and capitalism through the affective policing labor of white women is an affective economy in Ahmed's sense, one with a history.

It is in this affective economy that employs white women to produce affective provincialism and sympathy fatigue in the Global North that a First Lady's obliquely announced refusal to care about migrant children ("I really don't care, do u?") can function as pseudofeminism. This is a "feminism" that supports a US president whose rise was fueled by promises to build a wall and free Americans from political correctness with its liberal feeling rules that oblige compassion, to "make America great again" by running it like a business, kicking out "losers," and "be[ing] greedy for the United States."[56] I found myself reading Melania Trump's message somewhere between that of Madonna Massey and the Il Makiage woman: outraged that she should be expected to feel sorry for desperate immigrant children when we have plenty of blue-eyed American children patiently waiting at the front of the sympathy and privilege queue who deserve better than tinted chapstick. There is a form of global class constituted here that is also a form of colonial racism, and it is produced as affective status: Who is worthy of care and sympathy? And who, on the other hand, is disposable, a drain on our sympathy that must be walled out? In this affective economy, feminism equals self-care equals white women's tears[57] flowing toward ourselves and white children— not a sick African child, not the children of "blacks and immigrants and Syrian refugees,"[58] and not the children of desperate Central American migrants.

Thus, one way the affective economy that produces affective provincialism and sympathy fatigue in the Global North operates is through a global division of affective labor between women according to their race and class. One kind of affective labor has a history in the emotional work of white Southern women like Madonna Massey, and is now marketed (literally) to privileged women in the Global North as feminist agency, even as another kind of affective labor is passed down to poor and migrant women from the Global South. The latter is the affective labor, not only of care and reproductive service but also the affective labor I have termed "byproductive labor."[59] This is the labor of containing and metabolizing waste or unwanted affects, such as Vicky Diaz's sorrow about being separated from her own children or the contempt of the Il Makiage woman for unenlightened ladies who haven't climbed the ladder from domestic work to expensive mascara.

These two kinds of affective labor are connected: the type of labor expected of women in the Global North helps to create the burdens of the labor expected of women in the Global South. The demand for white affluent women to invest in self-care is also a demand to disinvest in the care of women below them in the hierarchies of race and class, to cultivate contempt for these women (even as they might hire them to clean their houses and care for their children). It doesn't merely pass down a care deficit and the exhausting burden of metabolizing affective byproducts. It also produces affective provincialism and sympathy fatigue that functions as sympathy border patrol.

The subsumption of feminism to capitalism in the Il Makiage ad and the economization of Vicky Diaz's isolation from her kin to produce displaced maternal affection—these are striking reminders that now, more than ever, we need an intersectional feminism that is alive, not only to the intersection of gender and race as forms of power but also the intersection of gender and race with the politics of labor and the emerging forms of global class. Affective economies are not independent of global political economies. The production and manipulation of affect is increasingly how we make a living, but also how we make ourselves and our social groups, how we empower our leaders, and how we make excuses for or pass down the increasingly dire human consequences of global capital.

Conclusion: From the Southern Strategy to the Northern Strategy

Hochschild proposes that, unlike Nixon's "Southern Strategy" which "appealed to white fear of black rise" in the South to get Southerners to follow Northerners away from the Democratic Party and into the Republican, there is now a "Northern strategy": one in which "conservatives in the North are following those of the [US] South."[60] The wealthy and "those identified with them," even if aspirationally, join Southern whites in "lift[ing] off the burden of help for the underprivileged."[61] I have traced the affective economy that produces sympathy fatigue through histories of coloniality that produce the affective weight of our places in line for the American Dream. But is this, too, a "Northern strategy" in Hochschild's sense? In what way is this affective investment in the moral authority of holding a place in line a (US) Southern gesture?

Hochschild relates an interview with a Louisiana Tea Partier named Lee Sherman who suggested that Syrian refugees should be sent to Guantanamo.[62] Another interviewee, Mike Schaff, explains this refusal to respond to refugees with compassion by comparing them unfavorably to US Southerners during the Civil War. While the Syrian refugees fled their country and homes,

Schaff says, US Southerners did not. They stayed and fought, even after the defeat of the Confederacy. Like the Confederates, Schaff reasons, "the Syrians should stay, take a stand, and fight for what they believe in. If you flee, in my mind, you're a traitor unto yourself."[63] Schaff's analogy between Syrian refugees and Southern Confederate sympathizers contrasts the quality and strength of their commitment to their own proper place in the world: their homes and provincial locations. It suggests an appeal to Global Northerners to displace sympathy from the refugees to the Southern Confederates (and contemporary US Southerners who identify with them): the Confederates are more deserving of our compassion because they refused to leave their homes. Migration itself is figured as line-cutting, giving up your place in the queue, and your claim to deserve sympathy and moral regard.

In an opinion column in the *New York Times* in the spring of 2019, Sindy Flores relates how she fled from Honduras when gangs threatened to kill her and her children. "When I asked to be let into this country because my family was in mortal danger," she writes, "a Border Patrol agent told me I was weak."[64] He scorned Flores for leaving her home, even in the face of mortal danger to her and her children. The resemblance between the agent's comments to Flores and those of Sherman and Schaff in Hochschild's interview is striking: both position those who flee their homes as cowards, not worthy of care, and even worthy of contempt.

When she was denied entry as a refugee, Flores sneaked herself and her children north across the border. When they were apprehended and detained, her eighteen-month-old baby was removed from her care. A month later, when Flores managed to find her infant daughter and demand her return, the baby's physical and emotional health was decimated. At the time Flores's story was published, the family's fate was uncertain.

Hochschild suggests that the "emotional deep story" of "line-cutters" and "sympathy fatigue" for them is exported from the US South to the US North.[65] I want to suggest that the affective economy of sympathy fatigue produces a form of subjectivity in Global Northerners characterized by an affective orientation toward the global world, and especially toward global phenomena of migration and dislocation, in which crossing borders is figured as line-cutting, cheating, giving up your place in line and becoming undeserving of sympathy and moral regard. There is a global economy of affects at stake.

Notes

1. Arlie Hochschild, "Global Care Chains and Emotional Surplus Value" in *On the Edge: Living with Global Capitalism*, ed. William Hutton and Anthony Giddens (New York: Vintage Books, 2000), 130–46.

2. Hochschild, "Global Care Chains," 130. This case is one Hochschild borrowed from Rhacel Parreñas's work on Filipino migrant domestic workers. "Vicky Diaz" is Parreñas's pseudonym for one respondent in her study, a 34-year-old mother of five with a college education who worked in the Philippines as a

schoolteacher and a travel agent before migrating to the United States. Parreñas's research was unpublished at the time of Hochschild's writing, but it formed part of the background research for Parreñas's *Servants of Globalization: Migration and Domestic Work* (Stanford, CA: Stanford University Press, 2015).

3. Sex work is another major global economy driving the migration of women from the Global South to the Global North. See Barbara Ehrenreich and Arlie Russell Hochschild, *Global Woman: Nannies, Maids, and Sex Workers in the New Economy* (New York: Henry Holt and Company, 2002).

4. See Hochschild and Ehrenreich, *Global Woman*.

5. Hochschild, "Global Care Chains," 130.

6. To think of this work as affective or emotional labor is to draw attention to the fact that the work consists—at least in part—in a uniquely affective or emotional expenditure. This may involve producing affects or affectively charged environments for consumers (for instance, administering attentive care or cultivating an environment of warmth and conviviality), but it may also involve the status confirmation labor of affording privileged weight to the customer's feelings (for instance, sympathizing with even the most trivial or petty concerns), and the *byproductive* labor of absorbing their negative affects (for instance, suffering rudeness with a smile). The unique kinds of exploitation to which the work is vulnerable cannot be understood except in light of this affective dimension. See Shiloh Whitney, "Byproductive Labor: A Feminist Theory of Affective Labor beyond the Production-Reproduction Distinction," *Philosophy and Social Criticism* 44, no. 6 (2018): 637–60.

7. Kalindi Vora, "The Transmission of Care: Affective Economies and Indian Call Centers," in *Intimate Labors: Cultures, Technologies, and the Politics of Care*, edited by Eileen Boris and Rhacel Salazar Parreñas (Stanford, CA: Stanford University Press, 2010), 33–48.

8. Vora, "The Transmission of Care," 34.

9. Vora, "The Transmission of Care," 36.

10. Vora, "The Transmission of Care," 36.

11. See Michael Hardt and Antonio Negri, "Biopolitical Production," in *Empire* (Cambridge, MA: Harvard University Press, 2000), 22–41.

12. Arlie Hochschild, *Strangers in Their Own Land: Anger and Mourning on the American Right* (New York: The New Press, 2016), 146.

13. Hochschild, *Strangers*, 226.

14. Hochschild, *Strangers*, 128.

15. Hochschild, *Strangers*, 139.

16. Hochschild, *Strangers*, 139.

17. The language of producing forms of subjectivity comes from Hardt and Negri's notion of biopolitical production: not only the production of affects but also of subjectivities (see Hardt and Negri, "Biopolitical Production"). Their approach is useful for linking up Marxian and Foucauldian analyses. But in my own research on affective labor and affective economies, I find myself increasing reluctant to conflate the production of what I call "affective agencies" with the production of forms of subjectivity. This is because capacities to affect or be affected may be produced in and through us without being correlated to the kinds of subjects we are, or take ourselves to be. Affective economies don't always or primarily work through how we are addressable as subjects.

18. Hochschild, *Strangers*, 22.

19. Hochschild, *Strangers*, 128.

20. Hochschild, *Strangers*, 128.

21. Hochschild, *Strangers*, 128.

22. For more on "feeling rules," see Arlie Hochschild, *The Managed Heart: Commercialization of Human Feeling* (Los Angeles: University of California Press, 2012).

23. Hochschild, *Strangers*, 226.

24. Hochschild, *Strangers*, 137.

25. Hochschild, *Strangers*, 135.

26. Hochschild, *Strangers*, 136, 137.

27. Hochschild, *Strangers*, 220.

28. Jeff Sessions, "Memorandum for Federal Prosecutors along the Southwest Border," Office of the Attorney General, April 6, 2018, https://www.justice.gov/opa/press-release/file/1049751/download.

29. Sara Ahmed, *The Cultural Politics of Emotion* (New York: Routledge, 2004), 44–49.

30. Ahmed, *Cultural Politics*, 8–12.

31. On the "Dumb View" of emotions, see also Elizabeth Spelman, "Anger and Insubordination," in *Women, Knowledge, and Reality*, edited by Ann Garry and Marilyn Pearsall (New York: Routledge, 1989); Alison Jaggar, "Love and Knowledge: Emotion in Feminist Epistemology," *Inquiry* 32, no. 2 (1989): 151–76.

32. Ahmed, *Cultural Politics*, 7.

33. Ahmed, *Cultural Politics*, 7.

34. Ahmed, *Cultural Politics*, 7.

35. Ahmed, *Cultural Politics*, 45.

36. Hochschild, *Strangers*, 128.

37. Hochschild, *Strangers*, 226.

38. Sara Ahmed, *The Promise of Happiness* (Durham, NC: Duke University Press, 2010), 123–33.

39. Ahmed, *The Promise of Happiness*, 124.

40. Ahmed, *The Promise of Happiness*, 124–25.

41. Ahmed, *The Promise of Happiness*, 130.

42. See Uma Narayan, "Sisterhood and 'Doing Good': Asymmetries of Western Feminist Location, Access, and Orbits of Concern," *Feminist Philosophy Quarterly* 5, no. 2 (2019): 1–26. Narayan offers a critique of contemporary discourses and practices among Western liberals that "construct Western subjects as entitled to and obligated to concern themselves with the world entire, while not extending this global scope of concern to non-Western subjects."

43. Ahmed, *The Promise of Happiness*, 126.

44. Kate Manne, *Down Girl: The Logic of Misogyny* (New York: Oxford University Press, 2018), 107, 111, 110, 201.

45. While Manne coins the term "himpathy" in *Down Girl*, she also wrote a widely circulated opinion piece for the *New York Times* using the notion to explain some of the reactions to the Kavanaugh hearings. Kate Manne, "Brett Kavanaugh and America's 'Himpathy' Reckoning," *New York Times*, Sept 26, 2018, https://www.nytimes.com/2018/09/26/opinion/brett-kavanaugh-hearing-himpathy.html.

46. Manne, *Down Girl*, 117.

47. Manne, *Down Girl*, 196–205.

48. Compare to Sandra Bartky's analysis of women's emotional labor in "Feeding Egos and Tending Wounds: Deference and Disaffection in Women's Emotional Labor," in *Femininity and Domination* (New York: Routledge, 1990), 99–119.

49. See Iris Marion Young's critique of "the distributive paradigm" in *Justice and the Politics of Difference* (Princeton, NJ: Princeton University Press, 1990).

50. See Shiloh Whitney, "Affective Intentionality and Affective Injustice: Merleau-Ponty and Fanon on the Theory of the Body Schema as a Theory of Affect," *Southern Journal of Philosophy* 56, no. 4 (2018): 488–515.

51. Il Makiage cosmetics advertisement, transcribed in New York City, July 11, 2018.

52. See Nina Power's trenchant monograph *One-Dimensional Woman* (Winchester, UK: Zer0 Books, 2009) for a vividly illustrated analysis of this capitalist pseudofeminism.

53. Hochschild, *Strangers*, 137.

54. See also the book accompaniment to the film, James Baldwin and Raoul Peck, *I Am Not Your Negro* (New York: Vintage Books, 2017), 11.

55. See Marilyn Frye, "A Note on Anger," in *The Politics of Reality: Essays in Feminist Theory* (Berkeley, CA: Crossing Press, 1983), 84.

56. Hochschild quotes Trump at a rally in Baton Rouge: "I've been greedy. I'm a businessman . . . take, take, take. Now I'm going to be greedy for the United States." Hochschild, *Strangers*, 224.

57. See Robin DiAngelo, "White Women's Tears," in *White Fragility: Why It's So Hard for White People to Talk about Racism* (Boston, MA: Beacon Press, 2018), 131–38.

58. Hochschild, *Strangers*, 226.

59. See Shiloh Whitney, "Byproductive Labor."

60. Hochschild, *Strangers*, 220.

61. Hochschild, *Strangers*, 220.

62. Hochschild, *Strangers*, 219.

63. Hochschild, *Strangers*, 219.

64. Sindy Flores, "We Fled the Gangs in Honduras. Then the U.S. Government Took My Baby," *New York Times*, April 3, 2019, https://www.nytimes.com/2019/04/03/opinion/border-honduras-separation-gangs.html?fbclid=IwAR0lDC_l1gHAjHS2oveAr0ZbNVJIaau-HkDnpWxVnxI-jcO3IQGuFMC9BTM.

65. Hochschild, *Strangers*, 220.

Bibliography

Ahmed, Sara. *The Promise of Happiness*. Durham, NC: Duke University Press, 2010.

Ahmed, Sara. *The Cultural Politics of Emotions*. New York: Routledge, 2004.

Baldwin, James, and Raoul Peck. *I Am Not Your Negro*. New York: Vintage Books, 2017.

Bartky, Sandra. "Feeding Egos and Tending Wounds: Deference and Disaffection in Women's Emotional Labor." In *Femininity and Domination: Studies in the Phenomenology of Oppression*, 99–119. New York: Routledge, 1990.

DiAngelo, Robin. "White Women's Tears." In *White Fragility: Why It's So Hard for White People to Talk about Racism*, 131–38. Boston, MA: Beacon Press, 2018.

Ehrenreich, Barbara, and Arlie Russell Hochschild, eds. *Global Woman: Nannies, Maids, and Sex Workers in the New Economy*. New York: Henry Holt and Company, 2002.

Frye, Marilyn. "A Note on Anger." In *The Politics of Reality: Essays in Feminist Theory*, 84–94. Berkeley, CA: Crossing Press, 1983.

Hochschild, Arlie. *Strangers in Their Own Land: Anger and Mourning on the American Right*. New York: The New Press, 2016.

———. *The Managed Heart: Commercialization of Human Feeling*. Los Angeles: University of California Press, 1983.

———. "Global Care Chains and Emotional Surplus Value." In *On the Edge: Living with Global Capitalism*, edited by William Hutton and Anthony Giddens, 130–46. New York: Vintage Books, 2000.

Jaggar, Alison. "Love and Knowledge: Emotion in Feminist Epistemology." *Inquiry* 32, no. 2 (1989): 151–76.

Lugones, María. "Heterosexualism and the Colonial/Modern Gender System." *Hypatia* 22, no. 1 (2007): 186–209.

Manne, Kate. *Down Girl: The Logic of Misogyny*. New York: Oxford University Press, 2018.

———. "Brett Kavanaugh and America's 'Himpathy' Reckoning." *New York Times*, Sept 26, 2018. https://www.nytimes.com/2018/09/26/opinion/brett-kavanaugh-hearing-himpathy.html.

Narayan, Uma. "Sisterhood and 'Doing Good': Asymmetries of Western Feminist Location, Access, and Orbits of Concern." *Feminist Philosophy Quarterly* 5, no. 2 (2019): 1–26.

Parreñas, Rhacel Salazar. *Servants of Globalization: Migration and Domestic Work*. 2nd ed. Stanford, CA: Stanford University Press, 2015.

Power, Nina. *One-Dimensional Woman*. Hants, UK: Zer0 Books, 2009.

Sessions, Jeff. "Memorandum for Federal Prosecutors along the Southwest Border." Office of the Attorney General. April 6, 2018. https://www.justice.gov/opa/press-release/file/1049751/download.

Spelman, Elizabeth. "Anger and Insubordination." In *Women, Knowledge, and Reality: Explorations in Feminist Philosophy*. Edited by Ann Garry and Marilyn Pearsall. New York: Routledge, 1989.

Vora, Kalindi. "The Transmission of Care: Affective Economies and Indian Call Centers." In *Intimate Labors: Cultures, Technologies, and the Politics of Care*, edited by Eileen Boris and Rhacel Salazar Parreñas, 33–48. Stanford, CA: Stanford University Press, 2010.

Whitney, Shiloh. "Affective Intentionality and Affective Injustice: Merleau-Ponty and Fanon on the Theory of the Body Schema as a Theory of Affect." *The Southern Journal of Philosophy* 56, no. 4 (2018): 488–515.

———. "Byproductive Labor: A Feminist Theory of Affective Labor beyond the Production-Reproduction Distinction." *Philosophy and Social Criticism* 44, no. 6 (2018): 637–60.

Young, Iris Marion. *Justice and the Politics of Difference*. Princeton, NJ: Princeton University Press, 1990.

6

✦

Altars for the Living

Shadow Ground, Aesthetic Memory,
and the US-Mexico Borderlands

Mariana Ortega

> This tombstone of the "world" . . . is situated at the edges of
> what exists, between the shadows and the light, between the
> conceived (abstraction) and the perceived (readable/visible).
> Between the real and the unreal. Always in the interstices, in
> the cracks. Between directly lived experience and thought and
> (a familiar paradox) between life and death.
> —Henri Lefebvre, *The Production of Space*

> I will etch visas on toilet paper and throw them from a lighthouse.
> —Javier Zamora, *Unaccompanied*

In a play of presence and absence, in the liminality between the public and the
private, we find spaces that have been produced explicitly to memorialize the
dead. Consider roadside memorials or what are now considered "grassroot
memorials"—those spaces marked by white crosses and all manner of unso-
phisticated memorial objects, the plastic flower, the discolored ribbon, the
tattered stuffed animal.[1] They are spaces produced by mourning and pain as
they are meant to remind us of that self that tragically died in ground that has
now become sacred. They are also performative as they have the function of a
making-remember, a bringing-to-light, and resisting—not only death but also
the traditional spatialities of mourning. Graves, cemeteries, obituaries, and
churches are not enough, however—not enough for those who have found
their being-in-the-world halted in an instant, an *Augenblick*, meaning not a
moment of conscience as in Heideggerian phenomenology but a moment of
finality, of the real end. These are the spaces of the dead for the dead and the
living that remain and find themselves angry, grieving, desperate.

Yet, in addition to being performative spaces of being and mourning, can these spaces be something else? Can they be more than shadowed grounds that have been marked by death, violence, or violence-to-be? And what are we to say of those who are able to walk on those grounds without collapsing to the unexpected finality of a flying bullet, or the violence of a coyote or an ICE soldier,[2] or to the wrath of the elements in a burning desert or an angry river, el Río Bravo del Norte or the Rio Grande that serves as a border between Texas and the Mexican states of Chihuahua, Coahuila, Nuevo León, and Tamaulipas?

In this chapter, I consider the production of spaces of mourning at the border of the US South and the Global South. I do so in connection to memory practices, but not for the dead; for the living. In so doing, I would like to honor border-crossers whose marginalized lives are such that their deaths are forgotten, made invisible, and their lives undermined, even when there are altars for them. As I examine the production of spaces of mourning, I draw from the work of Verónica G. Cárdenas, an artist from the border town of McAllen, Texas, specifically her series *Traveling Soles*, a series of photographs about detained undocumented immigrants, including many Central American children. I call for aesthetic memory as a way to honor all of those immigrants who have become invisible as humans and hypervisible as "criminals" and "illegals." I deliberately do not discuss grand memorials in honor of those who died in grand battles or events, memorials that are traditionally used to exalt nationalism, the use of *our* dead against "evil" forces. I instead discuss a particular kind of spontaneous memorial that is also an altar for the living: for undocumented border-crossers, especially children, whose names we do not even know and who do not fill the pages of our newspapers or social media or radio waves, unknown altars for those whose crossing is the result of a painful history connecting the United States, Mexico, and Central America.

In the first section, I present photographs from Cárdenas's *Traveling Soles* series. I analyze these photographs as well as the spatialities that Cárdenas creates in order to honor border-crossers and to highlight Central American children who have been apprehended at the US Border and put in detention camps.[3] I present the photographs and the spaces in which they were created as instances of spontaneous memorialization and as altars for the living. In turn, the photographs become *memento vivere*, reminders to live in such a way that we cannot forget the lives of these border-crossers. In the second section of the chapter, I discuss the role of the photographs as *memento vivere* and as aesthetic memories, thus opening the space for political possibilities mediated by what Ann Cvetkovich calls a sensational archive or an archive of feelings.[4]

Traveling Soles: Inferno

Let's think of traveling soles/souls in search for a better life, escaping violence in their land, wishing for a better economic future, wanting to meet a father, mother, or uncle who has gone to *el Norte* in order to be able to send the precious Dollar so the family can survive. Let us think of them going through what Jason de León describes as a "massive open grave," a space where he spots a complete tooth lying on top of a rock, where he picks up a small piece of bone, only for it to crumble to dust.[5] He is referring to the strip of desert south of Tucson, Arizona, the desert that has consumed 2,721 bodies between October 2000 and September 2014, eight hundred of which have not been identified—and these are only the deaths of this particular gravesite.[6] Imagine how many soles have traveled and continue to make the journey if between 2000 and 2013 approximately 11.7 million people were apprehended on their journey to a better life.[7]

No need to provide horrid details for the sake of pulling sentimental strings or engaging in "immigration pornography"—although I shall be writing about affect. I am interested in affect as a necessary element for understanding the possibility of bringing to memory the lives of border-crossers—or its impossibility. Suffice to say that the desert is highly efficient in pushing bodies to the limit, especially when they are not well prepared for such a treacherous journey—the scorching heat, the dust, the animals waiting patiently for the will to give up. Or the angry waves of an angry river, the Rio Grande, both respected and dreaded by those who know the stories of those who have managed to swim to their new land. And we cannot forget that an estimated 90 percent of women crossing the Rio Grande suffer from physical and sexual abuse. It is a hell of sand and water. But if you have heard about these "illegals," you have probably only heard about them as criminals and these loose women as creating "anchor babies." But mostly, you will not hear about them, especially the ones who have died—unless it is so tragic that television stations will not skip the opportunity to get more viewers.

In the border town of McAllen, in the southernmost region of Texas in general, however, it would be difficult not to hear about all of those border-crossers. They are part of the landscape, landscape-turned-passage to other worlds and to the so-called American Dream. Verónica G. Cárdenas hails from that region and her documentary photography serves as a small archive of documents written with light that indeed records one of the most important transnational and geopolitical events (and here I use event with the sense of disclosure) happening in front of our very eyes. As so many geopolitical events that are connected to forces of capital, the South-to-North migration of thousands looking for a better life, not to mention the many other migrations occurring globally now, disclose not only economic forces tied to power plays within corporations and governments but also histories of trauma, especially in connection to US-Mexico relations and US interventions in

Central America.[8] What would it mean for us to look at the history of modernization, colonization, and technocratization without an understanding of the pain that these have and continue to cause in many different populations, but especially in bodies of color?

Marx himself, the tireless teacher of materialist explanation, shows his human side and his attunement to sensation in his theory of alienation. While connected to forces of material production, his theory reveals the affective dimensions of not only being alienated ultimately from the product and the activity of labor but also being alienated from one's very species. It is not enough, however, citing Walter Benjamin, to be wary of the shock that the modern has imposed on dwellers of cities as beautiful as Paris but which hide mechanical rhythms that deny humanity.[9] What if Baudelaire had to run away from his beautiful but cruel city with all those crowds and tyrannical faces? What if Baudelaire had to cross the border? So many Europeans did at one point, and Benjamin himself took his life in his own border-crossing. All this movement to and from prompted by economic and political forces cannot simply be recorded in the way that one records how many containers have arrived at the dock. What does Cárdenas do, then, in the face of this voluminous movement of bodies and feelings, this migratory weeping full of desire and longing and pain and tears marked by US influence and exertion of economic, political, and military power in Mexico and Central America?

The answer is that Cárdenas creates an archive of feeling. I will call these archives altars for the living, which themselves will become *memento vivere*, or that which will remind us about the fragility of life being lived—not because we are going to die but because we need to live in such a way that we cannot forget. To say that Cárdenas's work produces an "archive" of feeling is to think of the archive beyond its traditional mode in which objects are classified for the purposes of tracking events. It is to understand the way in which the spaces created by Cárdenas and the photographs themselves do not merely index or record an event but also are engaged in the production of affect regarding the lives of border-crossers fleeing violence and danger or seeking a better life in *el Norte*.

Traveling Soles consists of a series of photographs of shoes. Not just any shoes but shoes that undocumented migrants were wearing as they entered the United States and that were discarded as they continued to move forward on their travel or as they were apprehended and put in *las hieleras*, or ice boxes, the name given to immigration detention centers because they are miserably cold. A shivering hell. Cárdenas takes these fragments of selves and places them in strategic spaces—the Humanitarian Respite Center at Sacred Heart Church in McAllen, Texas; near the Rio Grande River; the port of entry in Hidalgo, Texas; a water station at an immigration checkpoint in Falfurrias, Texas; the grave of an unidentified migrant in the cemetery in Falfurrias. Let us see the images:[10]

433 soles entering the United States through the Rio Grande or "El Río Bravo," as the river is known in México. Copyright © Verónica G. Cárdenas.

433 soles turning themselves in at the port of entry in Hidalgo, Texas. Copyright © Verónica G. Cárdenas.

433 soles getting water while avoiding the immigration checkpoint in Falfurrias, Texas. Copyright © Verónica G. Cárdenas.

433 soles visiting the remains of a migrant's unidentified body at the cemetery in Falfurrias, Texas. Copyrighte © Verónica G. Cárdenas.

I wish to start a discussion of these photographs by way of a discussion about the cross that the soles are visiting in the photograph directly above. I immediately wonder whether these soles will become crosses too, but I do not wish to dwell on that thought. For now, I think of the present, a present permeated by past injuries. I am reminded of the *descansos*, or roadside memorials, that are so prevalent in highways in Mexico but also closer by, the memorials we find along US highways where there has been a tragic death, what scholars formerly called "spontaneous memorials"[11] but are now referred to "grassroot memorials."[12]

Such memorials are found on highways but also in urban areas. They are called *descansos* and are found in various states in the United States, being particularly ornate in New Mexico. For example:

Roadside memorial, around mile marker 13 on US 550 west out of Bernalillo, New Mexico. Copyright © John Fowler, Wikimedia Commons [https://www.flickr.com/photos /snowpeak/3872188202/].

Roadside memorial, Riggs Road, Gila River Indian Reservation, Arizona. Copyright © Kevin Dooley, Wikimedia Commons [https://www.flickr.com/photos/pagedooley /13330451324/].

But there are also the less elaborate but no less important ones, simple white crosses growing from the ground like some type of strange plant looking for sun:

"andy kyle 1997" [https://www
.flickr.com/photos/15362885@N00
/3741673202] by vistavision [https://
www.flickr.com/photos/15362885@
N00] is licensed under CC BY-NC-
ND 2.0 [https://creativecommons.org
/licenses/by-nc-nd/2.0/]

Here I am interested in finding the nexus between *descansos* and *Traveling Soles* in terms of the production of a particular space, a space that is multifaceted insofar as it is "sacred space," "counter space" in the sense that Lefebvre notes,[13] a liminal space as Gloria Anzaldúa would have it. In particular, I am interested in the anamnetic powers of the production of the spaces as well as in the spatialities themselves, which, because they are between the public and the private, the sacred and the profane, the visible and the invisible, can be said to be haunting. Ultimately, I wish to show that what Cárdenas effectively does is not only to document, for the purposes of an archive of feeling, the history of Latinx migration in this country; she also produces altars for the living which are *memento vivere*, a combination of spaces and objects aimed at reminding us not just to live but to live in a particular way that does not forget the lives of those who have been injured. They have been injured not by tragic accidents but by tragic, yes, tragic, historical circumstances in which coloniality, empire, capitalism, and neoliberalism collide so as to force countless of people into dangerous migrations. While I do not have the time to dwell here on these historical circumstances, I do wish to remind the reader of the long history of US involvement in Latin America and specifically in Central America, a history marked by military interventions and support of oppressive governments. Take, for example, the US Marines' occupation in Panama from 1903 to 1914 to safeguard the interests of the United States during the construction of the Panama Canal; the occupation of Nicaragua from 1912 to 1933 and subsequent support of the Somoza family; the 1954 CIA-backed armed overthrow of Jacobo Arbenz Guzmán in Guatemala in order to protect landholdings of the powerful US corporation, the United Fruit Company; the 1980s involvement in the civil war in El Salvador, in which the United States fought against the rebel group FMLN (Farabundo Martí National Liberation Front); support of the Contras in order to destabilize the government of the Sandinistas in Nicaragua after the 1979 overthrow of the dictator Anastacio Somoza Debayle; and actions connected to the overthrow of Honduran president Manuel Zelaya in 2009.[14] Cárdenas's *Traveling Soles* thus honors those migrants, border-crossers, whose lives have been tragically impacted by US colonial and economic interests.

In the following section I discuss the act of the production of the space of *descansos* or roadside memorials in general, whether they are on country roads, highways, or in urban centers. This will help us understand the way in which *descansos* can inform a reading of *Traveling Soles*, despite the fact that *descansos* are spontaneous and result from the tragic loss of life while the events that *Traveling Soles* documents do not have that unexpected quality. I will then reflect on the altarity of these spaces.

Haunted and Haunting Spaces

In his analysis of roadside memorials, Robert M. Bednar quotes W. J. T. Mitchell's view of landscapes as constituting "a dynamic medium" and "a process by which social and subjective identities are formed."[15] Following Anna Petersson, we can see the material world as an "important media for expressing, communicating, and experiencing, understanding and even debating different experiences of loss and bereavement."[16] In a play of absence and presence, ritualistic practices are carried out to call forth the memory of a loved one lost too soon. A cross is placed where it is not supposed to be placed, and this very act designates sacred ground. Through symbolic elements, primarily the cross, public spaces become private spaces of mourning while at the same time remaining public in what, inspired by Barthes, we could call a public *punctum*[17] that calls us, those driving by that road, that street, to remember to stop drinking and driving, to stop texting and driving, or simply to remember the dead. The symbolism of the cross is powerful. It is thought to prevent the soul of the deceased from getting lost or staying at the place of death,[18] or to keep the ghost of the deceased from haunting the location. There is also the Spanish tradition in which crosses were used by the side of the road to mark resting places (*descansos*) for those carrying a coffin to burial ground. In the Catholic tradition, the cross is supposed to be a reminder for those walking by the site to pray for the deceased as souls in purgatory need the prayers of the living.[19]

Importantly, the production of this space of mourning and memory-making is marked by a disruption of instituted modes of spatiality. As Henri Lefebvre has argued, capitalist modes of production seep through all aspects of experience, including spatiality—thus leading to the imposition of homogeneity and transparency everywhere we go. Spaces are broken up for practicality and visibility, what Lefebvre calls the modernist trio of readability-visibility-intelligibility takes over, and logics of visualization and metaphorization rule.[20] Highways, become part of that modernist machinery of space with its specific functions. They are to transport us in our pilgrimages of productivity. They are not supposed to be places of mourning. Yet, Lefebvre calls for a

counter space, a space that, as he notes, "shakes existing space to its foundation."[21] I see *descansos* as radically rupturing established rules of the meaning
and purpose of specific spatialities while at the same time producing another
kind of space, an alternative liminal space suffused with anamnetic power.[22]

These spaces of memory are liminal in various ways. As such, they have
the quality of in-between space in the way they disrupt the distinction
between the public and the private (private rituals of mourning mark public
roads aimed for practical purposes); in the way they play with presence and
absence (present objects point to absent loved ones); in the way that they mix
the sacred and the profane (the spiritual is intertwined with the material);
and in the way that they problematize the distinction between the visible and
the invisible (what I see in these spaces is not what is there). Insofar as these
liminal spaces call for practices of mourning which both recall the spiritual
and the worldly they can be considered altars, and they are memento mori—
not the discrete death masks or pieces of bone or tufts of hair of the beloved
hidden inside a portrait but shifting, earthly yet sacred ground of prayer and
remembrance.

In these makeshift sacred grounds, there is a logic of spectrality—that is,
these are places haunted and haunting insofar as they are shadowed ground.
They are grounds that harbor within them a history of violence. Here I want
to think of a different kind of violence than is associated with the grassroot
roadside memorials. Not because I do not think they do not matter. Again,
they are in-between sites of memory. But I wish to go back to Cárdenas's
series. She has specifically chosen spaces that are indeed haunted, not just by
those who cross and do not make it but also by the histories of US imperialism in Latin America and histories of economic exploitation that have left
more people dead or in perilous circumstances, thus forcing them to engage
in hellish journeys colored by an imagined brightness of what is really a discolored American Dream. The Rio Grande, the immigration checkpoint in
Falfurrias—these are spaces haunted and haunting. While I am deeply aware
of the popularity regarding discourses about ghosts and haunting in part due
to Avery Gordon's moving and influential analysis in *Ghostly Matters* and, of
course, the work of Toni Morrison, Marx, Derrida, and others, I do not wish
to avoid these ghostly matters. As Gordon herself explains:

> The ghost, as I understand it, is not the invisible or some ineffable
> excess. The whole essence, if you can use that word, of a ghost is that
> it has a real presence and demands its due, your attention. Haunting
> and the appearance of specters or ghosts is one way I tried to suggest,
> we are notified that what has been concealed is very much alive and
> present.[23]

For Gordon, there are three important characteristics of haunting: (1) ghosts
add strangeness into a space, thus "unsettling the propriety and property

lines that delimit a zone of activity or knowledge"; (2) ghosts are symptoms of what is missing and, as such, they represent loss but also future possibilities (I will return to this point later); and (3) a ghost is alive and thus we "must reckon with it graciously, attempting to offer it a hospitable memory out of a concern for justice."[24]

Cárdenas's series of photographs enact a haunting. It presents us first with 250 and then 433 shoes that unsettle the chosen spaces as well as those who can visit the space and those who look at the photographs. They may represent a call to justice that is missing for these border-crossers in their journey as well as in their places of origin. And they call on us to *remember* them. No, they are not dead, although "social death" might apply in their future.[25] For Gordon, ghosts carry the departed in the present and point to a longing in the future. For me, the soles/souls animated in Cárdenas's photographs are alive. These are ghostly subjectivities that are being forgotten. So many have literally been left in limbo, in purgatory, stuck in *hieleras* with no knowledge of what will happen to them, unless the US immigration system decides to do justice to them. We have, then, these souls floating not in an ethereal, transcendent limbo but in real, brutal, inhumane spaces in which their health does not matter, and their futures even less. As Andrew Gumbel reports in an article for *The Guardian* regarding the quality of the US holding facilities for these immigrants, conditions are "grim," unhygienic, and inhumane, with reports of immigrants having only a thin metallic sheet to warm themselves, sleeping on the floor, being hungry, being maltreated and teased by guards, and many times having been separated from other family members due to the Trump presidency's "zero tolerance" policy implemented in April 2018 which called for the prosecution of all those crossing the border into the United States without documents.[26] Gumbel quotes Rafael Martinez's comment about his experience in the detention facility: "There we were, caged up like animals, and they were laughing at us."[27] Imagine, then, the horror of this cold, grim purgatory holding so many souls in need of altars.

As Laura Pérez notes in her influential analysis of Chicana aesthetics, Chicana altar art is *alter* art. Chicana altars are altars of alterity. As she claims, the altar has been "a site for the socially and culturally 'alter' or other, to express, preserve, and transmit cultural and gender-based religious and political differences."[28] They also disclose otherness. So, altar art is created by those considered to be other about their condition. It discloses the lives of Chicanas at the margins and their spiritual politics. When considering Amalia Mesa-Bains's altar art, Pérez explains that Mesa-Bains's table-like altars are places "for the care of the self."[29] For her series, Cárdenas constructed altars for the living who have been forgotten. The care of the self that is found in the spaces is not care of the individual self but communal care. Cárdenas makes art about that which matters to her, but she also produces a space of altarity, alterity, and in-betweenness that calls us to remember. She has created mnemonic sacred spaces but in the name of the living.

In order to create these spaces of alterity, Cárdenas started collecting shoes at the beginning of 2016 from the Humanitarian Respite Center in McAllen, Texas, which was opened in order to help the increasing number of asylum seekers entering McAllen after being processed by authorities. Volunteers usually take asylum seekers to the center, where they can shower and get clean clothes and shoes. Seeing that the old shoes were discarded, Cárdenas got the idea for the series early in 2014. With the aid of friends, she was able to place the shoes in the areas described, removing them as soon as the photographs were taken. She then gathered the shoes and stored them, thus keeping the now-sacred objects. Similar to grassroot memorials, the sites are filled with objects belonging to those whose memory needs to be honored. As Cárdenas states:

> I think that when the shoes are placed there, it is a way of making the place come back to life. By placing the shoes, missing their owners, it is a way of not showing their absence, but it is more of a reminder that there are people continuously taking the same paths. It is a non-stop flow of people coming seeking asylum, evading Border Patrol and also dying. So, when we place the shoes, I think of a large group of people that was passing by those places and then they stopped so that I could take their photo to document that small fragment of their journey. This would only apply to those that are seeking asylum. When I took the photo of the shoes gathered around the water barrel or the cross, I think of asylum seekers honoring those that had to take a different journey. So, by showing the shoes and imagining that the shoes' owners are present, it's my way of documenting that this is never ending.[30]

The spatialities produced, then, intertwine the individual and the communal, the sacred and the material, presence and absence, and memory and forgetting. They are altars for the living and for those who perish in their migration, and they are living paths insofar as they signal actual trajectories that forge possibilities of survival.

In addition, Cárdenas's photographs themselves are art objects that can be understood as forging aesthetic memory, a type of memory that is both prompted and preserved through the aesthetic work and its experience. Photographs of those shoes, those soles/souls waiting for water, looking at the waters of the Rio Grande, at the grave of an unidentified border-crosser, point to those who crossed, are crossing, and will continue to cross as the embodied consequence of the way in which capitalism, imperialism, and racism inform US practices and relations of power with Mexico and Central American countries. In my view, the function of the art object, in this case, photographic images, is not simply a recording of events that have clear indexical qualities. Rather, these photographs mark an *empty* index—empty because the border-crossers are no longer in the places photographed. The border-crossers are marked by empty soles. The index of these photographs cannot be simply, as Barthes would put it, the "that has been" of soles, of shoes.[31] Let's look at some of the other photographs in the series, along with the descriptions that Cárdenas includes about the owners of the shoes:

Luis, Honduran, age 8. His mother left him when he was only two years old. Luis's father says that "violence gets worse everyday." Gang members started recruiting him to work for them when he was only 10. His father opted to give him a better future by taking him to the United States. Since they did not have the economic means, they had to board *La bestia* (The Beast), the cargo train that some migrants take in order to get to the northern part of México. Copyright © Verónica G. Cárdenas.

Alondra, Honduran, age 3. There were complications while she was being born and as a result, she cannot walk, although the prognosis for the next two years is good. Her father lost a leg when he was run over by a vehicle. Alondra's mother along with her older sister moved to the United States three years ago. Her father did not tell her mother that he would embark on this journey along with their youngest daughter. Despite their physical limitations, they were able to get to the United States. Copyright © Verónica G. Cárdenas.

Fernando, Guatemalan, age 4. He and his mother left their country to seek a better life since they had lost their home and his father left them. They were able to escape alive after the *federales*, Mexican police, shot the trailer in which they were being transported. Fernando spent his fourth birthday hiding from the Mexican migration agents in the bushlands. Copyright © Verónica G. Cárdenas.

In addition to pointing to a border-crossing that has the possibility of material, living paths to a better future or perhaps to mere survival, Cárdenas's photos index a thereness of selves that are no longer in those spaces but in detention facilities, deported, or in the precarious condition of the undocumented self. The photographs point to the absence of these selves, these children who, as we can read from Cárdenas's explanation of the reasons for their migration, had painful, perilous journeys. But as Lisa Saltzman states in her powerful study on art, memory, and history, even when emptied, the index has a semiotic function and "emerges as a compelling form for concretizing and commemorating loss, for marking and memorializing absence."[32] Whereas art historians such as Saltzman concentrate on the empty index in works by well-known artists such as Glenn Ligon and Kara Walker, whose important work points to the loss of so many African American lives as they succumbed to slavery, I find that Cárdenas's photographs also point to "spectral presence."[33] As such, they point to an emptied index that nevertheless takes us to the presence, in this case, of those who are being forgotten and thus remain in cold purgatory—if they have not already been deported only to face the violence they were running from in the first place. They constitute aesthetic memories that perform memory work at a time when the usual practices of memory-making either fail or are not called upon, and what remains is a forgetting. This is a forgetting that thousands of Central Americans, most of them children, crossed the perilous border, many of them unaccompanied, and they remain in the United States waiting in their cold cells.[34]

In discussing her project, Cárdenas also explains, "I wanted for people to imagine what the owner of those shoes went through."[35] This is a particularly important point to remember as the single pairs of shoes above are those of children. We must imagine then what it took for young children, many of whom were suffering from hunger and dehydration, to arrive at the US-Mexico border after dangerous travel in northbound freight trains called *la bestia* and then walk miles and miles on different types of terrain.[36] Without wishing to reify the image of the child here (and thus a heteronormative understanding of the role of children), it is of the utmost importance that we consider these children's experiences in terms of the way their bodies and minds are being pushed to the limit. We must consider their exhaustion, hunger, thirst, confusion, fear, dread—a complete displacement of quotidian modes and spaces of comfort. It is not the case that the perilous travel that adult border-crossers experience is any less brutal. Yet, echoing the sentiment of Ivan Karamazov in *The Brothers Karamazov*, the suffering of children does not make sense. While in Dostoevsky's novel Ivan is concerned about the suffering of children in a religious context and thus explores the important problem of evil as understood in the philosophy of religion, we can still use his work to consider the suffering of children in any context and raise its utter incomprehensibility and injustice. We must then imagine *and* remember what the owners of these soles/souls have gone through in their perilous travel and crossing of the US-Mexico border.[37]

It is important to remember especially because the forgetting of not just their experiences but the border-crossers themselves, both those who survived and those who perished, identified and unidentified, is not a simple forgetting or failure of memory practices. It is a sustained forgetting. It is an intentional practice better understood as part of the project, yes, the active project of epistemic ignorance. It is also a deep forgetting as M. Jacqui Alexander would call it.[38] Knowledge of these selves as well as their imprisonment and their brutal deaths at the border is intentionally covered up. If it is not covered up, it is transformed and included in a different narrative, one that upholds hypernationalistic, xenophobic standards that consequently tell their story as that of "illegals" who come to this country to "milk" the United States. Think here of the unfortunate tale of mothers who are said to come here to have babies in order to drain the American system.[39] They are also described as criminals, gang members, and rapists. We thus encounter a double-edged process in the national imaginary regarding these border-crossers. On the one hand, they are made invisible, their lives and deaths of no consequence to the nation. And on the other hand, they are made hypervisible by way of a narrative of criminality.

Given this double-edged sword that doubly injures the border-crossers to whom Cárdenas builds altars and sacred grounds, the function of aesthetic memory becomes key as the photographs serve both to negate these narratives of invisibility and hypervisibility and to preclude the possibility of these beings and their stories being relegated to oblivion. Despite the fact that, as we have seen, the photographs index spectral presence, and a certain void and emptiness, they nevertheless carry with them crucial mnemonic possibilities. As the products and recorders of altars of alterity, they may help us—or rather, *haunt* us—not to forget. Such is the nature of spectrality.

And what remains when the shoes are removed from the sites chosen by Cárdenas? More voids. Yet, as Margry and Sánchez-Carretero point out in their analysis of grassroot memorials, a void—that is, the void of a nonpresent memorial that reflects absence—adds a powerful emotional indexical quality to the emptiness.[40] Such an indexical quality also carries with it the invitation to memory-making.

Through her work, Cárdenas produces particular spaces of mourning for border-crossers and altars for the living. Her photographs, in turn, can be understood as indexing a spectral presence, a play of both presence and absence, that serves to memorialize not the dead but the living—those who risk their lives in order to flee violence or find the so-called American Dream. As such they are also *memento vivere*. They are reminders of the lives of border-crossers, and reminders that we need to live in such a way so as to not forget.

There Is No Heaven

Cárdenas's photographs can be understood as sites of memory that are also calls for mourning of lives lost crossing the US-Mexico border and of the lives of those border-crossers who have been caught and remain in limbo under terrible conditions in *hielera*-like detention centers. Her photographs push us to confront a reality that in the current US imaginary has been relegated to forgetting. As we have seen, in their function as representing altars for the living and also for the dead who have died in their journey to the United States, Cárdenas's photographs may also function as aesthetic memories whose purpose is not only to record the lives and experiences of border-crossers but also to preclude the possibility of us forgetting their plight. Although these aesthetic memories and memorials are markers for the lives of the marginalized and in some cases may serve as a call to conscience, even if for an instant, or an archive of feeling, they are not to supplant the daily reality of those whose crossings are memorialized. Their mnemonic function is not a simple, "let's remember and life is better." Or, "art saves." Like my view of hometactics,[41] the production of spaces of memorialization in the in-between, between the shadow and the light, in the cracks, between life and death, are memorytactics à la de Certeau which we already enact as a way of dealing with the forgetting that is so much a part of worlds ruled by imperialism, colonization, and the rule of capital. This is a forgetting that remains etched in histories of violence. If only we could indeed etch visas[42] on whatever paper we find and give them to all those running for their lives and their children's lives, lives cut short not by death but by growing up too fast in a cold, brutal, and indifferent purgatory. There is no heaven for them.

Notes

1. Peter Jan Margry and Cristina Sánchez-Carretero, eds., *The Politics of Memorializing Traumatic Death* (New York: Berghahn Books, 2011).

2. "Coyote" is the term given to one who smuggles undocumented migrants across the US-Mexico border. An ICE agent is a US Immigration and Customs Enforcement officer.

3. For a discussion on the unaccompanied children arriving at the US Border see Fernanda Echavarri, "64,000 Kids Have Showed Up Alone at Our Border This Year. Filthy Cages Are Just Part of the Story," *Mother Jones*, July 10, 2019, https://www.motherjones.com/politics/2019/07/border-detention-unaccompanied-children-trump-minors-honduras/.

4. Cvetkovich describes the "archive of feelings" as "cultural texts as repositories of feelings and emotions, which are encoded not only in the content of the texts themselves but in the practices that surround their production and reception." Ann Cvetkovich, *An Archive of Feelings: Trauma, Sexuality, and Lesbian Public Cultures* (Durham, NC: Duke University Press, 2003), 7.

5. Jason de León, *The Land of Open Graves, Living and Dying on the Migrant Trail* (Berkeley: University of California Press, 2015), 25–28.

6. de León, *The Land of Open Graves*, 29. It is important to remember that for de León, this desert is not just a massive open grave but a "crime scene" because of the fact that the deaths of these immigrants are not merely due to the hostile terrain but to a strategic federal plan, "Prevention Through Deterrence (PTD)," that relies on the earth, on brutal terrain, to stop people from crossing into the US. PTD was first implemented in 1993 in El Paso, Texas. The strategy aims at funneling border-crossers into remote, inhospitable areas, where the cruelty of a harsh terrain will take care of the problematic intruders.

7. de León, *The Land of Open Graves*, 6.

8. A key point to remember is that the numerous South-to-North migrations, specifically migrations from Mexico and Central America, are a result of complex historical and economic factors prompted by various US interventions—political, military, and economic—that have had atrocious consequences for these areas and thus have contributed to the waves of migrations to the North. For an important discussion of how US involvement in Central America has led to instability, violence, poverty, and US domination in the area, see Walter LaFeber, *Inevitable Revolutions: The United States in Central America* (New York: W. W. Norton & Company, 1993). For a discussion of Central American migration to Mexico and the United States as a result of political and economic unrest in the 1980s and 1990s, see María Cristina García, *Seeking Refuge: Central American Migration to Mexico, The United States and Canada* (Berkeley.: University of California Press, 2006). For a historical account of the US-Mexico border, see Rachel St. John, *Line in the Sand: A History of the Western U.S. Mexico Border* (Princeton, NJ: Princeton University Press, 2011). For a narrative of asylum that includes first-person perspectives, see Eileen Truax, *We Built the Wall: How the U.S. Keeps Asylum Seekers from Mexico, Central America, and Beyond* (London, UK: Verso Books, 2018). For understanding the impact of NAFTA (North American Free Trade Agreement) on various facets of the lives of Mexicans, including migration practices to the United States, see Alyshia Gálvez, *Eating NAFTA: Trade, Food Policies, and the Destruction of Mexico* (Berkeley: University of California Press, 2018).

9. See Walter Benjamin, "On Some Motifs in Baudelaire," in *Illuminations, Essays and Reflections* (New York: Schocken Books, 1968). In this essay Benjamin discusses the notion of "shock" in the context of modernity. Shocks disrupt the linearity of history and make apparent one's dislocation within capitalist culture.

10. See the entire series, in color, on Cárdenas's website: http://veronicagabriela.com/traveling-soles/.

11. C. Allen Haney, Christina Leimer, and Juliann Lowery, "Spontaneous Memorialization: Violent Death and Emerging Mourning Ritual," *Omega* 35, no. 2 (1997): 159–71.

12. Margry and Sánchez-Carretero, *The Politics of Memorializing Traumatic Death*.

13. Lefebvre, *The Production of Space*, 383–85.

14. For a particularly influential critical account of US interventions in Central America with various editions, see Noam Chomsky, *Turning the Tide: U.S.*

Intervention in Central America and the Struggle for Peace (London: Pluto Press, 2015).

15. Robert M. Bednar, "Killing Memory: Roadside Memorial Removals and the Necropolitics of Affect," *Cultural Politics* 9, no. 3 (2013): 338.

16. Anna Petersson, "The Production of a Memorial Place: Materialising Expressions of Grief," in *Deathscapes: Places of Death, Dying, Mourning and Remembrance*, ed. Avril Maddrell and James D. Sidaway (Farnham, UK: Ashgate Publishing, 2010), 142.

17. For Barthes, the *punctum* is a highly subjective element in the photograph that moves the viewer to continue exploring the image. As Barthes states, the *punctum* is the element "which rises from the scene, shoots out of it like an arrow, and pierces me." Roland Barthes, *Camera Lucida: Reflecting on Photography* (New York: Hill and Wang, 1981), 26. Here, however, I am rethinking this idea of an individual subjective *punctum* and exploring the possibility of a communal *punctum* in light of experiences of public mourning.

18. Ana María Portal, "Las creencias en el asfalto: La sacralización como una forma de apropiación del espacio público en la ciudad de México." *Cuadernos de Antropología Social*, no. 30 (2009): 67.

19. Jon K. Reid and Cynthia L. Reid, "A Cross Marks the Spot: A Study of Roadside Death Memorials in Texas and Oklahoma," *Death Studies* 25, no. 4 (2001): 344.

20. Lefebvre, *The Production of Space*, 98–99.

21. Lefebvre, *The Production of Space*, 383.

22. Historian Pierre Nora's account of *"lieux de mémoire,"* or "sites of memory," may be helpful to understand these sites. As Nora states: "The *lieux* of which I speak are hybrid places, mutants in a sense, compounded of life and death, of the temporal and the eternal. They are like Mobius strips, endless rounds of the collective and the individual, the prosaic and the sacred, the immutable and the fleeting. For although it is true that the fundamental purpose of a *lieux de mémoire* is to stop time, to inhibit forgetting, to fix a state of things, to immortalize death, and to materialize the immaterial (just as gold, they say, is the memory of money)—all in order to capture the maximum possible meaning with the fewest possible signs—it is also clear that *lieux de mémoire* thrive only because of their capacity for change, their ability to resurrect old meanings and generate new ones along with new and unforeseeable connections . . ." Pierre Nora, *The Realms of Memory: The Construction of the French Past*, ed. Laurence D. Kritzman, trans. Arthur Goldhammer (New York: Columbia University Press, 1996), 15.

23. Avery F. Gordon, *Ghostly Matters: Haunting and the Sociological Imagination* (Minneapolis: University of Minnesota Press, 1997), xvi.

24. Gordon, *Ghostly Matters*, 63.

25. Orlando Patterson, *Slavery and Social Death: A Comparative Study* (Cambridge, MA: Harvard University Press, 1982). While Patterson develops the notion of social death in the context of slavery, this notion can be extended to lives which have been denied the possibility of identity and freedom within different contexts.

26. See Andrew Gumbel, " 'They Were Laughing at Us': Immigrants Tell of Cruelty, Illness, and Filth in US Detention," *The Guardian*, September 12, 2018,

https://www.theguardian.com/us-news/2018/sep/12/us-immigration-detention
-facilities. For information on the "zero tolerance" policy see Salvador Rizzo,
"The Facts about Trump's Policy Separating Families at the Border," *The Washington Post*, June 19, 2018, https://www.washingtonpost.com/news/fact-checker
/wp/2018/06/19/the-facts-about-trumps-policy-of-separating-families-at-the
-border/?noredirect=on&utm_term=.454f6880f686.

27. Gumbel, "'They Were Laughing at Us.'"

28. Laura E. Pérez, *Chicana Art: The Politics of Spiritual and Aesthetic Altarities* (Durham, NC: Duke University Press, 2007), 91.

29. Pérez, *Chicana Art*, 100.

30. Email correspondence with Cárdenas dated January 11, 2019.

31. For Barthes, the "essence" of photography consists in pointing to something "that has been." See Barthes, *Camera Lucida*, 76, 80.

32. Lisa Saltzman, *Making Memory Matter: Strategies of Remembrance in
Contemporary Art* (Chicago: University of Chicago Press, 2006), 20.

33. Saltzman, *Making Memory Matter*, 51.

34. For more information on the Central American Refugee Crisis, see Jonathan
T. Hiskey et al., "Understanding the Central American Refugee Crisis: Why They
Are Fleeing and How U.S. Policies Are Failing to Deter Them," American Immigration Council, February 1, 2016, https://www.americanimmigrationcouncil
.org/research/understanding-central-american-refugee-crisis; and "Fleeing for
Our Lives: Central American Migrant Crisis," Amnesty International, https://
www.amnestyusa.org/fleeing-for-our-lives-central-american-migrant-crisis/. For
information on the caravan of Central American refugees in the United States, see
Annie Correal and Megan Specia, "The Migrant Caravan: What to Know about
the Thousands Traveling North," *New York Times*, October 26, 2018, https://
www.nytimes.com/2018/10/26/world/americas/what-is-migrant-caravan-facts
-history.html.

35. Email correspondence with Cárdenas dated January 11, 2019.

36. For information on these trains, see Dominguez Villegas, "Central American Migrants and 'La Bestia': The Route, Dangers, and Government Responses,"
Migration Policy Institute, September 10, 2014, https://www.migrationpolicy.org
/article/central-american-migrants-and-%E2%80%9Cla-bestia%E2%80%9D
-route-dangers-and-government-responses.

37. See Fyodor Dostoevsky, *The Brothers Karamazov* (New York: W. W. Norton and Company, 1976), book 5, chapter 4. In this text one of the major issues
that Dostoevsky brings to light is the problem of evil (if God is omnipotent,
omniscient, and benevolent, why evil?), and in particular highlights the suffering
of children. Whether in a religious or philosophical context, understanding the
suffering of children presents a great challenge.

38. M. Jacqui Alexander, *Pedagogies of Crossing: Meditations on Feminism,
Sexual Politics, Memory and the Sacred* (Durham, NC: Duke University Press,
2005), 275. It is a forgetting that we have forgotten. It is also a wanting to forget.

39. For an analysis of "alien sexuality" and the notion of "anchor babies," see
Natalie Cisneros, "'Alien' Sexuality: Race, Maternity, and Citizenship," *Hypatia*
28, no. 2 (2013): 290–306.

40. Margry and Sánchez-Carretero, *The Politics of Memorializing Traumatic
Death*, 20.

41. Mariana Ortega, *In-Between: Latina Feminist Phenomenology, Multiplicity, and The Self* (Albany: SUNY Press, 2016), chapter 7. In my view, hometactics are everyday practices that allow for a sense of familiarity and a sense of "belonging" in various contexts, particularly in spaces in which we find ourselves alienated, othered, or unwelcomed.

42. Javier Zamora, *Unaccompanied*.

Bibliography

Alexander, M. Jacqui. *Pedagogies of Crossing: Meditations on Feminism, Sexual Politics, Memory and the Sacred*. Durham, NC: Duke University Press, 2005.

Amnesty International. "Fleeing for Our Lives: Central American Migrant Crisis." https://www.amnestyusa.org/fleeing-for-our-lives-central-american-migrant-crisis/.

Barthes, Roland. *Camera Lucida: Reflections on Photography*. Translated by Richard Howard. New York: Hill & Wang, 1980.

Bednar, Robert M. "Killing Memory: Roadside Memorial Removals and the Necropolitics of Affect." *Cultural Politics* 9, no. 3 (2013): 337–56.

Benjamin, Walter. "On Some Motifs in Baudelaire." In *Illuminations, Essays and Reflections*, edited by Hannah Arendt, 155–200. New York: Schocken Books, 1968.

Chomsky, Noam. 2015. *Turning the Tide: US Intervention in Central America and the Struggle for Peace*. London, UK: Pluto Press.

Cisneros, Natalie. "'Alien' Sexuality: Race, Maternity, and Citizenship." *Hypatia* 28, no. 2 (2013): 290–306.

Correal, Annie, and Megan Specia. "The Migrant Caravan: What to Know about the Thousands Traveling North." *New York Times*, October 26, 2018. https://www.nytimes.com/2018/10/26/world/americas/what-is-migrant-caravan-facts-history.html.

Cvetkovich, Ann. *An Archive of Feelings, Trauma, Sexuality, and Lesbian Public Cultures*. Durham, NC: Duke University Press, 2003.

de León, Jason. *The Land of Open Graves: Living and Dying on the Migrant Trail*. Berkeley: University of California Press, 2015.

Dostoevsky, Fyodor. *The Brothers Karamazov*. New York: W. W. Norton and Company, 1976.

Gálvez, Alyshia. *Eating NAFTA: Trade, Food Policies, and the Destruction of Mexico*. Berkeley: University of California Press, 2018.

García, María Cristina. *Seeking Refuge: Central American Migration to Mexico, the United States and Canada*. Berkeley: University of California Press, 2006.

Gordon, Avery F. *Ghostly Matters: Haunting and the Sociological Imagination*. Minneapolis: University of Minnesota Press, 1997.

Gumbel, Andrew. "'They Were Laughing at Us': Immigrants Tell of Cruelty, Illness, and Filth in US Detention." *The Guardian*, September 12, 2018. https://www.theguardian.com/us-news/2018/sep/12/us-immigration-detention-facilities.

Haney, C. Allen, Christina Leimer, and Juliann Lowery. "Spontaneous Memorialization: Violent Death and Emerging Mourning Ritual." *Omega* 35, no. 2 (1997): 159–71.

Hiskey, Jonathan T., Abby Córdova, Diana Orcés, and Mary Fran Malone. "Understanding the Central American Refugee Crisis: Why They Are Fleeing and How U.S. Policies Are Failing to Deter Them." American Immigration Council, February 1, 2016. https://www.americanimmigrationcouncil.org /research/understanding-central-american-refugee-crisis.

LaFeber, Walter. *Inevitable Revolutions: The United States in Central America.* New York: W. W. Norton & Company, 1993.

Lefebvre, Henri. *The Production of Space*, translated by Donald Nicholson-Smith. Oxford, UK: Wiley-Blackwell, 1991.

Margry, Peter Jan, and Cristina Sánchez-Carretero, eds. *Grassroots Memorials: The Politics of Memorializing Traumatic Death.* New York: Berghahn Books, 2011.

Nora, Pierre. *The Realms of Memory: Rethinking the French Past.* New York: Columbia University Press, 1996.

Ortega, Mariana. "Hometactics." In *In-Between: Latina Feminist Phenomenology, Multiplicity, and the Self*, 193–214. Albany: SUNY Press, 2016.

Patterson, Orlando. *Slavery and Social Death: A Comparative Study.* Cambridge, MA.: Harvard University Press, 1982.

Pérez, Laura E. *Chicana Art: The Politics of Spiritual and Aesthetic Altarities.* Durham, NC: Duke University Press, 2007.

Petersson, Anna. "The Production of a Memorial Place: Materialising Expressions of Grief." In *Deathscapes: Spaces of Death, Dying, Mourning and Remembrance*, edited by Avril Maddrell and James D. Sidaway, 141–60. Farnham, UK: Ashgate Publishing, 2010.

Portal, Ana María. "Las Creencias en el Asfalto: La Sacralización como una Forma de Apropiación del Espacio Público en la Ciudad de México." *Cuadernos de Antropología Social*, no. 30 (2009): 59–75.

Reid, Jon K., and Cynthia L. Reid. "A Cross Marks the Spot: A Study of Roadside Death Memorials in Texas and Oklahoma." *Death Studies* 25, no. 4 (2001): 341–56.

Rizzo, Salvador. "The Facts about Trump's Policy Separating Families at the Border." *The Washington Post*, June 19, 2018. https://www.washingtonpost.com/news /fact-checker/wp/2018/06/19/the-facts-about-trumps-policy-of-separating -families-at-the-border/?noredirect=on&utm_term=.454f6880f686.

Saltzman, Lisa. *Making Memory Matter: Strategies of Remembrance in Contemporary Art.* Chicago: University of Chicago Press, 2006.

St. John, Rachel. *Line in the Sand: A History of the Western U.S. Mexico Border.* Princeton, NJ: Princeton University Press, 2011.

Truax, Eileen. *We Built the Wall: How the U.S. Keeps Asylum Seekers from Mexico, Central America, and Beyond.* London: Verso Books, 2018.

Villegas, Dominguez. "Central American Migrants and 'La Bestia': The Route, Dangers, and Government Responses." Migration Policy Institute, September 10, 2014. https://www.migrationpolicy.org/article/central-american-migrants -and-%E2%80%9Cla-bestia%E2%80%9D-route-dangers-and-government -responses.

Zamora, Javier. *Unaccompanied.* Port Townsend, WA: Copper Canyon Press, 2017.

Part III

Southern Practices

7

✦

"I Ain't Thinkin' 'Bout You"

Black Liberation Politics at the Intersection of Region, Gender, and Class

Lindsey Stewart

"I have listened to the northern abstractions about justice, and seen the cold hardness to the black individual. Therefore I stick to my point that this thing is a national problem instead of a sectional one. As I said, in some instances, the South is kinder than the North. Then the North adds the insult of insincerity to its coldness."

—Zora Neale Hurston

Moving across the country multiple times has brought to the fore how issues of class, race, and region collide when a Black woman like me opens her mouth to say that she *prefers* to live in the South. With a roll of the eyes from many Northern-bred Black colleagues (who surely have a Southerner *somewhere* in their family closet) and disappointed looks from friendly white liberals who would *not* get Hurricane Katrina horror tales from me, I became attuned to the many ways that Black Southern life is dismissed, erased, or ignored in academia. While many have recognized the importance of analyses that engage the intersection of race, gender, and class, we have largely under-theorized the role of regional identity at these intersections.[1] As I will show in this chapter, region is often a specter in Black political thought, haunting as a shorthand for intraracial class and gender tensions. However, taking seriously Alice Walker's claim that "no one could wish for a more advantageous heritage than that bequeathed to the Black writer in the South,"[2] I argue that there are social-political resources that emerge in the dynamic intersection of race, region, class, and gender. My specific example will be what I call "principled indifference."

"My Daddy Said Shoot"

One place to start a foray into regional discourse at the intersection of gender, race, and class would be contemporary discourse on Southern Black women's political agency. For instance, Black women voters in Alabama are largely responsible for Democrat Doug Jones's senatorial seat, which he won in a special election in December 2017. While a welcome result to many, this local election has caused aggravated discussions of race, gender, and region to flare up. Many have analyzed one particular problematic response to this event: the utter surprise, and even condescending demonstrations of gratitude, toward Black women. Historian Cynthia Greenlee argues that these responses harbor problematic assumptions about Black women's political agency. "More to the point, the surprise and awe of Americans over the Alabama outcome reinforces the ludicrous notion," Greenlee writes, "that Black Southerners have been out here twiddling our thumbs and waiting for the liberation bus to stop in Dixie. *But we been here.*"[3] Greenlee points out that a narrative of total Black victimization in the South has caused some to assume that we would be unable to participate in the electoral voting process, "that Black Alabamians have been ground into passive dust by the potent and public racism for which their home state has long been known—and were going to be MIA at the polls."[4]

However, this assumption fails to register the Black Radical Tradition in which these Black Alabamian women are participating.[5] This is a tradition that not only reaches back into the heart of the Reconstruction era but also was brought to our attention over a century ago by Black feminist writer Anna Julia Cooper. Back in 1886, Anna Julia Cooper noted that the failure to grasp the complexity of Southern Black women's political agency is, like the heel of young Achilles, a "vulnerable point" in Black political discourse.[6] Cooper is well known for positioning herself as a Black female Southerner in her works, and she held an abiding interest in Southern Black cultural traditions.[7] "I speak for the colored women of the South because it is there that the millions of blacks in this country have watered the soil with blood and tears," Cooper writes, "and it is there too that the colored woman of America has made her characteristic history, and there her destiny is evolving."[8] As a result, the welfare of these women is the proper measure of the racial "progress" of the nation.[9]

For Cooper, not only do most Black people live in the South but the experiences of Southern Black women in particular include valuable resources for liberation. Much of her work points to the legacies of agency in the South. For instance, in "The Status of Woman in America," Cooper refutes the argument that Black women have no political interests in or important insights relevant to the current Black liberation movement of her day. As a counterexample to this claim, Cooper points to the Black women of the South who are responsible for preserving the political integrity of Black men in the voting polls. At this time, only Black men had the right to vote, and they received pressure (through their bosses and the Ku Klux Klan, for example) to cast their votes for the Democratic party, a practice they called "voting away." However, doing so would directly hinder Black liberation efforts (given that this was before the switch that resulted in the political parties we have today). Cooper points to the folklore, in songs and tales, which contained records of Southern Black women who would threaten their men to prevent them from "voting away"—by public shaming, physical violence, or even withholding sex.[10] They also would show up at the voting polls, weapons ready, to prevent the men from voting Democrat. One sheriff in Louisiana remarked during the time, "by God, I thought there was going to be a revolution here. . . . The democrats are armed, and the women are coming out with cane-knives and hoes and axes."[11]

Cases like these led Cooper to write the following: "Talk as much as you like of venality and manipulation in the South, there are not many men, I can tell you, who would dare face a wife quivering in every fiber of her being at the thought of her husband's cowardice."[12] While the assumption was that Black people in the South had a lack of political agency due to the severity of racial oppression, Cooper's example highlights a very specific tradition of political influence. While these women were barred from the political game (seeing that they had no right to vote), they still managed to shape the political landscape. "It is largely our women in the South today who keep men solid in the Republican party," Cooper asserts.[13] Far from total victim or passive bystander, Cooper concludes that "to be a woman of the Negro race in America, and to be able to grasp the deep significance of the possibilities of the crisis, is to have a heritage . . . unique in the ages."[14]

I have offered this sliver of Southern Black women's political history to shine a light on insights that appear to be lost to our current national political discourse. As Nancy Tuana writes on epistemologies of ignorance, knowledges can be actively erased, such that "what was once common knowledge or even scientific knowledge can be transferred to the realm of ignorance . . ."[15] For Tuana, this underscores that, concerning ignorance, "why we do not know something, whether it has remained or been made unknown, who knows and who is ignorant, and how each of these shifts historically or from realm to realm, are all open to question."[16] Within Black feminist philosophy, Kristie Dotson has also noted that Black women's contributions are often made invisible through "ignorance-producing practices" that she calls "process-based invisibilities."[17] In the next two sections, I provide an account of how Black Southern life gets erased in our social and political discourse in order to, as Dotson advocates, "identif[y] and unpack the many process-based invisibilities shrouding black theoretical production."[18] Doing so puts me in a position to consider, as a "deliberate act of inheritance," the valuable social and political contributions and resources of Black Southern women.

"Earned All This Money, but They'll
Never Take the Country Out Me"

While there are many more recent texts that illustrate the regionalism I am
analyzing, I have chosen Iris Marion Young's *Justice and the Politics of Difference* because it has become an important, well-known text in social-political
philosophy. This text offers an important critique of John Rawls's conception
of justice as fairness, in part by arguing for the recognition of group-based
identities and harms. While I find Young's critique insightful, for this essay I
am interested in her attempts to formulate (albeit partial) solutions, such as
in the chapter "City Life and Difference." What does her political-liberatory
imaginary tell us about region in social-political discourse? While in "City
Life and Difference" Young is mostly interested in outlining a model of
social interaction that does not fall into either the communitarian or liberal
shortcomings, I am interested in how her discussions of the "urban" and her
privileging of "city life" as a normative ideal of politics implicitly privileges
the North.[19]

Young's defense of the city as the ideal social arrangement is based upon,
in part, the assertion that the communitarian's model of society is "wildly
utopian."[20] This is because bringing the communitarian model into fruition
would "require dismantling the *urban character* of the US."[21] That is, "contemporary political theory must accept urbanity as a material given for those
who live in advanced industrial societies," as Young writes, and "urban relations define the lives not only of those who live in the huge metropolises, but
those who live in suburbs and large towns."[22] Since "models of a transformed
society must begin from the material structures (i.e. urban relations) that
are given to us," Young starts from the city to imagine ideal social arrange-
ments.[23] "City life" is, for Young:

> a form of social relations which [she] define[s] as the being together
> of strangers. In the city persons and groups interact within spaces and
> institutions they all experience themselves as belonging to, but with-
> out those interactions dissolving into unity or commonness.[24]

This definition compliments Young's larger, normative view of politics, which
"must be conceived as a relationship of strangers who do not understand
one another in a subjective and immediate sense, relating across time and
difference."[25]

For Young, this social arrangement yields certain virtues or normative
ideals, such as social differentiation without exclusion and publicity (in the
Kantian sense).[26] And Young is forthright that these virtues are *ideals*. However, this does not make them utopian on her account because the "ideals of
city life [she] ha[s] proposed are realized incidentally and intermittently in
some cities today."[27] The question we should ask, however, is *which* cities is

she talking about? In the passage defining city life as a normative ideal, the only cities mentioned by name are Boston, San Francisco, and New York.[28] In my view, the absence of Southern cities from her account is not accidental. Rather, her account of cities prevents it.

First, her assertion that the character of the United States is "urban" conflates cities with urbanity—a condition that does not hold in major cities of the South. That is, while cities like New Orleans may have *infrastructures* that are urban, there are norms of rurality that complicate their urbanity. For example, one social relation that prevails is that of the "neighbor," rather than stranger. The neighbor is someone who is worthy of a warm greeting in the street. Someone who can be tapped in church. Someone who shoulders the responsibility of rearing your child if needed. Though seldom reaching across racial lines, these norms extend over small towns, neighborhoods, cities, and state boundaries, forming part of a "unity or commonness" that Young denies of cities.[29]

Second, in *Black-majority* Southern cities (like Memphis and Atlanta), Black Southerners often fashion a regional identity that defies the urban–rural dichotomy.[30] As sociologist Zandria Robinson notes, many Black Southerners exhibit a "country cosmopolitan worldview" that "draws upon tropes of the rural South—like home, community, family, and food—but decenters, configures, and relocates them" in urban Southern cities.[31] More to the point, "the dialectal interplay of urban and rural cultures" is central to this worldview and "explains the existence of black folk's incorporation of rural and small-town practices into their urban traditions."[32] Thus, while these Black-majority Southern cities *are* urban cities in some respects, "the intersection of rural and urban cultures" creates a "fundamentally different urban experience that affects the way regional, racial, and spatial identities were and are formed."[33]

One example is the form of social relations pertinent to African American culture, termed "ancestry." In "Rootedness: The Ancestor as Foundation," Toni Morrison describes ancestors as "sort of a timeless people whose relationships . . . are benevolent, instructive, and protective, and they provide a certain kind of wisdom."[34] One reason I am interested in the ancestor is because of the stakes in material histories (forced migration, uprootedness, enslavement, and homemaking) that inform this social relation for African Americans. Put another way, the ancestor embodies racial memory and connection.[35] Building upon Morrison's discussion of ancestors, Farah Jasmine Griffin expands the notion of the ancestor by noting that "the ancestor is present in ritual, religion, music, food, and performance. His or her legacy is evident in discursive formations like the oral tradition."[36] In other words, those rural and small-town practices that Black folks bring into their cities.[37] While this relationship is often a tumultuous one—as tumultuous as African Americans' deeply complicated relationship to the South itself—"keeping in touch" with the ancestors is highly valued. Drawing upon James Baldwin's fiction, Morrison observes that "when [we] cannot [touch the ancestor], then and only then [are we] frustrated, devastated, and un-regenerated."[38] Yet, when in touch with the ancestor, [we are] "regenerated" and "balanced."[39] In contrast to the ancestor, as Griffin notes, stands the stranger, a "cosmopolitan figure"[40] who "exists in a dialectical relationship with the ancestor."[41] Moreover, this dialectical relationship is regionalized: "While the ancestor originates in the South and lives in the North, for the most part the stranger is a Northern phenomenon."[42] Or, as Morrison notes, the ancestor is "imagined surviving in the village but not in the city."[43]

With her privileging of the stranger relation that is prevalent in *Northern* cities, Young cannot explain why thousands of Black millennials are moving from (Northern) cities that *do* offer them the "cover of anonymity and a critical mass [of strangers]" to rural-urban, Southern, Black-majority cities that *do not*.[44] Reniqua Allen, in her "Racism Is Everywhere, So Why Not Move South?," notes a "loneliness" that many Black millennials feel in Northern cities, prompting (reverse) migration for a sort of "visible humanity" in Southern cities.[45] Namely, "the idea that black people can live in an area where blackness is seen as valuable, despite the horrific past, because of the legacy that black people have left in the region."[46] Indeed, in the South, who you are is where you are from, and the question granted most weight upon meeting is, "Who your people?" Buried within this question is the insistence upon honoring a legacy of those who have built a life here. As Jesmyn Ward writes in "My True South: Why I Decided to Return Home," "even as the South remains troubled by its past, there are people here who are fighting so it can find its way to a healthier future, never forgetting the lessons of its long brutal history . . ."[47]

"My Daddy Warned Me about Men Like You"

When it comes to Black liberation in the United States, the North is also often a privileged site in our political thought. This is due, in part, to the geography of freedom drawn during enslavement and the abolitionist campaign, where emancipation was often charted Northward. One example can be found in W. E. B. Du Bois's *The Souls of Black Folk*, where gender, class, and region interact in his analysis of Black life. In "Of the Faith of the Fathers," Du Bois turns to a "study of Negro religion" to answer questions about the meaning of slavery, life, ethics, and desire for African Americans.[48] Drawing a (Hegelian) dialectical relationship between two strains of Black spiritual traditions, "voodooism" and "radicalism" versus Christianity and "hypocritical compromise," Du Bois sketches the "ethical attitude[s]" of Black folk with regard to persistent problems that plague Black life.[49] Moreover, these responses stand as an exemplar of the double-consciousness within which we "must live, move, and have our being."[50] In this essay, I focus on the latest step of the dialectic, where these two responses—radicalism and hypocritical compromise—are crystalized in region, classed as well as gendered. "To-day the two groups of Negroes, the one in the North, the other in the South, represent these divergent ethical tendencies," Du Bois writes, "the first tending toward radicalism, the other toward hypocritical compromise."[51]

For Du Bois, "hypocritical compromise" in the South stems from patterns of survival developed during enslavement. While Blacks have since been emancipated, Du Bois argues that the white South has refused to accept this change in status.[52] As a result, hypocritical compromise becomes the political tactic of the day for Black folk in the South.[53] I quote Du Bois in full here:

> To-day the young Negro of the South who would succeed cannot be frank and outspoken, honest and self-assertive, but rather he is daily tempted to be silent and wary, politic and sly; he must flatter and be pleasant, endure petty insults with a smile, shut his eyes to wrong; in too many cases he sees positive personal advantage in deception and lying. His real thoughts, his real aspirations must be guarded in whispers; he must not criticize, he must not complain. Patience, humility, and adroitness must, in these growing black youth, replace impulse, manliness, and courage.[54]

By contrast, in the North, there's a tradition of "radicalism" that stems from the abolitionist campaign:[55]

> In the North, the tendency is to emphasize the radicalism of the Negro. Driven from his birthright in the South by a situation at which every fiber of his more outspoken being and assertive nature revolts, he finds himself in a land where he can scarcely earn a decent living amid the harsh competition and color discrimination. At the same time, through schools and periodicals, discussions and lectures, he is intellectually quickened and awakened. . . . What wonder that every tendency is to excess—radical complaint, radical remedies, bitter denunciation, or angry silence.[56]

For Du Bois, neither attitude is sustainable, as he aims to find a middle term between these two extremes.[57] However, I want to draw attention to the language in the Southern passage. The mannerisms are that of a Southern belle—a dainty silence, swallowing criticisms, polite flattery, deft pleasantries. Quite literally, the "manliness" of Blacks is prevented in the South.

Du Bois extends these themes in his "Of the Coming of John," a story of a young Black boy named John who is reared in the South, sent "up North" to school to "become a man,"[58] and upon his return to the South is lynched. John's entrance to manhood culminates in a double-consciousness that is stimulated through Northern education, as in the quote above about the North.[59] However, this newfound consciousness is buttressed with middle-class trappings: "He grew in body and soul, and with him his clothes seemed to grow and arrange themselves; coat sleeves got longer, cuffs appeared, and collars got less soiled."[60] Not only are "cuffs" a far cry from his "happy bare-foot" days as a rural youth, but along with his manhood came a constellation of affects and mannerisms. The "waves of merriment" and "good-nature and genuine satisfaction with the world" that he once felt in the South in his youth are now replaced with constant complaint, bitter sarcasm, and seeth-ing anger in the North as an adult.[61] In the North, John "first noticed now the oppression that had not seemed oppression before," Du Bois observes, "differences that erstwhile seemed natural, restraints and slights that in his boyhood days had gone unnoticed or been greeted with a laugh."[62] Similar to Du Bois's portrait of the development of Black religion, progress is marked by regional shifts: from South to North in the personal story of the coming of John, and, institutionally, from the "heathenism of the Gold Coast to the institutional Negro church of Chicago" in Black religion.[63]

"I Ain't Thinkin' 'Bout You"

I would like to revisit the phenomenon Du Bois describes in the South by considering a *Southerner's* perspective. Du Bois, after all, was from New England. Due to the confluence of region, class, gender, and affect in Du Bois's account of Black life, Zora Neale Hurston (a Floridian) went so far as to claim that the Du Boisian concept of "double-consciousness" itself is actually a Black, male, middle-class, Northern (New England) phenomenon. "[The Ivy League Black man] was told so often that his mentality stood him alone among his own kind and that it was a tragic accident that made him a Negro," Hurston writes, "that he came to believe it himself and struck the tragic pose."[64] That is, Hurston thought this double-consciousness was due to the internalized racism these young men experienced during their tenure at "New England colleges," where it was "assumed that no Negro brain could ever grasp the curriculum of a white college," and so "there was bound to be some conflict between his dark body and his white mind."[65] As for her own relationship to Blackness, Hurston remarks, "I am not tragically colored. There is no great sorrow dammed up in my soul, nor lurking behind my eyes. I do not mind at all."[66]

Concerning her relationship with whites, Hurston describes an encounter similar to Du Bois's "hypocritical compromise" in her *Mules and Men*:

> [Negroes] are most reluctant at times to reveal that which the soul lives by. And the Negro, in spite of his open-faced laughter, his seem-ing acquiescence, is particularly evasive. You see, we are a polite

people and do not say to our questioner, "Get out of here!" We smile and tell him or her something that satisfies the white person because, knowing so little about us, he doesn't know what he is missing. . . . That is, we let the probe enter, but it never comes out. It gets smothered under a lot of laughter and pleasantries.[67]

Where Du Bois reads this response as acquiescence, deceitfulness, and cowardice, I argue that, for Hurston, it is a kind of refusal that is based, in part, upon an acute awareness of and intimacy with white folk's racism.[68] Rather than seriously entertain this conversation with whites or use this interaction as a "teachable" moment, African Americans in this example give the bare minimum needed to keep their inner life moving and undisturbed by whiteness. I call this type of response "principled indifference," part of a political strategy that I term the "politics of joy."

One place where we see Hurston performing principled indifference herself is in her essay "The 'Pet Negro' System":

It has been so generally accepted that all Negroes in the South are living in horrible conditions that many friends of the Negro up North actually take offense if you don't tell them a tale of horror and suffering. They stroll up to you, cocktail glass in hand, and say, "I am a friend of the Negro, you know, and feel awful about the conditions down there." That's your cue to launch into atrocities amidst murmurs of sympathy. If, on the other hand, just to find out if they really have done some research down there, you ask, "What conditions do you refer to?" you get an injured, and sometimes malicious look. Why ask these foolish questions?[69]

In response to Northern white liberals asking about how horrible racism is in the South, Hurston counters by appearing indifferent. While this practice put Hurston at odds with many of her Black (male) contemporaries, many letters and essays of Hurston's that have surfaced over the past two decades demonstrate that her position was not as naive as once assumed.[70]

For instance, Hurston's response points out the dangers in a popular culture that siphons off the nation's racism into the South. In a letter to Alain Locke, she describes this phenomenon as "Them Southerners Done Snuck Up Here and Done It Logic."[71] When Northerners are forced to desegregate, Hurston notes, they find "that [they] are no more willing to live in close communion with a number of Negroes than the southerners."[72] (A sentiment, I would argue, that has been behind a number of contemporary white folks calling the police when Black folks are simply taking up spaces that they want to keep "white.") However, these Northerners do not want to admit that they feel this way, so "they take refuge in saying that southerners moving north did it."[73] Or when these Northerners want to hold onto cultural conventions that are racist, perhaps they invoke an imaginary Southerner.[74]And even Black folk, the "Negroes who have gloried in the North . . . also join the chorus," so that racism can be blamed on this mythic Southerner in the bushes.[75] In contrast, Hurston urges us to see that racism is a national, not regional problem. "We must come out of our rosy dream that [racism] is only a sectional thing," Hurston tells Locke; "it is national, and we ought to recognize it as such and attack it from that angle."[76]

On an interpersonal level, managing these interactions in a way that did not steal her own joy or wantonly waste her energy meant performing indifference. Rather than stew or correct whites on their racism, "I have laughed to myself watching northerners," Hurston admits, "after saying to Negro individuals how distressed they were about the awful conditions down South, trying to keep Negroes from too close a contact with themselves."[77] Moreover, as I have written elsewhere, her refusal to accept a narrative of Black Southern tragedy and white Northern progression allowed her to render visible the assumptions of Black pathology that frame progressive, liberal discourse.[78] "They get mad if I don't let them defend me, . . . they condescend, and then are infuriated if I don't like it," Hurston observes, "which is just another way of telling me that I am incompetent, and ought to be proud to let them stand watch-and-ward over me, and pity me. It feels so good to them. I say, to hell with it!"[79]

Principled indifference continues to be a method of response in the South today. In a recent study, Robinson observed this phenomenon when her respondents, Black Southerners, would often say they were "not studyin' them white folks" when faced with blatant racism. Robinson writes that this is meant to "supplant emotional reactions to everyday racialized injustice" by "appearing unfazed by negative interracial interactions."[80] Indeed, "many respondents indicated that they are neither surprised nor regretful when 'good' white folks go bad," notes Robinson, "nor do they demonstrate or express gratefulness or surprise when 'bad' white folks do good."[81] I argue that the indifference described here is employed, in part, to insist upon Black agency in response to the national narrative of Black Southern tragedy. Robinson writes: "These respondents and others minimized the negative interaction to emphasize their agency."[82] This response is tied to the ancestral relation mentioned earlier in that the "respondents pass down and draw on regionally ingrained folk wisdom about whites and situate this knowledge as key to knowing precisely how best to engage whites."[83] That is, this indifference is a tradition of response passed down *through generations*. In addition, there is often a religious component as well, belief in some power registry *other* than white supremacy, that enables the respondents to "study" something else besides white folk.[84]

Most recently, we can also find the performance of Southern Black female indifference in Beyoncé's visual album, *Lemonade*. Set in the South with flashbacks to the Reconstruction era, the presence of the ancestor is evidenced by an inundation of references to Black spiritual traditions, such as hoodoo, voodoo, and Yoruba religion, that drive the narrative. One song in particular, "Sorry," captures principled indifference with the posturing of the protagonist, a woman who has been deeply betrayed by her lover. When he comes to make amends, she responds, "I ain't thinkin' bout you." She refuses to "study" his apology not because she is unwilling to forgive him but because of the continuation of bad behavior in the present (he is still cheating on her).[85] As I have argued elsewhere, the backdrop of this song—Destrehan Plantation in Louisiana, where one of the largest slave revolts in the United States occurred—suggests that the song has larger social and political implications as well.[86] For instance, the song points to racist beauty standards that emerged during plantation life (i.e., "Becky with the good hair"). I want to emphasize that the site of Beyoncé's performance of indifference is Destrehan Plantation because this fact illustrates the stakes present in the ancestral relation as a touchstone of inheritances—of *both* traditions of agency *and* residues of oppression.

An implicit privileging of the North via a problematic catalog of Black responses, as in Du Bois's account, would cause us to miss the rich complexity of how Black Southerners navigate their oppression. My point is not that the South is the only place where principled indifference is practiced or liberatory resources can be found. Rather, I have shown how inclusion of region in our analyses of Black agency *matters*. Namely, I have demonstrated how implicit normalization of the North can cause us to miss resources in Black political thought. One way to disrupt this normalization is to refuse the narrative of Black Southern tragedy by principled indifference. As Greenlee advocates in "Just Say No Thanks to #ThanksAlabama and 'Magical Negro' Narratives," this would be to appear indifferent to white tokens of gratitude that belie astonishment at Black Southern agency. In this way, principled indifference can shift the conversation such that it allows us to address the real issues that corrode coalition building, making it a particularly apt tool in our current political moment.

Notes

Epigraph: Zora Neale Hurston, "Letters: The Forties," in *Zora Neale Hurston: A Life in Letters*, ed. Carla Kaplan (New York: Anchor Books, 2003), 477.

Section Titles:
"My Daddy Said Shoot." Lyrics from Beyoncé, "Daddy Lessons," by Wynter Gordon, Beyoncé Knowles-Carter, Kevin Cossom, Alex Delicata, track 6 on *Lemonade*, Parkwood Entertainment and Columbia Records, Visual Album, April 2016.
"Earned All This Money . . ." Lyrics from Beyoncé, "Formation," by Khalif Brown, Asheton Hogan, Beyoncé Knowles-Carter, Michael Len Williams II, track 12 on *Lemonade*, Parkwood Entertainment and Columbia Records, Visual Album, February 2016.

"My Daddy Warned Me . . ." Lyrics from Beyoncé, "Daddy Lessons."
"I Ain't Thinkin' 'Bout You." Lyrics from Beyoncé, "Sorry," Wynter Gordon, MeLo-X, Beyoncé Knowles-Carter, track 4 on *Lemonade*, Parkwood Entertainment and Columbia Records, Visual Album, April 2016.

1. See Zandria Robinson, *This Ain't Chicago: Race, Class, and Regional Identity in the Post-Soul South* (Chapel Hill: University of North Carolina Press, 2014), 26.

2. Alice Walker, "The Black Writer and the Southern Experience," in *In Search of Our Mothers' Gardens: Womanist Prose* (San Diego, CA: Harcourt Brace Jovanovich, 1983), 21.

3. Cynthia Greenlee, "Just Say No Thanks to #ThanksAlabama and 'Magical Negro' Narratives," Rewire.News, December 14, 2017, https://rewire.news/article/2017/12/14/just-say-no-thanks-alabama-magical-negro/.

4. Greenlee, "Just Say No Thanks."

5. See also Sarah Lazare, "Don't Thank Democrats. A Tradition of Black Radical Organizing Paved the Way for the Alabama Upset," *In These Times*, December 14, 2017, http://inthesetimes.com/article/20768/Alabama-Roy-Moore-Doug-Jones-Black-Freedom-Voting-Suppression-Organizing. Lazare writes: "Leading pundits and politicians are celebrating the upset by Democrat Doug Jones with deracialized platitudes about the 'triumph of decency.' But racial justice organizers say credit should go to Black Alabamians—specifically, to the hard-fought Black radical tradition, in a state where many have sacrificed their homes, jobs and even lives to fight the exclusion and suppression of the African-American vote."

6. See Anna Julia Cooper, "Womanhood: A Vital Element in the Regeneration and Progress of a Race (1886)," in *The Voice of Anna Julia Cooper: Including A Voice from the South and Other Important Essays, Papers, and Letters*, ed. Charles Lemert and Esme Bhan (Lanham, MD: Rowman and Littlefield Publishers, 1998), 62.

7. Vivian M. May, "'By a Black Woman of the South': Race, Place, and Gender in the Work of Anna Julia Cooper," *Southern Quarterly* 45, no. 3 (2008): 127.

8. May, "'By a Black Woman of the South,'" 127. This quote is from Cooper's speech, "Woman's Cause Is One and Universal," given on May 18, 1893.

9. See Cooper, "Womanhood: A Vital Element," 62–63. See also Brittany Cooper, *Beyond Respectability: The Intellectual Thought of Race Women* (Urbana: University of Illinois Press, 2017), 5–6.

10. See Anna Julia Cooper, "The Status of Woman in America (1892)" in *The Voice of Anna Julia Cooper: Including A Voice from the South and Other Important Essays*, ed. Charles Lemert and Esme Bhan (Lanham, MD: Rowman and Littlefield Publishers, 1998), 114–15.

11. John C. Rodrigue, *Reconstruction in the Cane Fields: From Slavery to Free Labor in Louisiana's Sugar Parishes, 1862–1880* (Baton Rouge: Louisiana State University Press, 2001), 171.

12. Cooper, "The Status of Woman in America (1892)," 115.

13. Cooper, "The Status of Woman in America (1892)," 115.

14. Cooper, "The Status of Woman in America (1892)," 117.

15. See Nancy Tuana, "Coming to Understand: Orgasm and the Epistemology of Ignorance," *Hypatia* 19, no. 1 (2014): 195. Tuana writes that ignorance is an "active production," which is "frequently constructed and actively preserved, and is linked to issues of cognitive authority, doubt, trust, silencing, and uncertainty" (195).

16. Tuana, "Coming to Understand," 196.

17. See Kristie Dotson, "Radical Love: Black Philosophy as Deliberate Acts of Inheritance," *The Black Scholar* 43, no. 4 (2013): 39. Dotson also writes: "Process-based invisibility, on my account, refers to manufactured forms of invisibility that can be traced by the very processes that affect the disappearances in question" (39).

18. Dotson, "Radical Love," 39.

19. One of the most common strains of this argument in black political thought is offered by Hazel Carby in "Politics of Fiction, Anthropology, and the Folk: Zora Neale Hurston," in *New Essays on Their Eyes Were Watching God*, ed. Michael Awkward (New York: Cambridge University Press, 1991), 71–94. Carby argues that we romanticize (a past) South in order to avoid the current problems of Black life that plague us in the present. However, as Robinson notes, this argument has allowed "a generation of black literature" to "strategically displac[e] rural folk, and by extension southerners, from the narrative of black political agency." See Robinson, *This Ain't Chicago*, 202.

20. See Iris Marion Young, *Justice and the Politics of Difference*, (Princeton, NJ: Princeton University Press, 1990), 234.

21. Young, *Justice and the Politics of Difference*, 234, italics mine.

22. Young, *Justice and the Politics of Difference*, 237.

23. Young, *Justice and the Politics of Difference*, 234.

24. Young, *Justice and the Politics of Difference*, 237.

25. Young, *Justice and the Politics of Difference*, 234.

26. Young, *Justice and the Politics of Difference*, 236–40.

27. Young, *Justice and the Politics of Difference*, 241.

28. Young, *Justice and the Politics of Difference*, 236–40.

29. Young, *Justice and the Politics of Difference*, 237.

30. It is important to note as well that a comparatively large portion of the nation's African American population still resides in the South.

31. Robinson, *This Ain't Chicago*, 21.

32. Robinson, *This Ain't Chicago*, 21.

33. Robinson, *This Ain't Chicago*, 21.

34. Toni Morrison, "Rootedness: The Ancestor as Foundation," in *What Moves at the Margins: Selected Nonfiction*, ed. Carolyn C. Denard (Jackson: University Press of Mississippi, 2008), 62.

35. Toni Morrison, "City Limits, Village Values: Concepts of the Neighborhood in Black Fiction," in *Literature and the Urban Experience: Essays on the City and Literature*, ed. Michael C. Jaye and Ann Chalmers Watts (New Brunswick, NJ: Rutgers University Press, 1981), 43.

36. Farah Jasmine Griffin, *"Who Set You Flowin'?": The African-American Migration Narrative* (New York: Oxford University Press, 1995), 5.

37. What Toni Morrison calls "village values." See Toni Morrison, "City Limits, Village Values," 37–38. Morrison writes, "in spite of their labor and enterprise—the Black-owned oyster houses of Wall Street, the Black stone masons of Manhattan, the iron workers of New Orleans—the affection of black writers (whenever displayed) for the city seems to be for the village within it: the neighborhoods and populations of those neighborhoods," 37–38.

38. Morrison, "City Limits, Village Values," 39.

39. Morrison, "City Limits, Village Values," 39.

40. Griffin, *Who Set You Flowin'?*," 7.

41. Griffin, *Who Set You Flowin'?*," 6. Griffin also notes, concerning her take on "the stranger": "My concept of the stranger is greatly influenced, but not circumscribed by, the stranger 'who stays' in the work of the German-Jewish sociologist Georg Simmel. Simmel's stranger is a figure whose membership within a group involves being at once outside and within its boundaries" (7).

42. Griffin, *Who Set You Flowin'?*," 6.

43. Morrison, "City Limits, Village Values," 39.

44. Young, *Justice and the Politics of Difference*, 238.

45. Reniqua Allen, "Racism Is Everywhere, So Why Not Move South?," *The New York Times*, July 8, 2017, https://www.nytimes.com/2017/07/08/opinion/sunday/racism-is-everywhere-so-why-not-move-south.html.

46. Allen, "Racism Is Everywhere."

47. Jesmyn Ward, "My True South: Why I Decided to Return Home," *Time*, July 26, 2018, http://time.com/5349517/jesmyn-ward-my-true-south/.

48. See W. E. B. Du Bois, *The Souls of Black Folk*, in *W. E. B. Du Bois: Writings: The Suppression of the African Slave-Trade/The Souls of Black Folk/Dusk of Dawn/Essays*, ed. Nathan Huggins (New York: The Library of America, 1986), 495. Du Bois writes: "What did slavery mean to the African savage? What was his attitude toward the World and Life? What seemed to him good and evil,—God and Devil? Whither went his longings and strivings, and wherefore were his heartburnings and disappointments? Answers to such questions can come only from a study of Negro religion as a development, through its gradual changes from the heathenism of the Gold Coast to the institutional Negro Church of Chicago" (495).

49. Du Bois, *The Souls of Black Folk*, 499–500, 504.

50. Du Bois, *The Souls of Black Folk*, 501.

51. Du Bois, *The Souls of Black Folk*, 503.

52. Du Bois, *The Souls of Black Folk*, 503.

53. Du Bois, *The Souls of Black Folk*, 503.

54. Du Bois, *The Souls of Black Folk*, 503–4.

55. Du Bois, *The Souls of Black Folk*, 500–501.

56. Du Bois, *The Souls of Black Folk*, 504.

57. Du Bois, *The Souls of Black Folk*, 504.

58. In the story, there is an association drawn between going "up North" for school and "becoming a man." See Du Bois, *The Souls of Black Folk*, 523.

59. See Du Bois, *The Souls of Black Folk*, 525–26.

60. Du Bois, *The Souls of Black Folk*, 525.

61. See Du Bois, *The Souls of Black Folk*, 502, 525.

62. Du Bois, *The Souls of Black Folk*, 525.

63. Du Bois, *The Souls of Black Folk*, 495.

64. Zora Neale Hurston, "Art and Such," in *Zora Neale Hurston: Folklore, Memoirs, and Other Writings: Mules and Men/Tell My Horse/Dust Tracks on a Road/Selected Articles*, ed. Cheryl Wall (New York: The Library of America, 1995), 907.

65. Hurston, "Art and Such," 907.

66. Zora Neale Hurston, "How It Feels to Be Colored Me," in *Zora Neale Hurston: Folklore, Memoirs, and Other Writings*, 827.

67. Zora Neale Hurston, *Mules and Men*, in *Zora Neale Hurston: Folklore, Memoirs, and Other Writings*, 10.

68. For a full development of this claim, see my forthcoming "'Tell 'Em Boy Bye': Zora Neale Hurston and the Importance of Refusal" in *Signs: Journal of Women in Culture and Society*, section titled "It's Exactly What You Get."

69. Zora Neale Hurston, "The 'Pet Negro' System," in *Zora Neale Hurston: Folklore, Memoirs, and Other Writings*, 918.

70. From foundational Black feminist texts that rediscovered Hurston, such as Alice Walker's 1975 essay "Looking for Zora," originally published in *Ms. Magazine*, to a number of anthologies in the 1990s that made available crucial essays of Hurston's (such as *Zora Neale Hurston: Folklore, Memoirs, and Other Writings* edited by Cheryl Wall or *Go Gator and Muddy the Water: Writings by Zora Neale Hurston from the Federal Writers Project* edited by Pamela Bordelon), to, most recently, *Zora Neale Hurston: A Life in Letters*, an anthology of Hurston's letters edited by Carla Kaplan.

71. Zora Neale Hurston, "Letter to Alain Locke," in *Zora Neale Hurston: A Life in Letters*, 491.

72. Hurston, "Letter to Alain Locke," 490–91.

73. Hurston, "Letter to Alain Locke," 491.

74. See Hurston, "Letter to Alain Locke," 491. Hurston writes: "All [Northerners] need to say when they wish to exclude us from hotels and neighborhoods is to say, 'I don't care myself, but some southerners will come along and object" (491).

75. Hurston, "Letter to Alain Locke," 491.

76. Hurston, "Letter to Alain Locke," 491.

77. Hurston, "Letter to Douglass Gilbert," in *Zora Neale Hurston: A Life in Letters*, 476.

78. See my forthcoming "'Tell 'Em Boy Bye': Zora Neale Hurston and the Importance of Refusal" in *Signs: Journal of Women in Culture and Society*, section titled "It's Exactly What You Get."

79. Zora Neale Hurston, "Letter to Burton Rascoe," in *Zora Neale Hurston: A Life in Letters*, 503.

80. Robinson, *This Ain't Chicago*, 94, 97.

81. Robinson, *This Ain't Chicago*, 94.

82. Robinson, *This Ain't Chicago*, 107.

83. Robinson, *This Ain't Chicago*, 96.

84. See Robinson, *This Ain't Chicago*, 94.

85. Beyoncé sings, "I see them boppers in the corner/They sneaking out the back door/He only want me when I'm not there." Lyrics from Beyoncé, "Sorry."

86. See my forthcoming "'Tell 'Em Boy Bye': Zora Neale Hurston and the Importance of Refusal" in *Signs: Journal of Women in Culture and Society*, section titled "It's Exactly What You Get."

Bibliography

Allen, Reniqua. "Racism Is Everywhere, So Why Not Move South?" *New York Times*, July 8, 2017. https://www.nytimes.com/2017/07/08/opinion/sunday/racism-is-everywhere-so-why-not-move-south.html.

Beyoncé. *Lemonade*. Produced by Beyoncé Knowles-Carter, Alex Delicata, Ben Billions, Boots, DannyBoyStyles, Derek Dixie, Diplo, Ezra Koenig, HazeBanga, Hit-Boy, Jack White, James Blake, Jeremy McDonald, Jonny Coffer, Just Blaze, Kevin Garrett, King Henry, MeLo-X, Mike Dean, Mike Will Made It, Pluss, Stuart White, Vincent Berry II, and Wynter Gordon. Parkwood Entertainment and Columbia Records. Visual Album, 2016.

Bordelon, Pamela. "Zora Neale Hurston: A Biographical Essay." In *Go Gator and Muddy the Water: Writings from the Federal Writers' Project*, by Zora Neale Hurston, 3–49. New York: W. W. Norton & Co, 1999.

Carby, Hazel. "The Politics of Fiction, Anthropology, and the Folk: Zora Neale Hurston." In *New Essays on Their Eyes Were Watching God*, edited by Michael Awkward, 71–94. New York: Cambridge University Press, 1991.

Cooper, Anna Julia. *The Voice of Anna Julia Cooper: Including a Voice from the South and Other Important Essays, Papers, and Letters*. Edited by Charles Lemert and Esme Bhan. Lanham, MD: Rowman and Littlefield Publishers, 1998.

Cooper, Brittany C. *Beyond Respectability: The Intellectual Thought of Race Women*. Urbana: Univerity of Illinois Press, 2017.

Dotson, Kristie. "Radical Love: Black Philosophy as Deliberate Acts of Inheritance." *The Black Scholar* 43, no. 4 (2013): 38–45.

Du Bois, W. E. B. *The Souls of Black Folk*. In *W. E. B. Du Bois: Writings: The Suppression of the African Slave-Trade/The Souls of Black Folk/Dusk of Dawn/Essays*. Edited by Nathan Huggins. New York: The Library of America, 1986.

Greenlee, Cynthia. "Just Say No Thanks to #ThanksAlabama and 'Magical Negro' Narratives." *Rewire News*, December 14, 2017. https://rewire.news/article/2017/12/14/just-say-no-thanks-alabama-magical-negro/.

Griffin, Farah Jasmine. *"Who Set You Flowin'?": The African American Migration Narrative*. New York: Oxford University Press, 1995.

Hurston, Zora Neale. *Zora Neale Hurston: A Life in Letters*. Edited by Carla Kaplan. New York: Anchor Books, 2002.

———. *Zora Neale Hurston: Folklore Memoirs and Other Writings*. Edited by Cheryl A. Wall. New York: The Library of America, 1995.

Lazare, Sarah. "Don't Thank the Democrats: A Tradition of Black Radical Organizing Paved the Way for the Alabama Upset." *In These Times*, December 14, 2017. http://inthesetimes.com/article/20768/Alabama-Roy-Moore-Doug-Jones-Black-Freedom-Voting-Suppression-Organizing.

May, Vivian M. ""By a Black Woman of the South": Race, Place, and Gender in the Work of Anna Julia Cooper." *Southern Quarterly* 45, no. 3 (2008): 127–52.

Morrison, Toni. "City Limits, Village Values: Concepts of the Neighborhood in Black Fiction." In *Literature and the Urban Experience: Essays on the City and Literature*, edited by Michael C. Jaye and Ann Chalmers Watts, 35–45. New Brunswick, NJ: Rutgers University Press, 1981.

Morrsion, Toni. "Rootedness: The Ancestor as Foundation." In *What Moves at the Margins: Selected Nonfiction*, edited by Carolyn C. Denard, 56–64. Jackson: University Press of Mississippi, 2008.

Robinson, Zandria. *This Ain't Chicago: Race, Class, and Regional Identity in the Post-Soul South*. Chapel Hill: The University of North Carolina Press, 2014.

Rodrigue, John C. *Reconstruction in the Cane Fields: From Slavery to Free Labor in Louisiana's Sugar Parishes, 1862–1880*. Baton Rouge: Louisiana State University Press, 2001.

Stewart, Lindsey. "'Tell 'Em Boy Bye': Zora Neale Hurston and the Importance of Refusal." *Signs: Journal of Women in Culture and Society*, forthcoming.

Tuana, Nancy. "Coming to Understand: Orgasm and the Epistemology of Ignorance." *Hypatia* 19, no. 1 (2014): 194–232.

Walker, Alice. "The Black Writer and the Southern Experience." In *In Search of Our Mothers' Gardens: Womanist Prose*, 15–21. San Diego, CA: Harcourt Brace Jovanovich, 1983.

Walker, Alice. "Looking for Zora." *Ms. Magazine*, 1975.

Ward, Jesmyn. "My True South: Why I Decided to Return Home." *Time*, July 26, 2018. http://time.com/5349517/jesmyn-ward-my-true-south/.

Young, Iris Marion. *Justice and the Politics of Difference*. Princeton, NJ: Princeton University Press, 1990.

8

✦

Black Ancestral Discourses

Cultural Cadences from the South

Devonya N. Havis

Oppressed blackness has long been the stand-in representing blackness writ large.[1] It has functioned this way both as spectacle and invoked through tropes of mournful immiseration. Those who struggle under the yoke of racialized oppression are constituted merely as suffering subjects who, despite best efforts, remain piteous, trapped creatures with a legacy that is only mourning and immiseration. Such framing often elicits sympathy or, occasionally, outrage, but it does little to fundamentally change the conditions under which Black peoples find themselves. In addition, and perhaps more importantly, this framing functions to effectively obscure the complex, rich histories of refusal evident in the creative rites, rituals, and practices that texture African diasporic peoples' modes of existence.

In contrast, when one resources Black Ancestral Discourses as a heterogenous archive for Blackness, it becomes possible to hear the ethico-political cadences that constitute Blackness as more than a legacy of lamentation and reconciled survival. ("Archive" may be understood here as a stand-in for actual or figurative collections and gathered material.) In this break, one can hear beyond mere suffering to the alchemical register attuned to the "tragic-comic." Drawing upon alchemy as a metaphor, I draw attention to those cultural processes where transformation, transposition, and transmutation take place. In traditional alchemy, transmutation comes about when "base elements" are put into relation with each other. The interaction between and among the elements transforms the relationships and thereby alters the content of everything that has been included in the "experiment." Taking up *practices of freedom under conditions of unfreedom* requires an experimental spirit and alchemical interventions. Such interventions problematize the uncomplicated quest for freedom along with the supporting presumption that securing freedom will produce justice as a by-product of the struggle.

The focus on historic, ancestral "practices of freedom under conditions of unfreedom" opens a clearing for registering different possibilities for Blackness.

This chapter will foreground Blackness as other than immiseration by juxtaposing Black Ancestral Discursive archives with the more visible archive of popular culture that far too often renders blackness, and thereby black peoples, as mere deficiency resulting from oppression. As I will demonstrate, Colson Whitehead's Pulitzer Prize–winning novel, *The Underground Railroad*, published in 2016, models this weary trope. Despite being touted for its nuanced treatment of race, the novel only shows blackness as suffering deficit. Drawing upon fictionalized history, Whitehead depicts slave life and the endeavor to secure freedom. This account, however, produces a "thin" conception of blackness and black cultures precisely because the view distills black culture under the narrow gaze of an oppression trope animated by plantation logics.[2] Whitehead's treatment of black agrarian life, along with its mischaracterization of the culturally significant Spirituals and Work Songs, paints a grim portrait of immiseration and violence. Not only is a hostile life of scarcity thrust upon those who have been enslaved, but the slave community also supposedly reproduces harm among its members without any motivation for doing so from masters and overseers. In disagreement with Whitehead, I argue that the Spirituals, Work Songs, Blues, and other forms of Black expressive culture operationalize "thick" conceptions of Blackness and Black cultures generated in those sacred liminal sites of Black Ancestral Discourses. Such "thick" conceptions transpose the racialized, gendered economy of the weary oppression trope, making it possible to hear Blackness in a different register—beyond the limited possibilities available when conceiving blackness as mere oppressed opposition or counterpoint to whiteness. One might, consequently, engage alchemical Blackness that is *otherwise* when sampling the "thick" cadences and inflections emerging in concert with Black ancestral archives and their associated *cultural harmonies*. Doing so traverses the discursive geography of the South, better attuning the ear to hear those harmonies, breaks, and dissonances as philosophical practice in and of the South.

Alchemy, the Tragic-Comic, and Black Ancestral Discourses

Black peoples' innovative, improvisational practices often function alchemically within the tragic-comic. Drawing attention to the "tragic and comic," Ralph Ellison articulates the transmutational capacity to embrace life in the midst of conditions that have prevented Black Americans from "celebrat[ing] birth or dignify[ing] death" while simultaneously maintaining an ability to embrace a will to life "despite the dehumanizing pressures of slavery." Ellison notes that this "profound sense of life" shared by many African diasporic peoples, a generative capacity, emerging in a "tragicomic attitude" that involves develop[ing] an endless capacity for laughing at . . . painful experience." Ellison makes clear that such an attitude is not about resignation but rather "has to do with a special perspective on the national ideals and the national conduct." The attitude, then, involves an affirmation of Black existence which includes one's relation to the community, critiques of injustice, and the tenacious insistence that ethico-political practice must refuse conditions as they are because they harbor injustice.[3]

Even under intensely unjust conditions, Black peoples have maintained an ability to embrace a will to life. This will to life is not sustained by a romanticized distance from the horrors experienced. Rather, it involves the capacity to simultaneously register such horrors as professed but repeatedly unmet democratic ideals while simultaneously insisting upon meaningful life. This type of Blues alchemy is a creative, improvisatory testament to Black experience as well as a transmutation of the everyday; transpositions by those without a certain kind of power who engage obliquely to "slip the yoke by changing the joke." The Blues, observes Ellison, carries with it "a sense of the excitement and surprise . . . of [the] enslaved and politically weak . . . successfully imposing their values upon a powerful society through song and dance. Not even a high degree of social or political freedom was required" to effect aesthetic alchemical transmutation.[4] These *cultural harmonies* speak to possible practices of freedom under conditions of unfreedom; something more than an aesthetics of survival.

The riffs—expressed in the Spirituals, Blues, Work Songs, and other forms of Black expressive culture—give rise to thick conceptions of Blackness that are inseparable from the communal ethico-political critiques of injustice that they also render. I use "thick" not in the way that anthropologist Clifford Geertz does but as a way to distinguish between accounts that attend to what often goes unheard but might be traced via the gaps, fissures, or displacements in typical accounts of Blackness versus those accounts framed primarily by what is externally imposed and popularly understood. In the sanctified space of thick Blackness, survival and struggle are by-products of the romance with being Black—an integral aspect of Black Ancestral Discourses.

I cannot imagine this work without also hearing my dad, who passed away in 2017. He was a father, a mentor, and a "possibility model" who in his theorizing, actions, and deeds unapologetically affirmed the power of Black community. These were critical lessons from a Black man whose intellectual and life journey traversed the cotton fields to the academy to the notorious Louisiana State Penitentiary—called Angola, after the former plantation that occupied its territory.[5] He spoke often about the ancestors, those underacknowledged Black Sisypheans whose toil came with alchemical return. He encouraged me to occupy those spaces—in his words, "where toughness of spirit is heard . . . seeking something known never seen before . . . a blues survival rejection of presence over absence and the analogical removal of

excess." This was a way of embracing the condition of, as his work characterized it, "being born under a bad sign."

I find myself constantly thinking with him and being challenged by his
guiding imperative to operationalize processes of theorizing so that they are
more than academic performance. In particular, "being nimble or not at all"[6]
takes place in dialogue with the ancestors—in an actual community—that
celebrates rites, rituals, and practices while simultaneously taking up the
ongoing ethico-political duty to engage in liberatory practices. Dad called
it "integrity." I would also characterize these modes of being as *practices of
freedom under conditions of unfreedom*. I am indelibly marked by Dad's
legacy as well as his caution that "sacrifice, to make sacred, requires loss."[7] As
Dad noted, such expenditures have a social-political function. They involve
alchemical processes inspired through Black ancestral discourses whose
"accumulated hope, longing, and aspirations," though unrealized, have been
vouchsafed to future generations so that they would not have "further need
for humiliating pleas to others for recognition or inclusion."[8]

Dad was one of my intellectual heroes and a frequent interlocutor. The fact
that he sat in an Arkansas waiting room anticipating my birth while reading
Heidegger's *Being and Time* provides a glimpse into his theoretical range.
A self-described "Blues Man," Dad never suggested that "literacy" could or
should displace Black ancestral discursive perspectives. These "nonliterate"
(rather than illiterate) archives inspired pride and formed the basis of a necessary critical attitude that I was always encouraged to embrace. Blackness,
nonliterate and beyond the literate, had the alchemical capacity to fashion
possibility from impossibility. Dad's encounters with "academic" philosophy
were a testament to such refashioning. He heard Heidegger, Sartre, Irigaray,
and others in the modal register tuned to Black Ancestral Discursive archives.
This juxtaposition transmuted the given theories into something *otherwise*;
beyond the uncomplicated embrace of Western theory.

Colson Whitehead's *The Underground Railroad*

Whitehead's novel *The Underground Railroad* begins with the protagonist
Cora rejecting an offer to run to the North to freedom. Implicated in this
denial is the backstory of her grandmother's enslavement. Ajarry (Cora's
grandmother), who was sold often, learns that "in America, the quirk was
that people were things."[9] With this realization, Ajarry comes to understand
that "things" are valued according to their possibilities. And since she understood herself as a thing, her value was bound by the logic of the plantation
and her ability to remain in that place—literally and figuratively. Accordingly, she teaches her children to obey as a means of survival conditioned by
her belief that "to escape the boundary of the plantation was to escape the
fundamental principles of your own existence: impossible." Hence, Cora's

initial impulse to decline an opportunity to flee the bounds of the plantation is driven by an inherited instrumental calculus of possibility and value.
In spite of Cora's eventual determination to seek the underground railroad,
Whitehead's novel never displaces plantation logics, even in the places and
spaces away from the masters' and overseers' gaze that allegedly depict life
among the community of the enslaved.

Whitehead plays on familiar, yet cringeworthy, habitual logics, making the
brutality of slavery's peculiar institution visible, and comfortably uncomfortable for white readers. While he deftly depicts slavery's pornographic levels
of violence, more problematic is the process by which his depictions simultaneously obscure the creation, critique, and contestation evident in practices
used by the enslaved to transpose and transmute existing conditions—namely,
practices of freedom under conditions of unfreedom. Such practices creatively
maintained rich community, forged a sustaining ethics, and engaged ongoing
philosophical critiques of an unjust system while simultaneously realizing
that it would be problematic to make "freedom" the ultimate goal.

Plantation logics are not only operative among "masters" and overseers
who impose such logics upon those who are enslaved. According to Whitehead, the enslaved also accept these same logics for themselves and their
communities. This depiction of the enslaved must be interrogated even though
it is presented by an African American author. As Ralph Ellison writes, "isn't
it closer to the truth that far from considering themselves only in terms of
that abstraction, [slaves] . . . really thought of themselves as men who had
been unjustly enslaved?" Following Ellison, we can affirm that the world
and community of the enslaved was not limited to the horizon, landscape,
and rhythms of plantation logics. Ellison makes clear that, despite being a
"most vicious system," slavery was not "a state of absolute repression. To
the extent that the [enslaved] was a *musician*, one who expressed himself in
music . . . [he was a person] who realized himself in a world of sound. For the
art—the blues, the spirituals, the jazz, the dance—was what we had in place
of freedom."[10] These insights differentiate conditions of unfreedom from
descriptions of oppression. Understanding that one exists under conditions
of unfreedom permits one to hear the practices of freedom left unregistered
when constraint is presumed to be absolute.

Vital to the texture of these practices of freedom under conditions of
unfreedom is a "critical attitude" deployed tactically by means of aesthetic
critiques that engage in parrhesia. Here parrhesia may be understood as a ver-
bal encounter by which someone reproaches the powerful and may compel
attention to the offense committed. "One in a profoundly unequal situation can do one thing: She can 'speak'—engage in a discursive act that calls
attention to the offense, that exposes injustice."[11] Spirituals, Work Songs, the
Blues, and Jazz are Black aesthetic modalities that assume a critical attitude,
engage in parrhesiastic practices, and thereby have the effect of transmut-
ing existing power relations. Since "parrhesia is the ethics of truth-telling

as an action which is risky and free,"[12] the performativity exemplified in Black improvisational production—in this case music understood broadly as innovative construction—constitutes a practice of freedom under conditions of unfreedom. By mobilizing a critical attitude, these Black aesthetic modalities also imply moral and political attitudes about "the art of not being governed . . . so much . . . like that and at that cost." The critical attitude in this respect invokes a "certain way of refusing, challenging, limiting . . . rule. Not [wanting] to be governed like that also means not wanting to accept these laws because they are unjust because . . . they hide a fundamental illegitimacy."[13] This attitude distinguishes what can be described as "conditions of *unfreedom*" from descriptions of oppressive conditions that presume an all-pervasive powerlessness for those who exist under oppression's yoke.

The Blues supported a Black phenomenal world where paradox and contradiction could be endured without negation. It was a world not intended for whites. Modes of existing in this world utilized aesthetic alchemies that involved aleatoric composition with indeterminacy and chance as pervasive organizing features. Taking place as co-occurrences, not antecedently calculated, a communal performativity disrupted popular racial reasoning that was underwritten by plantation logics. As such, the Blues fostered communities operating *otherwise* than under white logics of construction and white conceptions of blackness. As R. Havis noted, "a Blues composition might emerge from an intense moment along a long highway, or endless solitary field work, or miles of levee which have *common rhythms*. . . . The Bluesman, Noland Struck, for example, told me he took his stage name from the sound of a trailer truck rumbling past as he walked along a Louisiana highway longing for recognition. The Rolling Truck became Noland Struck. Notably, the name expresses an *Auditory Identity* rather than a visual one. [The] . . . *common rhythms* allow polar opposites to co-exist in the same word or image."[14]

The matrix of Blues experience emerges in the context of perilous conditions where a labor force, made servile, cultivated a place rich in natural resources (for example, the Southern Delta). Black labor did so via an existence that was materially constrained and marked by galling toil. "Confined by water and imprisoned by land," those who embraced the Blues fashioned possibility out of impossibility. Even though the Blues emerged from a crucible born of constraint, it cannot—or at least should not—be reduced to the merely tragic. It is this complex aspect of the Blues (and its corollary in the Spirituals and Work Songs) that Whitehead's novel misses.

Within Whitehead's framework, whites may glimpse the structural and systematic horror of the Atlantic slave trade without being at risk. They may be disturbed by the racialized politics and focused violence in the novel without simultaneously being pressed into unsettling the very logics that produce such heinous effects. There is an affective surrogacy via immiserated black bodies that fails to provoke or demand that whites take action to exorcise the ongoing ways that slavery still haunts the United States in the present.[15] Meanwhile, Blacks are bound to an identity that is only immiseration, mourning, and thingification. As Aimé Césaire explains, "thingification" is a process by which colonial practices construct African and Indigenous peoples as things to be managed rather than persons.[16] In a similar fashion, the geography of the plantation functions metonymically, leaving no room for understanding those who were enslaved as more than mere slaves.

While Whitehead gestures to the importance of music for slaves, he implies that it functions as a diversion granting temporary reprieve from misery. Or alternatively, in Whitehead's novel, music has an instrumental function in its use to secure steady production during work in the fields. Cora, for one, is suspicious of music. Cautious about the illusionary diversion it provides, the novel's protagonist observes that "all are put in servitude to the song," and should be "wary of how sometimes when the music tugged" they might be "pulled into the lively madness."[17] Cora views music as an opportunity for danger rather than an occasion for generative possibilities that might contest and displace plantation logics.

Whitehead further draws upon the instrumental function of music when he describes Blake, a newly acquired and much disliked slave on the plantation, leading a Work Song. Whitehead writes, "His voice boomed through the rows as he worked and even those who despised him couldn't help but sing along. The man had a terrible personality but the sounds that came from his body made the labor fly."[18] Contrary to customary Black communal practice, Blake serves as leader for the Work Song because of his nice voice. Whitehead does not attend to the fact that those who led Work Songs were also required to have ethical standing with and within the community. A good voice would not be sufficient for one who is reviled by the community to lead the song during work, nor would it be likely to compel members of the community to sing along, since this would signal an endorsement of the song leader's ethical transgressions. The scene is one of the few times that Whitehead deals with enslaved people laboring in the fields, yet the depiction harbors an insidious plantation logic that elides the ways that—despite galling toil—community could be forged in collective song and work with the soil. The Work Song could be wielded to produce alchemical effects so long as the song leader had experience cooperating with the people, cultivating community, and understanding communal rhythms. The quality of the leader's singing voice would not be paramount since the Work Song was not about the utility of production. Instead, it was about building communal practices of transmutation and communion. As such, any effective song leader would require ethical standing in the community and would have a keen understanding of the ancestral cadences that make it possible to engage in practices of freedom under conditions of unfreedom. In this context, those engaged in the collectivity of the Work Song transmute time and labor while also making an ethico-political demand, an intervention to disrupt injustice.

Conclusion

The picture of slave life drawn by *The Underground Railroad* is one of complete desolation. Given the novel's particular characterization of the enslaved as mere slaves, one might be prompted to ask if the slave quarter occupants even rise to the level of community, since they are continually depicted reproducing the violence of slavery. The utilitarian trajectory of slavery's violence is hardly a register that facilitates or cultivates any relationality that moves beyond use value. Whitehead, like many others, passes over the crucial ethico-political cadences echoed in Spirituals, Work Songs, and other modes of Black expressive culture that harness aesthetic performativity as a resource. He misrepresents vital elements utilized in the unique rites, rituals, and cultural practices that characterize Blackness and Black peoples. *The Underground Railroad*, consequently, leaves silent the salient philosophical critiques emanating from Spirituals and Work Songs—critiques that assert ongoing, oblique challenges to unrelenting demands for labor without return and that celebrate community forged in spite of hostile landscapes.

Resisting the characterization of Blackness as immiseration has important implications for how we understand not only Blackness but also Southernness in the United States. The complexities of both—which are intertwined with one another—must not be reduced to plantation logics. By hearing the literal and metaphorical music that emanates from Black Ancestral Discourses, one may avoid this reduction and affirm Southern Black practices of freedom under conditions of unfreedom.

Notes

1. This essay uses blackness with a lowercase *b* to indicate conceptions that come from the popular archive, as contrasted with notions generated via the archive of Black Ancestral Discourses, which are designated with an uppercase *B*.

2. I am indebted to Falguni Sheth's account of "the logics of exclusion" for the concept of "plantation logics"; see Sheth, *Toward a Political Philosophy of Race* (Albany: State University of New York Press, 2009).

3. Ralph Ellison, *The Collected Essays of Ralph Ellison*, ed. John F. Callahan (New York: Modern Library, 1995), 177–78, 286.

4. Ralph Ellison, *The Collected Essays of Ralph Ellison*, ed. John F. Callahan (New York: Modern Library, 1995), 286, 284–85.

5. My father was a forensic psychologist at the prison, and he developed Junglian influenced group models that used communal process to facilitate the continued personal development of those who were incarcerated. Dad's model allowed those who participated in "group" to chart their own development supported by a community lovingly invested in each person's success. Dad's model radically contrasted with the focus on punishment that was prevalent during his tenure at Angola.

6. Albert Murray's phrase, from Albert Murray, *Stompin the Blues* (New York: McGraw-Hill, 1976).

7. "Existence and Sound," Dr. Roland Havis's unpublished papers.

8. Author's commentary on "Born Dead in the House of Water," unpublished prose, 2005, by Dr. Roland Havis.

9. Colson Whitehead, *The Underground Railroad*, (New York: Doubleday, 2016), 6.

10. Ralph Ellison, *The Collected Essays of Ralph Ellison*, ed. John F. Callahan (New York: Modern Library, 1995), 284–85.

11. Devonya N. Havis, "The Parrhesiastic Enterprise of Black Philosophy," *Black Scholar* 43(4): 55.

12. Michel Foucault, *The Government of Self and Others: Lectures at the College de France, 1982–1983* (London: Macmillan, 2011), 44–46.

13. Michel Foucault, *Fearless Speech* (Cambridge, MA: Semiotext(e), 44–46.

14. . A reflection from Dr. Roland Havis's unpublished work on Delta Blues forms that included an interview with Nolan Struck.

15. . The same affective surrogacy may also be at work in the endless video loops that circulate when yet another Black person is killed by police officers or white citizens asserting their right to defend property. The prevalence and wide viewership of such video accounts prompts expressions of moral outrage. However, it is individuals who are highlighted, not the structural logics that tacitly sanction such violence.

16. Aimé Césaire, *Discourse on Colonialism*.

17. Whitehead, *The Underground Railroad*, 28–29.

18. Whitehead, *The Underground Railroad*, 17.

Bibliography

Césaire, Aimé. 2001. *Discourse on Colonialism*. Trans. Joan Pinkham. New York: Monthly Review Press.

Ellison, Ralph. 1995. *The Collected Essays of Ralph Ellison*. Ed. John F. Callahan. New York: Modern Library.

Foucault, Michel. 2001. *Fearless Speech*. Cambridge, MA: Semiotext(e).

Foucault, Michel. 2011. *The Government of Self and Others: Lectures at the College de France, 1982–1983*. London: Macmillan.

Havis, Devonya N. 2013. "The Parrhesiastic Enterprise of Black Philosophy." *Black Scholar* 43 (4): 52–58.

Havis, Roland. 2004. "Born Dead in the House of Water." A polymetaphotophonic blues symphony performed in Petersburg, Virgina. This was a multimedia performance that took place as part of a series at Richard Bland College of the College of William and Mary. The work is preserved in R. Haviss' electronic archives.

Havis, Roland. 2005. "Commentary on 'Born Dead in the House of Water.'" Unpublished essay.

Sheth, Falguni. 2009. *Toward a Political Philosophy of Race*. Albany: State University of New York Press.

Whitehead, Colson. 2016. *The Underground Railroad*. New York: Doubleday.

9

✦

Dumping on Southern "White Trash"

Etiquette and Abjection

Shannon Sullivan

In the United States, racists often are thought to be members of an uneducated white lower class. Their alleged stupidity is why they continue to think that white people are superior to nonwhite people. This assumption operates in the opposite direction as well: poor white people—so-called white trash, rednecks, and hillbillies—often are automatically assumed to be white racists, and if they aren't (yet) members of a white supremacist organization, then they are thought to be the best recruiting pool from which white supremacists can draw. As I will argue, both of these patterns tend to be implicitly—and sometimes explicitly—regionalized. White Southerners are thought of as the uneducated hicks who refuse to give up their racist beliefs, unlike white Northerners whose supposedly enlightened views on race make them morally superior to white Southerners. In this chapter, I demonstrate how corrosive divides between classes of white people help support racism against people of color. Examining race-class etiquette and the abjection of poor white people as mechanisms for the othering of white trash, I challenge the idea that (white) Southern practices necessarily are synonymous with racism.

Race, Class, and Etiquette

Etiquette concerns conventional requirements or expectations for social behavior. The word originated in eighteenth-century France, meaning "ticket" or "label." Small cards—*les étiquettes*—were printed with instructions for how a person was to behave in court or how a soldier was to behave in his lodgings.[1] *Les étiquettes* ensured that a visitor to the king wouldn't offend him and that a soldier obtaining lodging wouldn't harm the property or disturb its owners or other lodgers. Today, of course, we use the word more broadly. But in all cases, etiquette means the regulation of relationships between individuals by prescribing and proscribing particular forms of their conduct with one another.

Bertram Wilbur Doyle's classic study of the etiquette of race relations in the US South is useful not only for examining the role that etiquette played between white and Black people in antebellum and Jim Crow America but also for analyzing some of the general features of etiquette.[2] Etiquette is concerned primarily with personal relations, but its meaning and impact stretch far beyond the personal. At its heart, etiquette is a form of social control that defines and maintains social distances between people.[3] If a Black person routinely steps off the sidewalk to let a white person pass, this act is more than merely a private matter between the two people. It embodies, repeats, and supports social expectations of Black deference and subordination to white people. Even in a case involving two social equals, etiquette tends to regulate their behavior, including the degree of social distance that is supposed to exist between them. Thus, two academics at a conference might shake hands or kiss cheeks when greeting each other, depending on what country they are in (or what kind of philosophy they study). If one person refuses to do so, the breach of etiquette requires an explanation, such as having a bad cold and not wanting to spread germs, which has spawned new forms of etiquette such as the elbow bump. Absent an explanation, the breach of etiquette produces a rupture in social order—in this case, the person refusing the greeting asserts herself as superior to someone who was presumed to be an equal. This rupture in the social fabric leaves the offended party and those who witnessed the snub unsure of how to behave toward the person who violated a social code.

The emphasis on *social* distance here is important. Etiquette sometimes regulated physical distances between people, such as the sidewalk example above illustrates. But the physical distances prescribed by etiquette were and are always in the service of the more crucial matter of social distance. Etiquette is what makes possible physical proximity and intimacy between social superiors and inferiors without collapsing their social status.[4] For example, racial etiquette allowed white masters and Black slaves in the South to work side by side on the plantation and Black slaves to tend the most intimate matters of their white master's hygiene, all without any threat to the white person's status as superior. As long as both white master and Black slave observed the appropriate rules of address and gestural codes of behavior—etiquette is a code that binds both the dominant and subordinate, after all—then significant social distances could be maintained in the midst of intimate physical proximities.[5] What the example of racial etiquette from antebellum America shows is that "far more than physical separation, white southerners wanted social distance."[6]

For Doyle, etiquette is a form of government, and we can understand this term in a Foucauldian sense.[7] Michel Foucault understood government not as a top-down form of state power but as a horizontal form of social control embodied in institutions such as schools, medical facilities, and prisons. Governmentality combines strategies and technologies for influencing others with those of caring for or regulating the self.[8] In a similar fashion, Doyle argues that the government provided by etiquette is much more basic and extensive than that of legislation or political bodies. Etiquette operates throughout virtually all of our social relationships, and its "jurisdiction" often precedes and operates alongside official legislation and then continues after laws and other formal regulations have been abolished.[9] (This was the case after the Civil War, when slavery-era etiquette between white people and newly freed slaves continued in the South even though slavery legally had been abolished.) Etiquette governs informally, and this is precisely why its form of social control is incredibly effective.

Another way of approaching etiquette's informality—and thus also its effectiveness—is to understand etiquette as a form of habit. Habit is a predisposition for transacting with the world in a particular way. Habits operate on preconscious and sometimes even unconscious levels: they are what we do "without thinking." This doesn't mean, however, that habits necessarily are trivial or minor, as when for example a person absentmindedly twirls a lock of hair while reading. Just the opposite: some of the most complex skills that human beings acquire—such as playing the violin or driving a manual transmission automobile—are only fully acquired when they have become habit. But even these examples do not make the point about habit's ontological significance strongly enough, for habit is constitutive of the self. The gendered, raced, classed, and other patterns of transacting with the world that a person develops constitute who that person is.

Etiquette does not always take the form of habit. This is because it sometimes is an act that a person consciously decides to engage in. But when etiquette is at its most effective, it operates preconsciously or unconsciously. Quoting William Graham Sumner and using Sumner's "social ritual" as a synonym for "etiquette," Doyle explains that "ritual, as Sumner points out, 'is not something to be thought or felt. It is something to be done.' In fact, 'ritual is strongest when it is perfunctory and excites no thought.' "[10] As in the case of all habits, etiquette can become so ingrained in the self that it can seem instinctual, as if it were not learned behavior. This explains how Black slaves sometimes appeared "naturally" or "natively" deferential toward white people.[11] When it takes the form of habit, etiquette allows people to engage each other with the least expenditure of energy required by conscious thought. In this way, it facilitates smooth and easy transactions with one's environment.

As it does so, however, the social order preserved by etiquette also exerts its most effective—and thus potentially most harmful—control.[12] While some contemporary white philosophers have argued that etiquette must be part of attempts to defeat racism and thus that etiquette has a transformative role to play in an oppressive society, the forms of etiquette they describe tend to be mere pleasantries between people that eliminate social tension and for that reason don't bring about any substantial change.[13] (I'm reminded of Martin Luther King's criticism of "the white moderate, who is more devoted to 'order' than to justice; who prefers a negative peace which is the absence of tension to a positive peace which is the presence of justice."[14]) The primary function of etiquette remains the conservative one of protecting an existing social order by keeping people in different social groups in their "proper" place.[15] In the case of Jim Crow America, racial etiquette helped support white supremacy by securing racial hierarchy in situations of propinquity between white and Black people; by regulating affect and emotional expression on the part of white and Black people; and by reducing feelings of guilt on the part of white people about their domination of nonwhite people.[16] For example, white etiquette has included being pleasant, even gracious and generous, to Black people—when Black people remained "in their place," that is. If Black people became "uppity" through their speech or their unspoken body language, however, white etiquette required disregard, stinginess, and even violence on the part of white people to remind Black people of their supposedly inferior status.[17]

During Jim Crow, racial etiquette was (and to some degree, still is) a key method for training each new generation of white people into whiteness. With regard to white children, racial etiquette was "the closest thing to a 'core curriculum' that white southerners had," the main ticket to whiteness that white children needed to possess.[18] Learning habits of behavior toward nonwhite children and adults that would last them a lifetime, white children were less likely to question legal, institutional, and other forms of discrimination against Black and other nonwhite people. Those habits included different ways of addressing adults, for example, knowing which adult men you should call "Mister" (white men) and which you should call by their first name, or "boy," or worse (Black men). They also included "talking down" to Black people while assuming or insisting that Black people always talked "up" to white people.[19] Linguistic habits such as these were (and are) directly tied to the issue of who counted as a full person in a society. Racial etiquette's governance of interpersonal relationships thus had (and has) structural implications and effects. The central role that racial etiquette played in the education of white children also meant that racial etiquette had a special connection with white mothers, who were the primary source of their children's ticket to whiteness. Because of their key role in child-rearing, white mothers were the main adults who taught white children how to use bodily gestures and forms of address to maintain social distance between themselves and nonwhite people. Teaching racial etiquette to white children thus amounted to "one of white women's chief forms of collusion in the maintenance of white supremacy."[20]

Racial etiquette doesn't just operate interracially, however. It also governs intraracial behavior across class lines. This probably is true for most racial groups, but here I focus on intraracial white etiquette because it is one of the primary ways that white people shore up white racism.[21] As cultural anthropologist John Hartigan claims, "it is forms of etiquette—and importantly, their transgression—that maintain and reproduce the unmarked status of white identity."[22] White social etiquette crystallizes around the figure of white trash. White trash are the poor white people who fail to live up to middle-class expectations of white behavior, and their "failure" is at least threefold. First, white trash allegedly are uneducated and stupid. Epithets such as idiot, imbecile, and moron are regularly used to describe white trash, reflecting the influence of the eugenics movement on middle-class white people's views of race and class.[23] Second, the bodies of white trash are problematic. They yell and shout, talking too loudly and coarsely. They are unkempt and unclean, often barefoot and always dirty. And they are sluggish and lazy, which is why they are poor (and perhaps also why they are unclean). Across the board, their "actions, smells, and sounds . . . disrupt the social decorums that support the hegemonic, unmarked status of whiteness as a normative identity in [the United States]."[24] Finally—and intimately related to the first two "failures"—white trash share too many similarities of speech, behavior, diet, and lifestyle with Black people.[25] White trash are uncomfortably close to those whom they are supposed to be radically different from. Whether willfully or ignorantly, white trash fail to speak, eat, dress, and otherwise behave as proper (middle-class) white people are supposed to do, and their breach of white social etiquette threatens the boundary between white and nonwhite (especially Black) people.

This consideration of white etiquette brings out the bodily dimensions of class distinctions. While race often is examined in terms of bodily habits and behavior, class typically is not. Some critical philosophers of race even have claimed that "class is not inscribed on the body the way that race is."[26] But when etiquette has become sedimented into habit and operates without a person's thinking about its demands, then class has become part of the bodily self that one is. As Pierre Bourdieu's work in particular shows, "the body is the most indisputable materialization of class tastes. Bodies are the physical sites where the relations of class, gender, race, sexuality and age come together and are em-bodied and practiced."[27] In that case, class is not "just about the way you talk or dress, or furnish your home, it is not just about the job you do or how much money you make doing it; nor is it merely about whether or not you went to university, nor which university you went to. Class is something beneath your clothes, under your skin, in your psyche, at the very core of your being."[28] Incorporated into the self via its habits, white etiquette is constitutive of the self, in a complex dynamic relationship with raced, gendered, and other salient habits.

White social etiquette circulates within several race-class slurs for the white lower class, including "hillbilly," "redneck," and "cracker," but "white trash" carries a special significance. Unlike these other terms, which sometimes have been used to establish an antibourgeois identity, "white trash" generally has not been rehabilitated or reclaimed by the white lower class.[29] (Think here of the rehabilitation of "redneck" performed by Jeff Foxworthy's stand-up comedy and books, which focus on the one-liner, "You might be a redneck if . . ."[30]) In contrast, white trash "carries an irreducible debasing connotation," and the few "attempts to regard 'white trash' positively, to redeem it as a cultural identity, reveal an active remainder of social contempt and loathing that cannot be fully expelled."[31] The word "trash" helps explain why the term has remained irredeemable. "More than all these other labels, [white trash] articulates exactly what is at stake in intraracial efforts to maintain white racial identity—it encapsulates the self-conscious anxiety among whites over threats of pollution that threaten the basis for belonging within whiteness."[32] White trash is whiteness's dirty garbage, its refuse, its waste product. It is that which threatens whiteness with pollution and contamination from within.

Of course, whiteness also experiences itself as threatened from without—witness so-called yellow peril, Black peril, and all other sorts of "menacing" forces that other nonwhite races represent. Historically, miscegenation and immigration—the mixing of white and nonwhite "blood"—probably have served as the two greatest "threats" to the purity of whiteness. But especially with the rise of eugenics at the turn of the twentieth century, the white middle class became increasingly concerned about the threat to whiteness posed by (some) white people themselves. These were and are the people who count as white but do not uphold "proper" standards of whiteness. The danger posed by white trash is particularly alarming because "the source of the threat is depicted as arising from the allegedly purest of Anglo-Saxon strains, rather than through transgression of the color line."[33] Policing the color line between whites and nonwhites thus would not be sufficient to uphold white domination of nonwhite people, even when carried out by stronger means than racial etiquette, such as lynching. White social etiquette also was needed to internally discipline whiteness. White bodies and behavior had to be governed so that white superiority wouldn't destroy itself, and this meant "instilling [classed and raced] habits that are policed by concepts of disgust and embellished through ideas about pollution and dirt."[34]

Race, Class, and Abjection

Here we can see how white trash operates as the abject. As Julia Kristeva argues, the abject is crucial to societies and cultures that are based on rigid subject-object distinctions, but the abject itself is not an object completely other to the subject. The abject instead is what troubles sharp, clear boundaries between subject and object, self and other. The abject does have one but "only one quality of the object—that of being opposed to *I*."[35] The abject's opposition to the subject functions in a different way than that of the object.

Put another way, the differences between abjection and objectification demonstrate how othering can take place in related but different ways. Like the object, the abject is jettisoned from the subject, but "[the abject] lies there, quite close," threatening the dissolution of the bounded subject through its proximity.[36] In that sense, the abject is a different kind of threat to the subject than the definable object is. Even though the excluded object menaces the subject in its otherness, the sharp distinctions posited between subject and object provide a kind of safety and security for the subject. A gulf appears to exist between the subject and object that reassures the subject of its identity. Not so with the abject. The abject is uncanny, familiar in its strangeness. While the abject also safeguards the subject from its dissolution, the protection it offers is murkier, slipperier, and less firm than that which the object provides.

The division between white trash and proper white people also is slippery, revealing how white trash operates as whiteness's abject. White trash is opposed to the proper white subject, but its opposition is troublesome because it is not clear, sharp, or absolute. Like people of color and Black people in particular, white trash is excluded from whiteness proper. But the othering of people of color and of white trash tends to happen in different ways. White trash lies uncomfortably close to proper white people, threatening the dissolution of hegemonic forms of whiteness from within. Because of its whiteness, white trash threatens the coherence and identity of the proper white subject in a related but different way than people of color generally do. The presumed gulf between proper white people and people of color cannot be confidently assumed between proper white people and white trash. White trash is uncannily familiar to proper white people because of their shared race, and this murky point of contact is why white trash has to be forcefully expelled from whiteness. White trash thus becomes a "means of boundary maintenance through which white identity operates, containing or expelling certain whites from the social and political body of whiteness."[37]

The need to expel white trash demonstrates how white trash is considered to be repulsive, even as it, like a corpse, can be simultaneously considered horrifyingly fascinating. As Jim Goad argues, middle-class white people tend to have a "steaming liberal revulsion for white trash."[38] But this revulsion reveals more about middle-class white people than it does about any so-called objective features of white trash. Since white trash are not absolutely other to proper white people, the proper white person who attempts to jettison white trash from whiteness can never do so completely. As the proper white person expels white trash, she also expels herself. As Kristeva explains about abjection more generally, "I expel *myself*, I spit *myself* out, I abject *myself* within the same motion through which 'I' claim to establish '*myself*.' . . . 'I' am in the process of becoming an other at the expense of my own death."[39] For Goad, images of disease as well as death implicitly help illuminate white middle-class revulsion for white trash: "To the white elite white trash must seem like a disease in remission inside *all* whites, one that might flare up again given the right circumstances. When white blue bloods are repulsed by white trash, they are uncomfortably reminded both of what they used to be and what they may yet become."[40] White trash is not me—the proper white subject—and yet it is not safely not-me either. Like death and disease, white trash is what threatens proper whiteness with nonexistence. Ashes to ashes, dust to dust: what I used to be and what I might yet become is the dirty white trash that I am and the dirty white trash to which I shall return.[41]

The biblical reference to dust, or dirt, is particularly fitting for abjection since the abject often manifests itself as the unclean. Filth, waste, and excrement are common instances of the abject: "The repugnance, the retching that thrusts me to the side and turns me away from defilement, sewage, and muck."[42] As Kristeva documents, the Judeo-Christian Bible is permeated with strategies for managing the unclean and impure: certain foods, dead bodies (both human and nonhuman), diseases such as leprosy, and even speech.[43] But it is not the case that there is something "naturally" unclean or menacing to human health that then is repelled because of its "natural" threat. It may be that dead bodies can spread disease, for example, but this is not why they are considered abject. It is the ability of dead bodies, and other abject beings, to erase borders and boundaries that makes them repulsive. In Kristeva's words, "it is thus not lack of cleanliness or health that causes abjection but what disturbs identity, system, order. What does not respect borders, positions, rules."[44]

Above all—more than corpses, rotting food, or disease—what greatly disturbs identity, system, and order is the maternal body.[45] This is why the incest taboo is central to societies who found the subject on sharp subject-object dichotomies. "Abjection preserves what existed in the archaism of pre-objectal relationship, in the immemorial violence with which a body becomes separated from another body in order to be."[46] The other body from which I separated in order to be is the maternal body, which is a space (*chora*) where "I" did not yet exist as a distinct subject but was ambiguously merged with a being who was both me and not-me. The maternal body—and women more generally, along with menstrual blood and pregnant bodies—is what the (male) subject used to be a part of and what he may yet again become enmeshed with if he tries to return to it. Thus incest, especially between mother and son, is prohibited. Sexual relations between mother and son are repulsive and improper not because of a genetic health risk to any offspring they might produce, as we might try to explain the scientific reasons for prohibitions against incest. Rather, they are repulsive and improper because human existence inside the womb is a time of nonsubjectivity that should never be returned to, on pain of dissolution of human subjectivity as we know it.

We don't have to follow psychoanalysis all the way to the Oedipus complex to appreciate the way that the incest taboo functions in the abjection of

white trash. Perhaps more than anything, white trash are considered repulsive and objects of ridicule because they allegedly have sex with all sorts of
improper beings. Pointing out how rednecks and their hillbilly and white
trash kin are seen as intrinsically rapist, murderous, and otherwise violent,
Goad sarcastically jokes, "The hillbilly . . . serves all the functions of a modern
American scapegoat. And in the hillbilly, we receive an extra added bonus—a
scapegoat who also *fucks* goats."[47] Even more often than with nonhuman
animals, however, the improper beings that white trash allegedly have sex
with are their own nuclear family members. The alleged stupidity of white
trash is due to the fact that they breed with each other; white trash is "inbred,
degenerated, momma-impregnating vermin and scum." [48] As two of Jeff Foxworthy's jokes go, "you might be a redneck if you view the upcoming family
reunion as a chance to meet women" and "if your family tree doesn't fork."[49]
Goad claims that "the topic of inbreeding occurs with such frequency among
white-trash stereotypes that its symbolic function begs analysis,"[50] and while
I agree with him about the frequency of the stereotype, I think it benefits
from rather than begs the (psycho)analysis of abjection.[51] It is not merely
that proper white people "*need* to see hillbillies as stupid" in order to distinguish themselves as smart, as Goad rightly claims.[52] It is also that the alleged
incest on the part of white trash threatens fundamental structures of binary
divisions out of which white subjectivity is formed. Inbred white trash don't
just assure proper white people of their intelligence. They also threaten the
identity of proper white people because they show proper white people that
whiteness is no guarantee of subjectivity clearly distinguished from stupidity.

White trash also reveal that whiteness is no guarantee of subjectivity clearly
separated from people of color, and Black people in particular. As mentioned
earlier, white trash do not speak, eat, dress, and otherwise behave as proper
white people are supposed to do, and their breach of white social etiquette
threatens the boundary between white and nonwhite (especially Black) people. The geographical origins of white trash, and other related figures such
as the redneck and the hillbilly, help explain the powerful ability of white
trash to efface boundaries between white and Black. First circulating in popular discourse in the North of the United States in the 1850s and 1860s, the
term white trash was used to bolster antislavery sentiment.[53] "White trash"
captured the effects of slavery on poor whites living in the South. Because
Black slaves were used as laborers on Southern plantations and farms, the
poor white Southerner was denied the opportunity to develop the ability and
willingness to work. The result, as one nineteenth-century Northern scholar
wrote, was a class of white people who were "degraded, half-fed, half-clothed,
without mental or moral instruction, and destitute of self-respect and of any
just appreciation of character."[54] An outgrowth of the enslavement of Black
Americans, white trash was "a uniquely southern phenomenon."[55]

The distinction between white trash and hardworking, "respectable" poor
whites was and is difficult to maintain. This is because of "the lack of fixed,

distinguishing criteria" between the two groups and "the intense concerns generated by the need to keep whiteness and Blackness distinct."[56] No matter how hard one works, a poor white person is at risk of being viewed as lazy, ignorant, and morally deficient. Unlike the Black person who likely experiences racial discrimination in education and the labor market, a poor white person has no way to account for her poverty and related moral "failures." As one middle-class white person dismissively remarked to cultural anthropologist Kirby Moss, "for White people there is really no excuse [for poverty] because they are not treated differently because of their race."[57] Whether mental, moral, or financial, a poor white person's impoverished situation must be the result of her own failure: her refusal to work, her lack of intelligence, and her failure to adopt a proper work ethic. As Moss explains, to many middle-class white people in his study, "poverty was [merely] a ploy, an individual's excuse to not contribute to the progress of society."[58]

On the Tautology of Southern White Trash

Occasionally, the liminal position of white trash has been used to support rather than condemn a white person for his or her perceived proximity to Blackness. Writing about then-president Bill Clinton's 1998 impeachment due to the Monica Lewinsky sex scandal, Toni Morrison infamously claimed that Clinton was being attacked because of his Blackness. As Morrison argued, "white skin notwithstanding, this is our first black President. Blacker than any actual black person who could ever be elected in our children's lifetime. After all, Clinton displays almost every trope of blackness: single-parent household, born poor, working-class, saxophone-playing, McDonald's-and-junk-food-loving boy from Arkansas."[59] I'll set aside the question of whether Clinton is Blacker than Barack Obama, who was elected to the US presidency in Morrison's lifetime. What's important here is that Morrison is not trying to slander Clinton by emphasizing his trashiness. Reversing the usual valence given to Blackness, Morrison's comment is sympathetic to the president. Even more germane is that it is not the case that Morrison sees Clinton's Blackness as resulting from his particular views on race or white racism. As Morrison explained in the wake of Obama's 2008 election, her 1998 claim "was deploring the way in which President Clinton was being treated. . . . I said he was being treated like a black on the street, already guilty, already a perp. I have no idea what his real instincts are, in terms of race."[60] What Morrison's remark underscores is the blurring of boundaries between Black and white that white trash represents. Clinton's perceived Blackness comes from being white trash: white skinned and poor, with crude culinary tastes, and raised in a defective family in the South.

The seemingly small detail concerning Clinton's Southern roots is significant. Just as white trash and poor whites often are conflated, the distinction between white trash and Southern whites also tends to be blurry and difficult to maintain. The geographic origins of "white trash" continue to impact the connotations of the term: simply to be a white person from the South of the United States is to risk being considered white trash. As the old joke goes, "you can tell a Southern virgin . . . when you see a girl who's running faster than her father and brothers."[61] The joke doesn't have to specify that the Southern virgin is a white woman; the trope of inbred white trash conveys that message by itself. The joke also says nothing about the Southern virgin's economic status. Regardless of whether one is poor, to be a white person from the South is to be in an at least somewhat abject relationship to proper whiteness.

This, too, is the product of a distinctively Northern perspective on the legacy of Black slavery. White Southerners generally were seen as being too close to Black people. Whether poor or not, white Southerners were in closer physical proximity to Black slaves than white Northerners were, and they shared (too) many regional characteristics with them: similar accents and styles of speech, similar tastes in food, and similar sensibilities and life-styles.[62] We can see this perspective at work in 1940s and 1950s Detroit, where the label "hillbilly" was applied by Northern whites in an unreha-bilitated way to white people who transgressed white middle-class mores. "Hillbillies" began arriving in Detroit from the South in large numbers in the 1920s, and they soon were blamed for the decline in living conditions for working-class whites in the city.[63] In Detroit, the term hillbilly was used to "shor[e] up an imperiled sense of white identity that was challenged by the way shared traits of white and Black southerners undermined northern con-victions of a qualitative difference between the races."[64] In a similar fashion, Chicago complained of being invaded by Southern hillbillies, as the national publication *Harper's* documented in 1958: "The city's toughest integration problem has nothing to do with the Negroes. . . . It involves a small army of white Protestant, Early American migrants from the South—who are usually proud, poor, primitive, and fast with a knife."[65] Like white trash, hillbillies were seen by white Northerners as embodying characteristics that had been exclusively associated with Blacks. Admittedly, Southern heritage did not ensure that one would be called a hillbilly, and the term sometimes was used for non-Southern whites who transgressed standards of proper whiteness.[66] In other words, transgression of whiteness is what is central to the figures of the hillbilly and white trash. But Northern anxiety over that transgression was intensely focused on white Southerners, making white transgression and white Southernness difficult to untangle. It was white Southerners' cultural and physical proximities to Black people that tended to trouble Northerners' understanding of the color line between white and Black people.

These proximities weren't problematic in the same ways for white South-erners, but this is not because Southerners were less racist than their white Northern counterparts. An African American folk saying, still repeated today, captures the difference: "In the North, they don't care how high you get, as long as you don't get too close. In the South, they don't care how close you get, as long as you don't get too high."[67] The particular role of racial etiquette in the South is crucial to these regional differences. Southern racial etiquette maintained both white domination and white Southerners' sense of racial superiority as Blacks and whites mingled together in the South. Admittedly, sometimes etiquette was not enough to manage physical proximities between whites and Blacks, and legislation was needed to keep the color line in place. Mississippi's 1865 vagrancy law, for example, declared, "'all white persons assembling themselves with freemen, free Negroes, or mulattoes, or usually associating with freedmen, shall be deemed vagrants, and on conviction thereof shall be fined.'"[68] In this case, merely gathering with free or light-skinned Black people legally transformed a white person into a shiftless vagrant—into white trash, in other words. But generally, Southern racial etiquette worked to ensure that physical proximities and cultural similarities did not collapse racial hierarchies in Southern society. When proper etiquette was observed on all sides, Black slaves could serve white masters their food, for example, and it could be the same type of food from the very same pot, without blurring the boundary between master and slave. (Eating that food together was a different story. Racial etiquette made that act taboo during the days of slavery and Jim Crow.[69])

Likewise, today, as long as the proper forms of address are used and appropriate gestures are embodied, the Black "help" can work in the kitchen side by side with her white employer, preparing the Southern foods that they both love, without any serious threat to white racism. The taboo against interracial eating also has dissolved. But social rather than proximal distance between white and nonwhite people continues to be important in the post–Civil War South. Keeping Black people "in their place" is and has always been "more behavioral than spatial in nature. . . . Valuing hierarchy more than they feared propinquity, whites casually rubbed elbows with Blacks in contexts that sometimes startled northerners. Yet the requirements of caste . . . were zealously enforced" in the South nonetheless.[70] As a legacy of their proximity to Black slaves, white Southerners generally have available to them more nuanced—which is *not* to say less racist—forms of interacting with Black people than white Northerners do. Those nuances tend to allow for more intimate encounters between Black and white people without troubling white Southerners' sense of the color line between them.

There exists "a nebulous but enduring sense of cultural difference between northern and southern whites," and that difference expresses itself in Southern and Northern perspectives on white trash.[71] White Southerners use somewhat different characteristics than white Northerners to distinguish who counts as white trash. First and foremost—and somewhat obviously—for Southerners, the sheer fact of being a Southerner isn't relevant to distinguishing proper white people from white trash. Nor is sharing certain cultural traits with Black

Southerners, such as having a Southern accent, embodying a relatively slow pace of speech and movement, and enjoying Southern food. For Southerners, these traits do not indicate stupidity, laziness, or a boorish sense of taste.[72]

But this doesn't mean that Southerners don't worry intensely about hierarchical divisions between white and Black or the blurring of racial lines that white trash performs. For Southern, as for Northern, middle-class whites, white trash are those white people who "embod[y] a degraded form of whiteness—that is, whiteness without key forms of individual supports (striving for upward mobility) or institutional ones (from homeownership to political activity)."[73] For example, proper whiteness includes an appreciation of the aesthetics of restoring historical homes, including and perhaps especially ones from the antebellum era. In contrast, Black people often are perceived as uninterested in or even hostile to the activity of historical restoration—and perhaps for good reason, since this activity often involves an inchoate desire to restore an era of slavery or Jim Crow.[74] Thus, for a poor white person to be unable or unwilling to restore an historic home is for her to embody a degraded form of whiteness that shares problematic characteristics with Blackness. White trash represents the threatening possibility that a white person could slide into Blackness, which would mean for her to lose her racial status by means of losing her class status. Whether a white Southerner's regional identity increases the likelihood of this threat depends a great deal on whether one takes a Southern or Northern perspective on the question.

Conclusion

I have challenged the idea that white Southern practices are synonymous with racism, but this does not mean that there doesn't exist any racism on the part of white Southerners. There does, and plenty of it. Racism is not, however, concentrated exclusively in the beliefs and behaviors of poor white Southerners, and dumping full responsibility for racism on them is likely to be counterproductive for achieving any kind of racial justice in the United States. The so-called good white people of this nation—its Northerners as well as its middle-to-upper-class Southerners—have a great deal of work to do for the United States to someday "end the racial nightmare, and achieve our country."[75]

Notes

1. Dictionary.com, accessed March 21, 2013, http://dictionary.reference.com/browse/etiquette.

2. Bertram Wilbur Doyle, *The Etiquette of Race Relations in the South: A Study in Social Control* (Chicago: University of Chicago Press, 1937).

3. Doyle, *The Etiquette of Race Relations in the South*, xvii–xviii.

4. Doyle, *The Etiquette of Race Relations in the South*, xix.

5. Doyle, *The Etiquette of Race Relations in the South*, xx.

6. Jennifer Ritterhouse, *Growing Up Jim Crow: How Black and White Southern Children Learned Race* (Chapel Hill: University of North Carolina Press, 2006), 15.

7. Doyle, *The Etiquette of Race Relations in the South*, xvii, 172.

8. Ladelle McWhorter, *Bodies and Pleasures: Foucault and the Politics of Sexual Normalization* (Bloomington: Indiana University Press, 1999), 211. See also Michel Foucault, *The History of Sexuality*, vol. 1, trans. Robert Hurley (New York: Vintage, 1978), and Foucault, "The Ethics of the Concern for Self as a Practice of Freedom," in *Ethics: Subjectivity and Truth*, vol. 1 of *The Essential Works of Foucault, 1954–1984*, ed. Paul Rabinow (New York: New Press, 1997), 281–301.

9. Doyle, *The Etiquette of Race Relations in the South*, 11.

10. Doyle, *The Etiquette of Race Relations in the South*, xviii.

11. Doyle, *The Etiquette of Race Relations in the South*, 12.

12. Doyle, *The Etiquette of Race Relations in the South*, 159.

13. See Joseph Margolis, "Personal Reflections on Racism in America," in *On Race and Racism in America: Confessions in Philosophy*, ed. Roy Martinez (University Park: Pennsylvania State University Press, 2010), 29–37. In apparent contradiction with the conclusion of his essay, Margolis himself says that the "well-intentioned, natural etiquette that I've learned to share with all my neighbors . . . mediates every encounter along the street (and leaves the world unchanged). It exacts no tribute, and it has no deeper purpose. But it fills the air very nicely," 31–32.

14. Martin Luther King Jr., "Letter from a Birmingham Jail," 1963, accessed March 21, 2013, www.africa.upenn.edu/Articles_Gen/Letter_Birmingham.html.

15. Doyle, *The Etiquette of Race Relations in the South*, xviii–xix.

16. Ritterhouse, *Growing Up Jim Crow*, 15, 32–33, 48.

17. Ritterhouse, *Growing Up Jim Crow*, 69.

18. Ritterhouse, *Growing Up Jim Crow*, 54.

19. Ritterhouse, *Growing Up Jim Crow*, 1.

20. Ritterhouse, *Growing Up Jim Crow*, 19. See also Kristina DuRocher, *Raising Racists: The Socialization of White Children in the Jim Crow South* (Lexington: University Press of Kentucky, 2011).

21. John Hartigan Jr., *Racial Situations: Class Predicaments of Whiteness in Detroit* (Princeton, NJ: Princeton University Press, 1999), 17, 46–47.

22. John Hartigan Jr., *Odd Tribes: Toward a Cultural Analysis of White People* (Durham, NC: Duke University Press, 2005), 19.

23. Hartigan, *Odd Tribes*, 90.

24. Hartigan, *Odd Tribes*, 110.

25. Hartigan, *Racial Situations*, 28, 33, 88–90.

26. Charles Mills, "Comments on Shannon Sullivan's *Revealing Whiteness*," *Journal of Speculative Philosophy* 21, no. 3 (2007): 225. This is why, according to Mills, the eradication of class can be more radical than the eradication of race.

27. Beverley Skeggs, *Formations of Class and Gender: Becoming Respectable* (London: Sage Publications, 1997), 82.

28. Quoted in Steph Lawlor, "'Getting Out and Getting Away': Women's Narratives of Class Mobility," *Feminist Review* 63 (1999): 5.

29. Hartigan, *Odd Tribes*, 124.

30. See, for example, Jeff Foxworthy, *You Might Be a Redneck If . . . This Is the Biggest Book You've Ever Read* (Nashville, TN: Thomas Nelson Publishers, 2004).

31. Hartigan, *Odd Tribes*, 122.

32. Hartigan, *Odd Tribes*, 99.

33. Hartigan, *Odd Tribes*, 78; see also 85 and 103–4.

34. Hartigan, *Odd Tribes*, 18.

35. Julia Kristeva, *Powers of Horror: An Essay on Abjection* (New York: Columbia University Press, 1982), 1.

36. Kristeva, *Powers of Horror*, 1.

37. Hartigan, *Odd Tribes*, 113; see also Matt Wray, *Not Quite White: White Trash and the Boundaries of Whiteness* (Durham, NC: Duke University Press, 2006), especially page 2.

38. Jim Goad, *The Redneck Manifesto: How Hillbillies, Hicks, and White Trash Became America's Scapegoats* (New York: Simon and Schuster, 1997), 22.

39. Kristeva, *Powers of Horror*, 3.

40. Goad, *The Redneck Manifesto*, 100.

41. See Genesis 3:19: "For dust thou art, and unto dust shalt thou return."

42. Kristeva, *Powers of Horror*, 2.

43. Kristeva, *Powers of Horror*, 90–132.

44. Kristeva, *Powers of Horror*, 4.

45. Kristeva, *Powers of Horror*, 14.

46. Kristeva, *Powers of Horror*, 10.

47. Goad, *The Redneck Manifesto*, 100.

48. Goad, *The Redneck Manifesto*, 76.

49. https://www.amazon.com/You-Might-Be-Redneck-If/dp/1401601952/ref =sr_1_14?dchild=1&keywords=Jeff+foxworthy&qid=1597338109&s=books& sr=1-14, accessed August 13, 2020; Goad, *The Redneck Manifesto*, 90.

50. Goad, *The Redneck Manifesto*, 91.

51. Here I also disagree with John Hartigan in *Odd Tribes* when he claims the following: "It is not clear that psychoanalysis has any effective insight into collective processes, especially the intense contests over belonging that are constitutive of cultural orders," 13. Hartigan's concern is that psychoanalysis cannot deal with the classed and raced complexities of white identity and that it lumps together white people "as uniform ideological subjects all operating under a shared perception of Difference" (13).

52. Goad, *The Redneck Manifesto*, 91.

53. Hartigan, *Odd Tribes*, 61.

54. George Weston, quoted in Hartigan, *Odd Tribes*, 63.

55. Hartigan, *Odd Tribes*, 67.

56. Hartigan, *Odd Tribes*, 68.

57. Kirby Moss, *The Color of Class: Poor Whites and the Paradox of Privilege* (Philadelphia: University of Pennsylvania Press, 2003), 53.

58. Moss, *The Color of Class*, 52.

59. Toni Morrison, "The Talk of the Town: Comment," *The New Yorker*, October 5, 1998, accessed March 21, 2013, http://www.newyorker.com/archive /1998/10/05/1998_10_05_031_TNY_LIBRY_000016504?currentPage=all.

60. Andrea Sachs, "10 Questions for Toni Morrison," Time.com, May 7, 2008, accessed August 13, 2020, http://www.tufs.ac.jp/ts/society/masaaki/kyositu/espanol/grabacion/ToniMorrison_interview_080508.pdf.
61. Quoted in Goad, *The Redneck Manifesto*, 90.
62. Hartigan, *Racial Situations*, 28.
63. Hartigan, *Racial Situations*, 27–28.
64. Hartigan, *Racial Situations*, 88.
65. Quoted in Hartigan, *Racial Situations*, 33.
66. Hartigan, *Racial Situations*, 88, 89.
67. Thanks to Samuel Findley for sharing this saying with me at the March 2012 meeting of the West Virginia Philosophical Association.
68. Quoted in Doyle, *The Etiquette of Race Relations in the South*, 120. South Carolina and North Carolina had similar codes as well (138).
69. Doyle, *The Etiquette of Race Relations in the South*, 150. See also Ritterhouse, *Growing up Jim Crow*, 30, 42.
70. Neil McMillen, quoted in Ritterhouse, *Growing Up Jim Crow*, 15.
71. Hartigan, *Racial Situations*, 28.
72. See Daniel Hundley's account of "poor white trash" in his 1860 *Social Relations in our Southern States*: "They are about the laziest two-legged animals that walk erect on the face of the Earth. Even their motions are slow, and their speech is a sickening drawl . . . while their thoughts and ideas seem likewise to creep along at a snail's pace. . . . [They show] a natural stupidity or dullness of intellect that almost surpasses belief'" (quoted in Goad, *The Redneck Manifesto*, 81).
73. Hartigan, *Racial Situations*, 90.
74. Hartigan, *Racial Situations*, 197, 198, 206.
75. James Baldwin, *The Fire Next Time* (New York: Dell Publishing, 1963), 141.

Bibliography
Baldwin, James. *The Fire Next Time*. New York: Dell Publishing, 1963.
Doyle, Bertram Wilbur. *The Etiquette of Race Relations in the South: A Study in Social Control*. Chicago: University of Chicago Press, 1937.
DuRocher, Kristina. *Raising Racists: The Socialization of White Children in the Jim Crow South*. Lexington: University Press of Kentucky, 2011.
Foucault, Michel. *The History of Sexuality*. Vol. 1. Translated by Robert Hurley. New York: Vintage, 1978.
Foucault, Michel. "The Ethics of the Concern for Self as a Practice of Freedom." In *Ethics: Subjectivity and Truth*. Vol. 1 of *The Essential Works of Foucault, 1954–1984*, edited by Paul Rabinow, 281–301. New York: New Press, 1997.
Foxworthy, Jeff. *You Might Be a Redneck If . . . This Is the Biggest Book You've Ever Read*. Nashville, TN: Thomas Nelson Publishers, 1994.
Goad, Jim. *The Redneck Manifesto: How Hillbillies, Hicks, and White Trash Became America's Scapegoats*. New York: Simon and Schuster, 1997.
Hartigan, John, Jr. *Odd Tribes: Toward a Cultural Analysis of White People*. Durham: Duke University Press, 2005.
Hartigan, John, Jr. *Racial Situations: Class Predicaments of Whiteness in Detroit*. Princeton, NJ: Princeton University Press, 1999.

King, Martin Luther, Jr. "Letter from a Birmingham Jail." 1963. Accessed March 21, 2013. www.africa.upenn.edu/Articles_Gen/Letter_Birmingham.html.

Kristeva, Julia. *Powers of Horror: An Essay on Abjection.* New York: Columbia University Press, 1982.

Lawlor, Steph. "'Getting Out and Getting Away': Women's Narratives of Class Mobility." *Feminist Review* 63 (1999): 3–24.

Margolis, Joseph. "Personal Reflections on Racism in America." In *On Race and Racism in America: Confessions in Philosophy*, edited by Roy Martinez, 29–37. University Park: Pennsylvania State University Press, 2010.

McWhorter, Ladelle. *Bodies and Pleasures: Foucault and the Politics of Sexual Normalization.* Bloomington: Indiana University Press, 1999.

Mills, Charles. "Comments on Shannon Sullivan's *Revealing Whiteness*," *Journal of Speculative Philosophy* 21, no. 3 (2007): 218–30.

Morrison, Toni. "The Talk of the Town: Comment." *The New Yorker*, October 5, 1998. Accessed March 21, 2013. http://www.newyorker.com/archive/1998/10 /05/1998_10_05_031_TNY_LIBRY_000016504?currentPage=all.

Moss, Kirby. *The Color of Class: Poor Whites and the Paradox of Privilege.* Philadelphia: University of Pennsylvania Press, 2003.

Ritterhouse, Jennifer. *Growing Up Jim Crow: How Black and White Southern Children Learned Race.* Chapel Hill: University of North Carolina Press, 2006.

Sachs, Andrea. "10 Questions for Toni Morrison." Time.com, May 7, 2008. Accessed March 21, 2013. http://www.time.com/time/arts/article/0,8599 ,1738303,00.html.

Skeggs, Beverley. *Formations of Class and Gender: Becoming Respectable.* London: Sage Publications, 1997.

Wray, Matt. *Not Quite White: White Trash and the Boundaries of Whiteness.* Durham, NC: Duke University Press, 2006.

10

✦

On Being Slow

Philosophy and Disability in the US South

Kim Q. Hall

In *The Mind of the South*, W. J. Cash is unequivocal about what he perceives as the impossibility of philosophy in the US South. For Cash, the Southern mind's tendency to drift, along with its conformity, ignorance, intolerance, and paucity of imagination, make the region and its people downright hostile to philosophy. Cash's characterization of the Southern mind resonates with contemporary stereotypes of white, especially rural, Southerners as "dumb rednecks." While Cash focused on "the Southern mind," my focus in this paper is on the ableist temporality that informs abiding assumptions about the extent to which Southern body-minds[1] are fit for philosophy and whether the US South is hospitable to philosophy.[2] Much of the perception of the US South as counter to the cultivation of philosophical habits of mind is, I argue, a consequence of its association with the slow and backward. From a Southern drawl to a presumed general dull-mindedness, Southerners are frequently stereotyped as slow. A central question in this paper thus is: What does it mean to be or be perceived to be slow?

In addition to offering a critique of the perceived slowness of the South and Southerners, I offer a critically queer crip reframing of what it means to be slow, focusing in particular on the sort of institutional work slowness performs as well as the sort of work it might do. A critically queer crip approach challenges the naturalization and normalization of ableist binaries, like the abled-disabled binary. In addition, queer crip theorizing critiques additive and assimilationist approaches to disability and ableism, focusing instead on how the diversity of disability experience and the entanglement of all forms of oppression trouble conventional parameters of disability's meaning. Within queer crip critique, disability, like queerness, is a site to think with, from, and against.[3] While slowness is often offered as evidence of a lack of reasoning and speech capabilities deemed necessary for academic success in general and philosophical success in particular, I seek to reframe slowness as a critical resource for cripping philosophy in and of the South. Among its many meanings, "slow" is a word that refers to being disabled, and being deemed slow in some contexts is to be characterized as disabled. Whether in one's speech, gait, development, or cognitive processing, to be categorized as slow is to be judged as behind where one is "supposed" to be vis-à-vis prevailing norms of human body-mind development and functioning. The queer crip framework offered here considers how thinking about the slow can further understanding of institutionalized ableism, particularly by focusing on the ableist temporality in which slowness is either pathologized or normalized in ways that ultimately sustain rather than expose, resist, or undermine ableism.

In what follows, my discussion of slowness aims to make visible and trouble the normalizing temporality at the heart of the ableist structure of institutionalized philosophy in the United States and academia more generally. My approach is indebted to Fiona Kumari Campbell's argument about the importance of shifting from focusing only on the meanings of disability to exposing and troubling the workings of ableism that produce and maintain body-mind norms through the production and management of disability.[4] As Campbell explains, one of the ontological effects of ableism is its creation of "constitutional divide[s]," establishing the matter of difference such as the difference between the human and the nonhuman and the normal and the abnormal.[5] The distinction between the slow and the fast, I contend, is another site of ableism's production and management of difference. In stating this, I do not mean to suggest that ableism is intrinsic to all distinctions between being fast and being slow. Indeed, it is only by contextualizing these distinctions that one can hope to understand the extent to which they sustain or challenge the ableist structure and imaginary of philosophy. Instead, I offer a crip critique of presumed connections between slowness and Southernness that seeks to understand how ableism is embedded in the rhythms of institutionalized philosophy, orienting how body-minds are positioned in, jettisoned from, or kept out of its hallowed halls and canon. As a result of ableism's embeddedness in philosophy's institutionalized flow, critically intervening in and ultimately eliminating philosophy's ableism requires more than demographic change; it requires a reframing of philosophy itself. Because this paper is specifically interested in the ableist dimensions of how slowness sticks to the US South, what do geographies of the fast and the slow suggest about ableist imaginaries that inform institutionalized philosophy in the United States? How does slowness circulate in ways that normalize distinctions between where philosophy happens and where it does not? My consideration of these questions is not merely a correction of misunderstandings or false impressions of the US South (though, of course, there are certainly plenty of those). Instead, my analysis points to the embeddedness of ableism in institutionalized philosophy, and the consequence is that eliminating ableism requires more than demographic change. Given its embeddedness, meaningfully addressing ableism in the hopes of eliminating it necessitates a reframing of philosophy itself.

My aim is not merely to weigh in on the veracity of stereotyped connections between slowness, the US South, philosophy, and disability. Furthermore, I'm not suggesting that the marginalization and exclusion of people, cultures, and places deemed slow is the only site of philosophy's ableism. Instead, I focus on the entanglement of dominant discourses of slowness, disability, and Southernness in order to reveal its role in sustaining and normalizing the ableist rhythms of institutionalized philosophy. In part, discourses of slowness, disability, and Southernness converge within dominant, mainstream philosophy to define *real* philosophy over and against people, places, and cultures characterized as slow and Southern. As a result, whole geographies are marginalized and even dismissed within the field's mainstream.

My discussion will proceed as follows. First, I will explore associations between being Southern and being slow. Second, I will consider some implications of the South's imagined slowness for assumptions about the possibility of philosophy in and of the South. In the third and final section, I will first consider contemporary calls to return to slowness, including calls for a "slow philosophy."[6] I will conclude by contrasting the mainstream, commodified notion of slowness with a queer crip conception of being slow as a philosophical attunement in times of derangement.[7]

Slow as Molasses

Along with "racist," "slow" is a word that sticks to the US South. Indeed, one could say that the storied slowness of Southerners is part of how it is characterized as racist. Among its numerous entries for slow, the *Oxford English Dictionary* offers the following: "Not quick or clever in apprehending or understanding a thing; obtuse"; "naturally disinclined to be active or to exert oneself; constitutionally inert or sluggish; lacking in promptness or energy"; "not quick, ready, prompt, or willing to do something"; "tardy or dilatory in action; displaying a lack of promptitude or energy under particular circumstances; spending a comparatively long time in the performance of some act; doing something in a slow, deliberate manner." The *Oxford English Dictionary* entry also notes that the "slow learner" or "slow starter" in the context of education connotes an "educationally subnormal" student who lags behind others of the same age, someone who is "not only expected to remain [a] slow [learner] but also to be unable to learn as much as others."

The US South is imagined as slow in all these respects. Film is replete with images of the South as a hot, hazy, rural region where both speech and movement are slow. The South is also imagined as rooted in the past in ways that reflect an unwillingness or even inability to move forward. In the words of a well-known joke: How many Virginians does it take to change a lightbulb? Answer: four—one to change the lightbulb and three to remark on how much better the old lightbulb was! As slow, the South is imagined as the antithesis of progress. Mired in the past and attached to their monuments, many white Southerners are still fighting the US Civil War. Furthermore, educational achievement in red states in the South lags behind that of non-Southern blue states. With the exception of a few of its cities, the South is imagined as a dusty region that has been slow to modernize.

In a repudiation of this presumed slowness, many Southerners have proclaimed the arrival of a new South. In contrast to the provincial, racist Old South, the new South is characterized as refined, tolerant, and cultured. Interestingly, such pronouncements are not really new. For instance, in 1961 James Baldwin wrote about hearing from white residents of Charlotte, North Carolina, that their city "is not the South," that he hadn't "seen the South yet'"[8] For his part, Baldwin described Charlotte as "Southern enough," noting nonetheless that the South is neither monolithic nor different from the North in its "racial setup."[9] More recently, in his efforts to establish distance between the so-called new South and the old South, Shawn Chandler Bingham points out that Asheville, North Carolina, has become (depending on who you ask) the Paris or the San Francisco of the South, and according to *Rolling Stone* magazine, "America's New Freak Capital."[10] No longer a "cultural backwater," Bingham proclaims that "outside fixation now shines much brighter on Southernness, focusing on cities like Asheville, Austin, and Nashville; but a bohemian South has long existed in ways that contest views of a region lost in time, fossilized in traditionalism."[11]

I agree that the complexity of life in the US South challenges the rigidity of the stereotypes that stick to it. For example, as Linda Martín Alcoff demonstrates, the assumption that being white is synonymous with being racist eclipses the important historical and contemporary reality of white resistance to racism, especially poor white resistance to the intertwined forces of racism and capitalism, including in the US South.[12] While this fact certainly does not minimize the ongoing violence of white racism and white complicity with white supremacy, it does serve as an important reminder that white racism is not inevitable, that white people can and have resisted it. Furthermore, as Alcoff points out, it is important to remember how much of this antiracist work has happened in the rural US South.[13]

For different reasons, both Bingham and Alcoff emphasize how lived realities in the South defy stereotypes of it as irrevocably racist. Nonetheless, I find it interesting that in his efforts to distinguish between a more bohemian South and stereotypes of the South as backward and without culture (or slow), Bingham reinforces the very stereotypes he wants to challenge. There seems to be no way in which the South can, on its own, signify the contemporary, the cultured, or progress, as evidenced by the fact that Bingham resorts to comparisons to non-Southern cities to make his point, that is to materialize the South as new or a site of creativity and culture. Asheville can't be simply Asheville; it must be the Paris or the San Francisco of the South. It is as if in order to cease to be slow and to catch up with the rest of the times, the South and its cities must become non-Southern.

While the South is frequently characterized as slow, one might nonetheless wonder about the accuracy of this characterization. After all, automobile racing originated and remains very popular in the US South, especially among white Southerners. Wouldn't this fact indicate that the South is not only slow but also quite fast?[14] As the second-most-popular sport in the United States, NASCAR (National Association for Stock Car Auto Racing) has become mainstream, and with racetracks on the west coast and in the midwest and northeast, as well as tremendous corporate sponsorship, one might wonder if it is still accurate to characterize the sport as Southern.[15] According to Rebecca Scott, the connection between speed and corporate sponsorship situates NASCAR as an American (and even global) sport rather than a regional form of entertainment.[16] Moreover, Scott contends, speed and the centrality of the automobile link NASCAR to the whiteness and mobility of neoliberal subjectivity in a context of global capitalism.[17] Fast driving simultaneously insulates and removes the driver from specific environments and provides a feeling of access to all spaces;[18] in other words, fast driving situates the driver as everywhere and nowhere. The link between whiteness, speed, and mobility reflected in NASCAR is another example of the "ontological expansiveness" that is a feature of whiteness.[19] For Scott, the speed of the automobile in car racing enables the expansion of the Southern white masculine subject to the subjectivity of the nation itself.[20] While the roots of the sport are Southern, speed, mobility, and corporate sponsorship have facilitated the ontologically expansive whiteness of the sport, enabling the transcendence of regional boundaries in order to become another national pastime. Thus, the speed of NASCAR does not contravene the persistent association of slowness and Southernness. Speed is central to the temporal and spatial politics of nationalism, imperialism, and global capitalism that incorporates the Southern in a process of assimilative erasure.

The temporal politics of racism and antiracism is an important theme in Martin Luther King Jr.'s 1963 "Letter from Birmingham Jail" and James Baldwin's 1956 response to William Faulkner's observations about the South and desegregation published that same year. King and Baldwin demonstrate that slowness is a feature of Southern white racist resistance to Black demands for citizenship rights. In response to Faulkner's suggestion that civil rights leaders should stop, wait, go slow, and be patient if they wanted real change in the South, Baldwin replied, "After more than two hundred years in slavery and ninety years of quasi-freedom, it is hard to think very highly of William Faulkner's advice to 'go slow.' 'They don't mean go slow,' Thurgood Marshall is reported to have said, 'they mean don't go.' "[21] Similarly, King critiqued white paternalism, arrogance, and entitlement that characterized attempts to "set the timetable for another [person's] freedom."[22] King famously wrote, "we have waited for more than three hundred and forty years for our God-given constitutional rights. The nations of Asia and Africa are moving with jet-like speed toward the goal of political independence, and we still creep at horse-and-buggy pace toward the gaining of a cup of coffee at a lunch counter."[23] As Baldwin and King point out, the South is, in part, a temporal zone in which a paternalistic, infantilizing white racism is characterized by white desire for slowness in the face of antiracist demands for social change.

Lest one assume that such calls for slowness pertain only to the mid-twentieth-century South, it is important to note that similar concerns about moving too fast have been voiced by some white Southerners in response to demands to remove Civil War monuments. For example, on August 14, 2017, after activists toppled a Confederate statue in Durham, North Carolina, Governor Roy Cooper called for patience, saying that even though he, "unlike an African American father," would never have to explain the monuments in the same way to his daughter, "there is a better way to remove these monuments."[24] Whatever Cooper's intentions, the pattern critiqued by Baldwin and King remains the same: white Southerners proclaim to know best and assert that patience and going slow are the best courses of action for those who are oppressed by, oppose, and demand accountability for the persistence of white supremacy.

Nonetheless, the political significance of pace is not inherent to being fast or slow. Within the temporal politics of racism in the US South, both speed and slowness have informed white indifference. The temporal politics of racism in the South is fungible, governed by a timetable oriented toward the preservation of white supremacy. Time and tempo are neither politically neutral nor singular, and understanding the political significance of the multiplicity of temporalities requires grappling with their relationship and attunement to context. In fact, King's discussion of temporal politics refers to two types of slowness. Just as there are just and unjust laws, there are, for King, destructive and constructive (or creative) tempos in the work of justice.[25] Thus, the white, self-serving, "mythical concept of time" informs belief in the inevitability of progress but, in reality, signals a "wait" that "almost always" means "never."[26] At the same time, there is the hurried condemnation expressed by white moderates who, if they wish to be on the side of justice, must take time to think things through and patiently read King's letter that he took time to write while doing time in jail. King writes, "I'm afraid [this letter] is much too long to take your precious time."[27] King's carefully crafted, sharp letter demands to be read, slowly. White moderates have rushed to condemn antiracist, nonviolent civil disobedience. Justice requires whites to slow down and listen to the perspectives of Black people who are harmed by the status quo. In this context, being slow can inform an ethics and politics of white refusal to be complicit with racism. Without the hard work of justice, time "becomes an ally of the forces of social stagnation,"[28] but time coupled with the work of justice is the ally of social transformation. Rather than a condemnation of slowness (including slowness in the South) itself, I read King's powerful critique of white moderate desire for more time as a critique of white inertia. As both Baldwin and King note, when white people say "slow down" or "be patient" in response to antiracist demands for justice, they "almost always" mean "never." At the same time, the possibility of white antiracism requires a slowness that avoids a rush to judgment and tunes in to perspectives that have been distorted and squelched by centuries of racism's white noise.

Philosophy and the South

Slowness is a significant part of the US national imaginary concerning the South. Does slowness also play a meaningful role in academic philosophy? How does slowness appear in the discipline? What temporal politics inform distinctions between "good" and "bad" philosophy? In examining the stickiness of "the Southern" and "the slow," what might be learned about the ableist structure of institutionalized philosophy's disciplinary time?

For W. J. Cash, it is the South's slowness and religiosity that make it particularly inhospitable to philosophy or any of the "finer" habits of thinking. Cash's reasons for the absence of philosophy in the South include: a preference for immediate action rather than contemplation; the control of schools by ministers; the lack of complexity in the environment and in attitudes that obstructs the cultivation of a life of the mind; a religiously influenced hostility to new ideas; and the white Southerner's tendency toward feeling rather than thinking.[29] Importantly, for Cash, white Southern hostility to philosophy, to the life of the mind, served as a shield against criticism of slavery. He writes, "the defense of slavery not only eventuated . . . in a taboo on criticism [of it]; in the same process it set up a ban on *all* analysis and inquiry, a terrified truculence toward every new idea, a disposition to reject every innovation out of hand and hug to the whole of the status quo with fanatical resolution."[30] In fact, Cash's description of the Old South is remarkably similar to contemporary characterizations of white voters in the rural South.

For Cash, philosophy is a constitutional impossibility in the US South because the region and its people remain stuck in the past.[31] In the South, according to Cash, progress is delayed due to the persistence of attitudes shaped by the lingering effects of plantation slavery in rural, isolated areas. It seems that, even today and despite its cities and changing demographics, the South continues to be conceived as slow and rural in the way that Cash described in the 1940s, and that this slowness often symbolizes white Southern racism. For example, when talking about the violent clash between white supremacists and antiracist protesters in Charlottesville, Virginia, in August 2017 and the history of the city's Confederate monuments, Jalane Schmidt observed, "people like to think that we're this progressive university place. At the end of the day, we're just a small Southern town."[32]

Let me be clear that in using this example, I am not defending Confederate monuments. I agree that they are monuments to white supremacy and, thus, should be removed. I share Schmidt's critique of them. What interests me is the distinction between being a progressive university place and a small Southern town. Could a small Southern town in the United States ever be considered a progressive university place, or do the words "small" (that is, rural) and "Southern" signify the incongruity of that idea? Does the presence of white racism in the South render a place "small" no matter what size city it is? What does it mean that "small Southern town" stands in for white racism—an example of slowed progress in the United States, a region that holds back the rest of the nation? For Cash, it seems that the South, as imaginatively stuck in its past in ways that profoundly shape a white Southern mind and habitus, remains tied to the slow temporality of isolated rurality, and such ties render the South unfit for philosophy. Within the US national imaginary, the South (including, especially, small Southern towns) is considered synonymous with racism in ways that other US regions are not, despite their own racist histories and contemporary realities. In fact, I suggest that the conception of the South as slow is part of an ableist logic that shores up an exceptionalist understanding of the United States (especially its non-Southern regions), the university, and philosophy as progressive sites of antiracism.

These days it seems that many non-Southerners are perplexed by rural white Southerners, an observation that led Arlie Hochschild, as recounted in *Strangers in Their Own Land*, to travel south to try to understand the "empathy wall" between red states and blue states.[33] Most red states are in the South, and Hochschild went to bayou country in Louisiana in order to understand "red state logic"—that is, why those who are the most disadvantaged by cuts to social programs and environmental regulations nonetheless vote against their own interests by supporting candidates for whom these cuts are political priorities. Hochschild certainly does not claim that all white Southerners subscribe to red state logic, but she nonetheless reproduces a sense of the South's backward otherness that ultimately (even if unintentionally) reinforces the assumption that progressive universities are located elsewhere.

In comparisons of UC Berkeley (her campus) and Louisiana State University, Hochschild notes the greater variety of student social clubs and academic programs at UC Berkeley. She also lists some student clubs at Louisiana State University that do not exist at UC Berkeley: the Oilfield Christian Fellowship, the Agribusiness Club, the Air Waste Management Association, and the War Gaming and Role Playing Society.[34] Having taught *Strangers in their Own Land* in my environmental ethics course, I can attest that the implied suggestion that a better education and extracurricular university experience might be had outside the South does not escape my students' notice. The part of the South that Hochschild visits stands in for all red states and is defined by what it lacks: the *New York Times*, bookstores, and vibrant, diverse university campuses. While many of the people Hochschild interviews have been disabled by the slow violence of toxic environments and workplaces, they are also ill served by the region's educational system that has been negatively impacted by diverting money from educational spending to provide incentives to polluting industries.

Imagining that "real" universities exist outside the South is a distancing strategy that denies complicity with racism. However, as Jay Dolmage points out, wherever they are located, Western universities have always been settler-colonial projects; many North American universities have provided support for racist and ableist scientific research; they were built on stolen lands; and they were often built with slave labor.[35] Thus, despite all their diversity programs, marketing strategies, and ramps, North American universities, regardless of their location, have long been institutions for marking, sorting, and containing difference.[36] And, as Dolmage points out, one border that has been especially central to educational discourse is that between the slow and the promising student.

Recall that for Cash, the South is a place where philosophy is not. Hochschild reveals how being slow is part of what the South means—slow progress, slow speech, slow movement. In being slow, one is unprepared for educational success, delayed, behind where one should be—all of which stand in stark contrast to the characteristics that define philosophical brilliance. In listening to academic presentations—outside the context of disability-themed conferences where accommodations of various kinds are more likely to exist—it is as if the faster one speaks and reads, the more brilliant one is assumed to be. As slow, being Southern is equated with stupidity. Consider how many times "dumb" or "ignorant" are used as modifiers for Southerners. I've lost count.

Philosophy's Ableist Temporality

Within educational contexts, slow is another word for disabled, and, just as philosophy and the humanities more generally are perceived by some as wasteful compared to more deserving and "useful" disciplines, disabled students are often portrayed as a drain on resources at the expense of more deserving students. As Jay Dolmage points out, academic ableism has long relied on a stock of imaginary students, including the slow learner.[37] The specter of the slow learner often appears in critiques of pedagogical efforts to better accommodate disabled students for fear that such accommodations will unfairly hold back (or slow down) exceptional, bright students. Two such characters in the ableist imaginary are "super Samantha" and "slow Samantha." Super Samantha, Dolmage writes, is "totally flexible to a wide range of uses and values within capitalism"; she "is not molded by education, but rather bursts through the doors of the classroom and demands its reshaping."[38] As the student with a bright future who is more tech savvy than her professors, "super Samantha [is] a product or even a flag-bearer of fast capitalism, a logic stressing the need for constant change, flexibility, and adaptation, particularly in modes of expression."[39] In other words, it is education that must catch up to super Samantha. At the opposite end of the educational spectrum is "slow Samantha," who "is a kind of human vacuum . . . defined by what she can't do—and what she can't do stands in for deficits of the entire educational system."[40] Neither imagined Samantha represents the actual complexity of students' educational talents and needs. Nonetheless, both are central to the ableist educational project of sorting students in ways that fail students deemed slow, which is another word for students the educational system and the society it serves cannot and will not use.[41] Denied meaningful participation in school, slow students are deemed a "drain" on scarce educational resources, a threat to the nation's future, and, thus, "disposable."[42]

To be perceived as slow is to be perceived as delayed or unable to meet norms of human development and learning. One is deemed slow in relation to a norm whose meaning has long been shaped by racism and classism. As Nirmala Erevelles and Mel Chen argue, disability functions as more than a mere descriptive term for physical and mental impairments; its meanings are forged within racist, sexist, classist, ableist institutions in order to distinguish between those body-minds deemed useful and those body-minds deemed disposable. For example, students of color are disproportionately categorized as learning disabled, revealing how racialized disability is central to ongoing segregation of students of color in school and the school-to-prison pipeline.[43] Further, the definition of Down syndrome was informed by and helped to reinforce the assertion of Western supremacy, exemplifying the coconstitutive relationship between disability, race, and empire.[44]

Assumptions about disability are also central to various forms of sorting that occur in institutionalized philosophy in the United States. Certainly, self-identified disabled people are a demographic minority in the discipline.[45] Furthermore, as Licia Carlson argues, disabled people, when they appear in Western philosophy, have most often appeared as case studies or objects of philosophical analysis rather than as subjects with a point of view that orients philosophical discussion.[46] How might lingering with the concept of the slow reveal other ways that institutionalized philosophy works as an ableist sorting mechanism with implications for how people and geographical regions are imagined either as full of philosophical promise or as antithetical to philosophy?

Jay Dolmage proclaims that the university is a "thoroughly ableist institution," a claim that includes its various disciplines, such as philosophy.[47] In characterizing institutionalized philosophy as ableist, I am not suggesting that it should not be studied or dismissing the important work of disability in philosophy that aims to transform the field. Instead, I intend to highlight the persistence of institutionalized patterns of ableist sorting that, as Dolmage points out, continue to define the discipline (and the university) even as previously marginalized areas, like philosophy of disability, become incorporated into it. Consider studies about the gendered tendency to describe some students as brilliant and others as perhaps eager or hard workers but who are nonetheless slow to catch on.[48] In her discussion of the gendered consequences of implicit bias and stereotype threat in philosophy, Jennifer Saul recounts her experience as a graduate student overhearing faculty categorizing students according to "who's smart" and "who's stupid."[49] Saul cites Eric Schwitzgebel's 2010 analysis of characteristics that are associated with intelligence in philosophy; "seeming smart" in philosophy includes characteristics such as "whiteness, maleness, a certain physical bearing, a certain dialect (one American, one British), [and] certain patterns of prosody . . ."[50] US Southern accents are not associated with seeming smart, as evidenced by a recent study that showed that a Northern accent is associated with being smart and in charge and a Southern accent is associated with being nice.[51] Building on Dolmage, one might say that "bright Ben" plays the imaginative sorting role in philosophy. Bright Ben is an inspiration to his colleagues. There seems to be nothing that he can't master; he possesses boundless energy and a mythic, machinelike rate of productivity. He is white, male, ablebody-minded, and he does not have a Southern accent. Like "super Samantha," he is an ideal flexible cog in the machine of fast capitalism. He stands in contrast to those deemed slow and lazy, a drain on resources, and ultimately disposable. As an important gendered, racialized, and ableist sorting category in philosophy, seeming smart distances the truly philosophical from the Southern.

Focusing on the meanings of the institutional work of slowness can unearth the ableist structure of the university in general and philosophy in particular. Following Foucault, disciplinary power is shaped in part by a "temporal imperative" that is attuned to the arrangement of space, the organization of bodies, and the correlation between bodies and gestures.[52] This correlation of bodies and gestures, Foucault writes, aims at the maximization of speed and efficiency—in other words, the maximization of productivity. For example, Foucault discusses practices designed to regulate every minute movement and positioning of the body in order to produce good handwriting. To write well, Foucault explains, one must be correctly positioned: from the direction of one's feet, to the distance between one's torso and the desk, the way one holds a pen, and the fluency[53] (or speed) with which one writes.[54] Good handwriting involves the seamless coordination of all these elements to allow for fluency in writing that appears as one's natural, rather than a practiced or disciplined, rhythm. As Foucault contends, power pervades the temporal containment and regulation of bodies within institutions. The temporal discipline that manages the movements of bodies within institutions establishes "speed as a virtue."[55] Foucault's description of the timetable as a technique of disciplinary power illuminates the ableist structure it helps to maintain, produce, and naturalize, especially what Fiona Kumari Campbell describes as the ontological and epistemological dimensions of ableism.[56] I suggest that the distinction between the fast and the slow is a feature of disciplinary time that depoliticizes and normalizes ableism at the heart of institutionalized philosophy.

It is not simply that good philosophy is fast and bad philosophy is slow. Instead, the structure of ableism determines whether and how tempo matters. The imagined slowness of the US South is part of how ableism works to relegate the US South to the periphery of the imagined map of where philosophy happens or is possible. Understanding the relation between philosophy's disciplinary time and the structure of ableism requires consideration of the relationship between tempo and normalcy. Does the tempo interrupt or sustain gendered, racialized, classed, ableist rhythmic norms of being a good philosopher?

What about a Slow Philosophy?

Despite the negative connotations of being slow, these days there seems to be a new imperative to be slow. There is slow travel, slow narrative, slow reading, slow food, and the slow professor—to offer a partial list. The current emphasis on slowing down is an effort to resist the ever-accelerating pace of life in the context of global fast capitalism. This accelerated pace has changed the expectations of professorial work. One is expected to do more and to read, write, and publish quickly.[57] In any given week, there seem to be at least three new books that one needed to read the week before. As Maggie Berg and Barbara Seeber explain, the new culture of speed in academia is a result of "the corporatization of the university" in which [market] values of productivity, efficiency, and competition" prevail.[58] In particular, they claim, "productivity is about getting a number of tasks done in a set unit of time; efficiency is about getting a number of tasks done quickly; and competition, in part, is about marketing your achievements before someone else beats you to it."[59] But academia's culture of speed has damaging effects on the health of professors.[60] The institutional response to elevated stress is to blame individuals and emphasize time management. Far from shirking professional responsibility, Berg's and Seeber's slow professor resists the pressures to accelerate that threaten to undermine the value of higher education for faculty, students, and society. The slow professor, they proclaim, takes time to "read the institution."[61]

There have been some similar calls for a slow philosophy. For example, in *Slow Philosophy: Reading Against the Institution*, Michelle Boulous Walker traces the theme of slowness in some Western philosophical texts and argues for the importance of slow reading in the cultivation of philosophy as a way of life. She writes,

The instituting moment of philosophy as a love of wisdom involves the patient work of thought. It is first and foremost the patience involved in "sitting with" the world and being open to it; not merely for the sake of being patient but, rather, for engagement with the complexity of the world that this slow and open process of thought permits. Philosophy, at its best, involves judgment, but not the fast and furious judgment of a final verdict. Rather, it is the judgment that comes from suspending certainty, from hesitating, deliberating and taking time.[62]

As a practice of slow reading and writing, slow philosophy is a practice of wonder. A slow philosophy not only reads words but searches behind, under, and through them for deeper meaning. Such reading requires time and patience.

Friedrich Nietzsche's preface to *Daybreak* is another example of a call for philosophy to be slow. Nietzsche writes, "Nowadays it is not only my habit, it is also my taste—a malicious taste, perhaps?—no longer to write anything which does not reduce to despair every sort of man who is 'in a hurry.' "[63] He continues, "in the midst of an age of 'work,' that is to say, of hurry, of indecent and perspiring haste, which wants to 'get everything done' at once, including every old or new book—this art does not so easily get anything done, it teaches to read *well*, that is to say, to read slowly, deeply, looking cautiously before and aft, with reservations, with doors left open, with delicate eyes and fingers."[64] In his reading of Nietzsche's preface to *Daybreak*, John Sallis describes Nietzsche's work as "subterranean activity."[65] Sallis argues that Nietzsche tunnels under philosophical foundations of truth and morality, destabilizing the edifice of philosophy and its founding assumptions of truth and morality.[66]

From one perspective, this way of being slow seems to have much potential for cripping philosophy in and of the South. Nietzsche's untimeliness opens the possibility of a transformed practice of philosophy, not the edification of the canon. Nietzsche was, and in some quarters is still considered to be, a figure who is at best marginal to and at worst not even a part of the discipline of philosophy. Nietzsche's untimeliness takes aim at unquestioned values and assumptions in the field, and ableism is certainly one of philosophy's edifying values. But while Nietzsche's delicate eyes and fingers suggest a perspective from which philosophy can be cripped, reading Nietzsche slowly is no guarantee of transformation of philosophy's ableist, racist, sexist, Eurocentric edifice. The possibility of such transformation depends on the orientation of one's practice—namely, the extent to which one's engagement is oriented toward an unsettling or a straightening (or normalization) of institutional philosophy's disciplinary time. As Robert McRuer puts it, " 'To crip,' like 'to queer,' gets at processes that unsettle, or processes that make strange or twisted. . . . Cripping always attends to the materiality of embodiment at the same time that it attends to how spaces, issues, or discussions get 'straightened.' "[67] Being slow becomes straightened and folded into dominant institutional rhythms to the extent that its pace is orientated toward achieving greater fluency with philosophy's disciplinary time. In other words, it is only by attending to the context of philosophical engagement that one can ascertain the extent to which slowing down performs the subterranean work of destabilizing the edifice of institutionalized Western philosophy or is yet another disciplinary skill that reinforces rather than questions dominant notions of the boundary that defines what is taken to be the properly philosophical.

Returning to King and Baldwin, being slow has no value in itself. One form of slow philosophy is seamlessly folded into the pace that privileges some body-minds and geographies over others, and another form of slow philosophy interrupts the dominant rhythms of institutional philosophy in ways that enable the reconceptualization and transformation of the field through participation of body-minds and geographies deemed unfit for philosophy. Constituted as a new philosophical skill, the edifice-destabilizing potential of slow philosophy is disciplined, tamed, defused, assimilated, straightened. While Walker's analysis aims at reframing slowness in order to rehabilitate philosophy, my aim is to consider how ableist assumptions about slowness define the institutionalized mainstream of philosophy. Both speed and slowness can serve ableist disciplinary aims. Ableist institutions can cast out those deemed slow while simultaneously incorporating slowness as a new, better philosophical ability over and against a delay that interrupts or obstructs disciplinary aims.

Being slow can also be a mark of privilege, especially given the neoliberal global capitalist pressures of acceleration. The ability to slow down can be an indication of the extent to which one's time is one's own, that one's labor in the university (for example) is free of constant supervision. Furthermore, being slow, like the notion of "free time," can be folded into and support, rather than unsettle, a neoliberal global capitalist pace oriented toward greater efficiency and productivity.[68]

Consider the ableist structures that function to mark some body-minds as disabled because slow and others as abled because more efficient, skilled, and productive, regardless of the pace of their performance. In his essay "Too Dumb for Complex Texts?," Mark Bauerlein presents slow reading as a "slow cure" for students who are unable to perform as expected at the college level.[69] Due to the negative influence of technology-driven forms of multitasking, students today, Bauerlein argues, lack the attention span necessary to read complex texts that "require single-tasking, an unbroken and unbothered focus."[70] However, technology, as Julie Cosenza points out, can allow for greater visibility of invisible disabilities, such as learning disabilities.[71] Cosenza utilizes technology in her performance piece SLOW as a form of crip resistance that disrupts normalizing academic flows that negate multiple sites of learning and knowledge generation and makes visible her experience of dyslexia.[72]

As a practice of cripping philosophy, being slow involves much more than individual acts of focused, uninterrupted reading and writing. Cripping philosophy "reads against the institution" and, in so doing, destabilizes its historical, conceptual, methodological, and architectural edifice. Being slow, from this perspective, thinks on and against the "steep steps" that continue to keep out those deemed unfit for philosophy because slow and delayed.[73] Philosophy slowed in this way can offer a philosophy in and of the US South that critically intervenes in the racism and ableism that form the edifice of institutionalized philosophy. To disrupt the rhythms of dominant philosophy's ableist structures, a slow philosophy must not only read against the accelerated pace of neoliberal global capitalism that threatens the existence of philosophy and the humanities generally. It must also read against itself, both by resisting privileged geographies of where the best philosophy happens and seriously engaging and thinking from the perspective of body-minds and geographies deemed unfit within dominant disciplinary temporal frames. Oriented toward undoing philosophy's ableist temporalities, slow philosophy positions "the Southern" and "the disabled" as subjects rather than objects of transformed philosophical practice.[74]

Notes

1. Eli Clare, *Brilliant Imperfection: Grappling with Cure* (Durham and London: Duke University Press, 2017, xvi). Here I make use of Clare's hyphenation of "body-mind." The hyphen acknowledges the inseparability of the body and mind, as well as the hierarchal distinction between them in the western philosophical tradition, a distinction that continues to have profound, harmful implications for assumptions about disability and difference. In addition, the hyphen in "body-mind" resists collapsing differences between physical and mental disabilities.

2. Geopolitically of course, "the South" is not restricted to the United States, and my specific focus in this paper on the southern region of the United States in no way means to collapse differences between the many Souths in the world. Instead, I consider a particular set of assumptions about the US South and their implications for the possibility of philosophy in and of the US South.

3. See Alison Kafer, *Feminist, Queer, Crip* (Bloomington: Indiana University Press, 2013); Robert McRuer, *Crip Theory* (New York: NYU Press, 2006); and Robert McRuer, *Disability, Globalization, and Resistance* (New York: NYU Press, 2018, especially 19–20). As Kafer and McRuer point out, the point of an expansive approach to disability is not the sort of universalization of disability reflected in the claim that everyone is or eventually will become disabled. For more about queer disidentification as a critical strategy that thinks on and against (rather than rejects) identity, see E. Patrick Johnson, "'Quare' Studies or (Almost) Everything I Know about Queer Studies I Learned from My Grandmother," *Social Text* 21, no. 1 (2001): 1–25, and José Muñoz, *Disidentification: Queers of Color and the Performance of Politics* (Minneapolis: University of Minnesota Press, 1999).

4. Fiona Kumari Campbell, *Contours of Ableism: The Production of Disability and Abledness* (New York: Palgrave Macmillan, 2009), 4.

5. Campbell, *Contours of Ableism*, 6.

6. See Michelle Boulous Walker, *Slow Philosophy: Reading against the Institution* (London: Bloomsbury, 2017).

7. See Amitav Ghosh, *The Great Derangement: Climate Change and the Unthinkable* (Chicago: University of Chicago Press, 2016). Ghosh offers the concept of derangement to characterize the unpredictability that results from climate change. The change to the chemistry of the planet means that we can no longer take for granted the environmental norms that have long been assumed. Here, I extend Ghosh's idea of derangement to include the unpredictability brought about by the defunding of higher education, cuts to the humanities, and the growing contingency of academic labor.

8. James Baldwin, "Nobody Knows My Name: A Letter from the South," In *Collected Essays*, ed. Toni Morrison (New York: Library of America, 1998), 203.

9. Baldwin, "Nobody Knows My Name," 203. Baldwin's discussion of Charlotte, North Carolina, also critiques the resistance of white leaders who argued that integration had to proceed slowly in order to be successful but who simultaneously did what they could to legally obstruct integration (202). Later in the essay, I will return to Baldwin's and Martin Luther King Jr.'s critique of white liberal demands for slowness as a feature of white racism.

10. Shawn Chandler Bingham, "Bohemian Groves in Southern Soil," in *The Bohemian South: Creating Countercultures from Poe to Punk* (Chapel Hill: University of North Carolina Press, 2017), 1.

11. Bingham, "Bohemian Groves in Southern Soil," 2.

12. Linda Martín Alcoff, *The Future of Whiteness* (New York: Polity, 2015).

13. See Alcoff, *The Future of Whiteness*.

14. Thanks to members of the audience at UNC Charlotte for challenging me to think about these questions when I presented an earlier version of this paper in November 2018. My aim is neither to propose a reversal in which the slow is deemed better than the fast nor to suggest that crip time is necessarily slow time. As Margaret Price notes, because a "psychotic break" can happen in a flash, "crip time is not necessarily time slowed down." See Price, "The Bodymind Problem and the Possibilities of Pain," *Hypatia: Journal of Feminist Philosophy* 30, no. 1 (2015): 273.

15. See Neal Thompson, *Driving with the Devil: Southern Moonshine, Detroit Wheels, and the Birth of NASCAR* (New York: Broadway Books, 2009). See also Rebecca R. Scott, "Environmental Affects: NASCAR, Place, and White American Cultural Citizenship," *Social Identities* 19, no. 1 (2013): 13–31.

16. Scott, "Environmental Affects," 16.

17. Scott, "Environmental Affects," 18.

18. Scott, "Environmental Affects," 18.

19. See Shannon Sullivan, *Revealing Whiteness: The Unconscious Habits of Racial Privilege* (Bloomington: Indiana University Press, 2006), 144.

20. Scott, "Environmental Affects," 22.

21. James Baldwin, "Faulkner and Desegregation," in *Collected Essays*, ed. Toni Morrison (New York: Library of America, 1998), 209.

22. Martin Luther King Jr., "Letter from Birmingham Jail," In *The Radical King*, ed. Cornel West (Boston, MA: Beacon Press, 2015), 135.

23. King, "Letter from Birmingham Jail," 131.

24. Benjamin Wallace-Wells, "The Fight over Virginia's Confederate Monuments: How the State's Past Spurred a Racial Reckoning," *The New Yorker*, November 27, 2017, https://www.newyorker.com/magazine/2017/12/04/the-fight-over-virginias-confederate-monuments.

25. King, "Letter from Birmingham Jail," 136. See also King's distinction between reasonable, legitimate, unavoidable, and unreasonable forms of patience and impatience (127, 132, 144). As King demonstrates, slowness and hurry, patience and impatience, are relational terms with no intrinsic meaning or value.

26. King, "Letter from Birmingham Jail," 131, 135, 136.

27. King, "Letter from Birmingham Jail," 144.

28. King, "Letter from Birmingham Jail," 136.

29. Cash, *The Mind of the South*, 97, 9, 95, 98, 99.

30. Cash, *The Mind of the South*, 98, my emphasis.

31. Despite his critique of Southern white racism, Cash's discussion of philosophy in the South ignores Southern Black intellectual traditions, presenting the possibility of a philosophy in the South as solely determined by white Southern preferences and habits.

32. Jalane Schmidt, quoted in Benjamin Wallace-Wells, "The Fight over Virginia's Confederate Monuments: How the State's Past Spurred a Racial Reckoning."

33. Arlie Russell Hochschild, *Strangers in Their Own land: Anger and Mourning on the American Right* (New York: The New Press, 2016).

34. Hochschild, *Strangers in Their Own Land*, 19–20.

35. Jay Dolmage, *Academic Ableism: Disability and Higher Education* (Ann Arbor: University of Michigan Press, 2017), 13–21 and 49–51. See also Michael Gill and Nirmala Erevelles, "The Absent Presence of Elsie Lacks: Hauntings at the Intersection of Race, Class, Gender, and Disability," *African American Review* 50, no. 2 (2017): 132–34.

36. Dolmage, *Academic Ableism*, 21. Here, Dolmage characterizes the university as "a sorting game" and "a holding pen."

37. Dolmage, *Academic Ableism*, 103–14. My discussion of the distinction between students classified as slow and exceptional is indebted to Dolmage's analysis of "slow Samantha" and "super Samantha."

38. Dolmage, *Academic Ableism*, 103, 104.

39. Dolmage, *Academic Ableism*, 105.

40. Dolmage, *Academic Ableism*, 110.

41. Dolmage, *Academic Ableism*. See also Iris Marion Young's discussion of marginalization as a form of oppression in *Justice and the Politics of Difference* (Princeton, NJ: Princeton University Press, 1990).

42. Dolmage, *Academic Ableism*, 103.

43. Nirmala Erevelles, "Crippin' Jim Crow: Disability, Dis-Location, and the School-to-Prison Pipeline," in *Disability Incarcerated: Imprisonment and Disability in the United States and Canada*, ed. Liat Ben-Moshe, Chris Chapman, and Allison C. Carey (New York: Palgrave Macmillan, 2014).

44. Mel Y. Chen, "'The Stuff of Slow Constitution': Reading Down Syndrome for Race, Disability, and the Timing That Makes Them So," *Somatechnics* 6, no. 2 (2016): 235–48.

45. Shelley Tremain, "Introducing Feminist Philosophy of Disability," *Disability Studies Quarterly* 33, no. 3 (2013): http://dsq-sds.org/article/view/3877/3402.

46. Licia Carlson, *The Faces of Intellectual Disability: Philosophical Reflections* (Bloomington: Indiana University Press, 2009).

47. Dolmage, *Academic Ableism*, 7.

48. Jennifer Saul, "Implicit Bias, Stereotype Threat, and Women in Philosophy," in *Women in Philosophy: What Needs to Change?*, ed. Katrina Hutchison and Fiona Jenkins (New York: Oxford University Press, 2013), 54.

49. Saul, "Implicit Bias, Stereotype Threat, and Women in Philosophy," 53.

50. Saul, "Implicit Bias, Stereotype Threat, and Women in Philosophy," Schwitzgebel quoted on 54.

51. Katherine D. Kinzler and Jasmine M. DeJesus, "Northern = Smart and Southern = Nice: The Development of Accent Attitudes in the United States," *The Quarterly Journal of Experimental Psychology* 66, no. 6 (June 1, 2013): 1146–58.

52. Michel Foucault, *Discipline and Punish: The Birth of the Prison*, trans. Alan Sheridan (New York: Vintage, 1979), 149–52.

53. My thinking about ableist temporality and cripping fluency is indebted to Joshua St. Pierre's analysis of fluency, compulsory ablebodiedness, and the phenomenology of the stuttering masculine body in his excellent 2015 essay "Distending Straight Masculine Time: A Phenomenology of the Disabled Speaking Body," *Hypatia: A Journal of Feminist Philosophy* 30, no. 1 (2015): 49–65. In this essay, St. Pierre critiques the normalized ableist "choreography" that pervades institutions and communicative interaction and offers a queer crip temporal reframing of the speaking body.

54. Foucault, *Discipline and Punish*, 152.

55. Foucault, *Discipline and Punish*, 154.

56. Campbell, *Contours of Ableism*, 4.

57. For a critique of the disabling effects of the acceleration of academic life, see Ashely Taylor, "Slow(ed): Lessons on Slowness within Projects of Inclusivity," *Philosophy of Education Yearbook* (2019): 625–38. Taylor explores the transformative possibilities "doing slow" in the classroom as a mode of resistance to academic demands for speed.

58. Maggie Berg and Barbara K. Seeber, *Slow Professor: Challenging the Culture of Speed in the Academy* (Toronto: University of Toronto Press, 2017).

59. Berg and Seeber, *Slow Professor*, 8.

60. Berg and Seeber, *Slow Professor*, 8.

61. Berg and Seeber, *Slow Professor*, 9.

62. Walker, *Slow Philosophy*, 8–9.

63. Friedrich Nietzsche, *Daybreak: Thoughts on the Prejudices of Morality*, trans. R. J. Hollingdale (New York: Cambridge University Press, 1997), 5.

64. Nietzsche, *Daybreak*, 5.

65. John Sallis, "Doubly Slow Reading," *International Yearbook for Hermeneutics*, 12 (2013): 30.

66. Sallis, "Doubly Slow Reading," 30–31.

67. Robert McRuer, *Crip Times: Disability, Globalization, and Resistance* (New York: NYU Press, 2018), 23–24.

68. For more about acceleration, the politics of time, and the possibilities of resistance to the expansion of work into all aspects of human life, see John-Patrick Schultz, "Social Acceleration and the New Politics of Time," *Radical Philosophy Review* 20, no. 2 (2017): 329–54.

69. Mark Bauerlein, "Too Dumb for Complex Texts?," *Educational Leadership* 68, no. 5 (2011): 28–33.

70. Bauerlein, "Too Dumb for Complex Texts?," 31.

71. Julie Cosenza, "SLOW: Crip Theory, Dyslexia and the Borderlands of Disability and Ablebodiedness," *Liminalities: A Journal of Performance Studies* 6, no. 2 (2010): 1–10.

72. Cosenza, "SLOW," 5–7.

73. Dolmage, *Academic Ableism*, 44–48, 59. Dolmage uses the metaphor of steep steps to describe the myriad barriers that impede the mobility of body-minds deemed unfit for university life.

74. Many thanks to Shannon Sullivan, Jill Ehnenn, audiences at UNC-Asheville and UNC-Charlotte, and the anonymous peer reviewers for helpful comments on earlier versions of this essay.

Bibliography

Alcoff, Linda Martín. *The Future of Whiteness*. New York: Polity, 2015.

Baldwin, James. "Nobody Knows My Name: A Letter from the South." In *Collected Essays*, edited by Toni Morrison. New York: Library of America, 1998.

Baldwin, James. "Faulkner and Desegregation." In *Collected Essays*, edited by Toni Morrison. New York: Library of America, 1998.

Bauerlein, Mark. "Too Dumb for Complex Texts?" *Educational Leadership* 68, no. 5 (2011): 28–33.

Berg, Maggie, and Barbara K. Seeber. *Slow Professor: Challenging the Culture of Speed in Academia*. Toronto: University of Toronto Press, 2017.

Bingham, Shawn Chandler. "Bohemian Groves in Southern Soil." In *The Bohemian South: Creating Countercultures from Poe to Punk*, edited by Shawn Chandler Bingham and Lindsey A. Freeman, 1–19. Chapel Hill: University of North Carolina Press, 2017.

Campbell, Fiona Kumari. *Contours of Ableism: The Production of Disability and Abledness*. New York: Palgrave Macmillan, 2009.

Carlson, Licia. *The Faces of Intellectual Disability: Philosophical Reflections*. Bloomington: Indiana University Press, 2009.

Cash, W. J. *The Mind of the South*. New York: Vintage Books, 1991.

Chen, Mel Y. "'The Stuff of Slow Constitution': Reading Down Syndrome for Race, Disability, and the Timing That Makes Them So." *Somatechnics* 6, no. 2 (2016): 235–48.

Clare, Eli. *Brilliant Imperfection: Grappling with Cure*. Durham, NC: Duke University Press, 2017.

Cosenza, Julie. "SLOW: Crip Theory, Dyslexia, and the Borderlands of Disability and Ablebodiedness." *Liminalities: A Journal of Performance Studies* 6, no. 2 (2010): 1–10.

Dolmage, Jay. *Academic Ableism: Disability and Higher Education*. Ann Arbor: University of Michigan Press, 2017.

Erevelles, Nirmala. "Crippin' Jim Crow: Disability, Dis-Location, and the School-to-Prison Pipeline." In *Disability Incarcerated: Imprisonment and Disability in the United States and Canada*, edited by Liat Ben-Moshe, Chris Chapman, and Allison C. Carey, 81–99. New York: Palgrave Macmillan, 2014.

Foucault, Michel. *Discipline and Punish: The Birth of the Prison*. Translated by Alan Sheridan. New York: Vintage, 1979.

Ghosh, Amitav. *The Great Derangement: Climate Change and the Unthinkable*. Chicago: University of Chicago Press, 2016.

Gill, Michael and Nirmala Erevelles, "The Absent Presence of Elsie Lacks: Hauntings at the Intersection of Race, Class, Gender, and Disability," *African American Review* 50, no. 2 (2017): 123–37.

Hochschild, Arlie Russell. *Strangers in Their Own Land: Anger and Mourning on the American Right*. New York: The New Press, 2016.

Johnson, E. Patrick. "'Quare' Studies or (Almost) Everything I Know about Queer Studies I Learned from my Grandmother." *Social Text* 21, no. 1 (2001): 1–25.

Kafer, Alison. *Feminist, Queer, Crip*. Bloomington: Indiana University Press, 2013.

King, Martin Luther, Jr. "Letter from Birmingham Jail." In *The Radical King*, edited by Cornel West. Boston, MA: Beacon Press, 2015.

Kinzler, Katherine D., and Jasmine M. DeJesus. "Northern = Smart and Southern = Nice: The Development of Accent Attitudes in the United States." *The Quarterly Journal of Experimental Psychology* 66, no. 6 (2013): 1146–58.

McRuer, Robert. *Crip Times: Disability, Globalization, and Resistance*. New York: NYU Press, 2018.

McRuer, Robert. *Crip Theory: Cultural Signs of Queerness and Disability*. New York: NYU Press, 2006.

Muñoz, José. *Disidentification: Queers of Color and the Performance of Politics*. Minneapolis: University of Minnesota Press, 1999.

Nietzsche, Friedrich. *Daybreak: Thoughts on the Prejudices of Morality*. Translated by R. J. Hollingdale. New York: Cambridge University Press, 1997.

Price, Margaret. "The Bodymind Problem and the Possibilities of Pain," *Hypatia: Journal of Feminist Philosophy* 30, no. 1 (2015): 262–84.

Sallis, John. "Doubly Slow Reading." *International Yearbook for Hermeneutics* 12 (2013): 27–34.

Saul, Jennifer. "Implicit Bias, Stereotype Threat, and Women in Philosophy." In *Women in Philosophy: What Needs to Change?*, edited by Katrina Hutchison and Fiona Jenkins, 39–60. New York: Oxford University Press, 2013.

Schultz, John-Patrick. "Social Acceleration and the New Politics of Time," *Radical Philosophy Review* 20, no. 2 (2017): 329–54.

Scott, Rebecca R. "Environmental Affects: NASCAR, Place, and White American Cultural Citizenship." *Social Identities* 19, no. 1 (2013): 13–31.

St. Pierre, Joshua. "Distending Straight Masculine Time: A Phenomenology of the Disabled Speaking Body." *Hypatia: Journal of Feminist Philosophy* 30, no. 1 (2015): 49–65.

Sullivan, Shannon. *Revealing Whiteness: The Unconscious Habits of Racial Privilege*. Bloomington: Indiana University Press, 2006.

Taylor, Ashley. "Slow(ed): Lessons on Slowness within Projects of Inclusivity," *Philosophy of Education Yearbook* (2019): 625–38.

Thompson, Neal. *Driving with the Devil: Southern Moonshine, Detroit Wheels, and the Birth of NASCAR*. New York: Broadway Books, 2009.

Tremain, Shelley. "Introducing Feminist Philosophy of Disability." *Disability Studies Quarterly* 33, no. 4 (2013). http://dsq-sds.org/article/view/3877/3402.

Walker, Michelle Boulous. *Slow Philosophy: Reading against the Institution*. London: Bloomsbury, 2017.

Wallace-Wells, Benjamin. "The Fight over Virginia's Confederate Monuments: How the State's Past Spurred a Racial Reckoning," *The New Yorker*, November 27, 2017, https://www.newyorker.com/magazine/2017/12/04/the-fight-over-virginias-confederate-monuments.

Young, Iris Marion. *Justice and the Politics of Difference*. Princeton, NJ: Princeton University Press, 1990.

Afterword

Philosophizings in/of/regarding "the South(s)"

A New Field of Discourse in US American Philosophy?

Lucius T. Outlaw (Jr.)

As far as I have been able to determine, this is the first publication in the twentieth and twenty-first centuries of a book-length collection of writings in which US-based, professional, academic philosophers have made the foci of their concerns "the South(s)": according to certain considerations, a historically and culturally distinct region encompassing a collection of states of ongoing significance to the United States of America, and to North America generally; by still other considerations, historically and culturally distinct regions formed by particular neighboring nation-states and peoples on other continents that, considered collectively, are regarded as constituting "Global Souths" directionally south of continental North America and south of continental Europe. By contrast, before and during the nineteenth century, particular North American philosophers and other thinkers devoted considerable discursive and practical efforts to rationalizing and justifying, to legitimating and institutionalizing, the formation and preservation of distinctive modes of economic and sociopolitical life based on racialized plantation capitalism. This included a complex worldview of White Racial Supremacy further bolstered by a racialized philosophy of history, according to which it was the "manifest destiny" of the white race to order and rule the North American continent and, in partnership with racial white peoples of the mother countries of Europe, to rule globally over virtually all racialized, nonwhite, *colored* peoples.

Academic philosophy, often not separate from disciplinary enterprise(s) of religion or theology, has centuries-long histories in colleges, universities, and seminaries in various states in the US South, with persons of note having forged or otherwise contributed to intellectual histories of consequence for religious, political, social, economic, and cultural life generally in a number of these states, with regard to rationalizing and justifying the organization and management of polities (i.e., states) and the lives of the different races living within the polities by way of programs of White Racial Supremacy. Michael O'Brien's *Intellectual Life and the American South, 1810–1860* is an important historical recounting of such institutionalized intellectual endeavors and enterprises in particular states during the critical years leading up to the fateful Civil War of 1860–65, especially "Philosophy and Faith."[1] O'Brien documents the contributing efforts of philosophers to the formation and articulation of "conceptual machineries" put in service to rationalize and legitimate the modes of life—the racialized political economy and institutionalization of enabling formations of white supremacist cultural norms and practices—that have long been regarded as formative of a distinctive US "South." Of course, W. J. Cash's *The Mind of the South* is a now-classic effort of identifying, characterizing, explaining, and assessing the formation and significance of a distinctive mode of mindedness and the complementary patterns of sociality shared by white folks that were constitutive of the *Southernness* of the states comprising the US South. According to Cash:

> If it can be said there are many Souths, the fact remains that there is also one South. That is to say, it is easy to trace through the region (roughly delimited by the boundaries of the former Confederate States of America, but shading over into some of the border states, notably Kentucky, also) a fairly definite mental pattern, associated with a fairly definite social pattern—a complex of established relationships and habits of thought, sentiments, prejudices, standards and values, and associations of ideas, which, if it is not common strictly to every group of white people in the South, is still common in one appreciable measure or another, and in some part or another, to all but relatively negligible ones.[2]

Though Cash mentions Negroes numerous times in his book, the Southern-mindedness to which he refers is that of white folks, such exclusivity having long been the tradition of white writers, especially, who deliberated on "the South" of the United States. Attention, then, to the formation of modes of mindfulness (of philosophic mindfulness in particular) characteristic of, or concerned with, a more or less distinctive *South* in the United States, modes of mindfulness of intellectuals and ordinary folks of *all* racial and ethnic groupings, is worthy of the overdue attention of philosophers who are committed to critical explorations of the mindful makings of shared life in a region so consequential for life. This is likewise true regarding the mindful makings of life in "the Souths" south of the United States and Europe.

Why then, it seems, has it been the case that for more than a century, US-based professional academic philosophers have not devoted critical attention to "the South(s)," though all of the regions and peoples considered under organizing notions of *South(s)* have been and continue to be of significance and consequence in many regards? Why only now a collection such as this? What about agendas for and praxes of professionalized academic philosophizing, and about various practitioners' concerns regarding professionalized academic philosophizing, has set conditions such that these regions of profound consequence for the ongoing history of the United States of America and other regions of "the North(s)" have not been the focus of philosophical attention while having long been the concern of critically minded professional knowledge producers and artists in other knowledge-producing enterprises? Why has this been the case even when, for example, some notion of *Southern* has long been used to title a disciplinary professional journal, *The Southern Journal of Philosophy*? In reviewing the titles of the articles published in each issue of this journal, from the first (volume 1, issue 1, Spring 1963) to the most recent (volume 57, issue 4, December 2019), I did not find a single article the title of which announces that the writer will address the meaning and significance of "Southern," not even from editors regarding the journal's name.

This continues to be the case even though the journal's editorial base is a philosophy department in a public university that is located in a city in and of the US South—Memphis, Tennessee—that is widely and enthusiastically proclaimed as being an iconic city of *Southernness* manifested in the very best instances of definitive cultural creations: foods, music, religion, and forms of social engagement ("Southern hospitality"). Regarding all of these, however, there are still diversities that are at once old and continuous; long-shared, crosscutting, even contradictory; newly emergent; and all conditioned, more or less, by constellations and traditions of meaningfulness fostered by a political economy and cultural economy, and thus by social class– and gender-conditioned racial and ethnic populations, old and new. Such diversities, as well as pronounced intensified changes currently underway, have compelled Southern writer Tracy Thompson to revisit Cash's "mind of the South" project and to produce another assessment, *The New Mind of the South* (2013), in which she recounts a contemporary US South subjected to historic, dynamic forces of political, social, and cultural changes due in no small part to unprecedented demographic changes that are ushering in new patternings of life and mindedness.[3] Against the backdrop of even these considerations and writings regarding the US "South," the publication of this collection as a venture in academic philosophy is a milestone.

It is more than ironic that the efforts culminating in the publication of this collection came to a first important moment of realization as a panel of presentations that was organized for, and took place during, the annual meeting of an organization of professional academic philosophers—The Society for Phenomenological and Existential Philosophy—that was held *in Memphis* in 2017. The convener of that panel session and the organizing editor of this collection, like a number of the contributors, myself included, lives—on varying terms, in various ways, and to varying extents—through legacies and identities, personal and shared, as an imagined and felt "Southerner," even as a professional academic philosopher. *Especially* as a professional academic philosopher for the purposes of this now-published philosophizing project. Accordingly, this collection brings together individual efforts of philosophizing devoted, in part, to renouncing the apparent, more-than-a-century-long failure by US-based, professional, academic philosophers, possibly even of refusal in some cases, to take up for consideration "the South(s)." Yet another milestone for this collection: taking up and contributing to efforts by US-based, professional, academic philosophers to renovate professional, academic philosophy by initiating and sustaining new modes, foci, and networks of discourse that usher in greater intellectual diversity, freedom, creativity, and epistemic justice, in this case by liberating thinking and speaking about "the South(s)" *as philosophers.*

Belatedly, though. For, as noted, in a significant number of other disciplinary enterprises in the United States, and in "the Global South(s)," explorations of many matters "Southern" and of "the South(s)" have long been the concern of thoughtful, professional knowledge producers and artists in history, literature and literary studies, religion and theology, political science, sociology, music, art, cuisine, and architecture, among others; in interdisciplinary ventures in this country such as American Studies and African American and Diaspora Studies; and in inter- and transdisciplinary studies of "the Global South." Consequently, in a number of these disciplinary and interdisciplinary ventures, novel traditions and schools of critical thought have been forged while devoting attention to the formations of distinctive regions within which relatively distinct peoples and people-projects have come to be identified as "Southern." Furthermore, a number of prominent institutions of higher education in the US have established units devoted to studies of the US "South": for example, the Center for the Study of Southern Culture at the University of Mississippi; the Center for the Study of the American South at the University of North Carolina at Chapel Hill; the American Studies Program at the University of Virginia, which offers a concentration in "Southern Studies"; and *Southern Studies: An Interdisciplinary Journal of the South* (which, according to the journal's website, began publication in 1962 as "Louisiana Studies"; the title was changed to "Southern Studies" in 1977), hosted by Northwestern State University of Louisiana. Particularly noteworthy: there are no philosophers among the listed faculty of the two university centers, the "Southern studies" concentration at the University of Virginia, or the editorial board of *Southern Studies.*

These glaring absences do not, of course, tell the whole story, for there are more than a few philosophers in this country who have long drawn upon and contributed to the enterprises of American Studies, African American and Diaspora Studies, cultural studies, and other such ventures of critically minded knowledge production. This is also true of studies in aesthetics, of literature, music, other art-making enterprises. But, to my knowledge, the contributions by philosophers have been made with little focused, thematized attention on "the South(s)." Consequently, the belated focusing of attention on "the South(s)" in this collection might well have been hampered, as is true in my case certainly, by limited knowledge of how, and with what productive outcomes, productive thinkers in other disciplinary enterprises have already forged and put to work critically oriented projects of knowledge production that identify, characterize, and explain the modes of reproductive organization of shared living in historically consequential distinctive regional constellations that should and do matter to our living as "South(s)."

Indeed, my ignorance was made apparent when, in preparing for this piece by searching for publications with titles that included "south" and "philosophy," I discovered that there has been, and continues to be, much published philosophizing and theorizing regarding parts, and the whole, of "the Global South" by philosophers and other critically minded scholar-intellectuals in other disciplines in and beyond the United States of America, particularly by way of organized enterprises of trans- and interdisciplinary collaboration in knowledge production, the World Social Forum being but one institutionalized example. I learned of, and began studying, writings by one of the participants in and creative contributors to these international efforts of new ventures in social critique, Boaventura de Sousa Santos, whose provocative *Epistemologies of the South: Justice Against Epistemicide* and *The End of the Cognitive Empire: The Coming of Age of Epistemologies of the South* are opening me to new considerations that will influence how I endeavor to philosophize about matters of "the South(s)."[4] For example, in *Epistemologies of the South*, Santos expounds on the need for a new mode of and agenda for a critical theory of society that effects an "epistemological break . . . from the Western-centric critical tradition . . . of which the most brilliant exemplar is the Frankfurt School . . . [which] has failed to account for the emancipatory struggles of our time, in part at least because it shares with the bourgeois thinking it criticizes the same epistemological foundations that suppress the cognitive dimension of social injustice and thus renders universal the Western understanding and transformation of the world."[5] For my own reeducation, Santos's books are now high on my agenda of works-to-be-read (and reread) in their entirety.

Thus, while the publication of this collection is, I believe, a significant milestone, one that might well be an opportunity to forge a new field of discourse regarding "the South(s)" for interested professionals in academic philosophy in North America, I am now mindful that exploiting this opportunity will require new learning, and that participants who wish to contribute will need to get up to speed, as it were, on existing contributions from other fields of knowledge production. Further, I am convinced (but can be persuaded otherwise) that the intellectual resources required to effect an "epistemological break," as called for by Santos, and engage in needed creative reconstructions of knowledge production can be created in part by bringing to consideration and respectful appreciation instances of knowledge production in traditions of struggle against and endurance of various forms of oppression heretofore not thought worthy of attention by professional academic philosophers. Such new orientations to and practices of knowledge production are not widely ready to hand in academic philosophy, though we have examples in this collection—contributions from Havis, Stewart, and Farr, for example—that expose the lie of W. J. Cash's presumption that Southern black folks lacked any shared, discernable, let alone critical, mindedness worthy of serious critical attention, even by philosophers.

In order to fulfill the discursive promises of the contributions to this collection, much more work along these lines will be needed and, for philosophers especially, will require organized and sustained tapping of the resources already cultivated in other knowledge-producing enterprises that have long been about the work of attending thoughtfully and critically to "the South(s)" of the United States and beyond. An important need will be to become well informed of the formation and histories of the various "Southern" regionalities, of the more or less shared mindedness of the various—and changing—people and cultural groupings constitutive of these regions. The theoretical and empirical resources are not readily available to us by way of our training; this is also true, I believe, of much of our philosophizing that will be needed to engage in the work of producing critical, historically informed accounts of regionally shared similarities and differences of instantiations of racialized and ethnicized plantation, industrial, finance, and twentieth- and twenty-first-centuries advanced technological capitalist political economies, as well as the complementary sociocultural repertoires that, in each historical phase, made, and continue to make, regional lifeworlds while taking full account of important diversities within the same.

The publication of this collection makes evident that such efforts are under way. Still, there is a great need for bringing better inter- and transdisciplinary organization and focus to the thematizing of appropriate objects of inquiry, and for refining appropriate modes of inquiry and critique. Such efforts will require new forms and schedules of organized gatherings to foster shared efforts of critical philosophizing. The initial panel presentation that led to this collection will not suffice to sustain the mobilization of creative energies that will be required to maintain an ongoing venture of shared, focused intellectual work ordered by shared agendas regarding what is to be done. For many participants, those vital energies will have to be continuously remobilized and recharged by very real prospects for, and actual instances of, returns on investment that not only help sustain and advance their professional lives but nourish their individual souls as intellectuals concerned with a "South" of personal significance. To this end, there will also need to be assurance that the likes of the publisher of this collection will continue to print new writings of philosophizing that, in focusing on "the South(s)," help to effect Santos's needed "epistemological break" by contributing to whatever reformations, renovations, and creative developments in philosophizing are needed and made possible by the "break."

The publication, then, of this collection of writings on "philosophy in/of the South" by a highly regarded university press provides a not insignificant degree of recognition of the distinctive philosophical efforts of the organizing editor of the collection, the contributing writers, and the subject matter(s) addressed, thereby adding further legitimation to the discursive efforts that began as a panel of four presentations during a professional meeting. Worth noting, too, is that this panel came to be in response to concerns of a particular graduate student expressed to a particular professor, for both of whom regional identities as "Southern" became salient for philosophizing—though not by way of the education and legitimation of courses in philosophy or by way of writings on "the South(s)" by canonical or prominent, contemporary, US-based philosophers. According to the analyses of Randall Collins, legacies of the relations and practices cultivated and engaged in by networks of key philosophizing groups of intellectuals, including teacher-intellectuals and their students, have been foundational to the making and perpetuation of traditions of philosophizing.[6] To be appreciated, then, currently and in the future, will be the various ways, and extents to which, recognition and legitimation have (or have not!) been garnered by the production of philosophical articulations that have "the South(s)" as the foci of concern, and the extent to which this publication has fostered ongoing discourses sufficient to make a "field" of philosophical discourse regarding "the *Souths*."

Also noteworthy is the diversity (in terms of demographics and the foci of their philosophizings) of the persons invited to participate in the original panel session. To prepare contributions to this collection, each person was invited to consider intellectual concerns as well as personal experiences, elements of character and social being (e.g., class or geopolitical origin or residence), racial, ethnic, gendered, or ability identities, cultural background(s), and so forth, as these have been and are conditioned by "the South(s)" and, in turn, to draw on these as motivational resources for the subject matter(s) of their reflections and articulations. Taking the authors' responses as a whole, this collection provides a rich collection of articulations that might well serve as an initial contribution to the formation of a new field of discourse in academic philosophy in the United States of America: "Philosophy in/of/regarding the South(s)."

Will that be the case? How to continue the bringing together of persons in philosophy with resources and legacies of knowledge production from other regional, national, and transnational disciplinary and interdisciplinary discursive enterprises in order to further exploit the possibilities this collection has brought to the fore? Are the possibilities sufficiently discernable to persuade the publisher of this collection, if not other publishers, to serve as the publisher of articulations to come out of an organized, ongoing enterprise of efforts devoted to critical philosophical explorations of "the South(s)"?

Perhaps, for example, by way of a new journal or a well-considered, well-produced series of monographs on focal subjects such as the formation and foundations of particular regional "Souths" and associated identities; philosophical critiques of efforts to sustain or dismantle the various identities and their sociocultural bases; critical explorations of models of collaboration of philosophers with other disciplinary enterprises in producing various focal studies of "Southern" histories, cultures, demographies, etc.?

Or, will the publication of this collection be but a notable one-off instance of successful efforts by an organizer of a panel of presentations during an annual meeting of a professional organization of philosophers with overlapping intellectual interests and commitments, followed by success in persuading the panel presenters to refine their considerations into anthology-worthy contributions while expanding the project to include additional articulations by persons recruited to enrich the collection such that, as a publication, the anthology will constitute success for all involved in gaining yet another "publication" that adds to each contributor's professional standing?

It remains to be seen.

Notes

1. Michael O'Brien, *Intellectual Life and the American South, 1810–1860: An Abridged Edition of Conjectures of Order* (Durham: University of North Carolina Press, 2010), 259–313.
2. W. J. Cash, *The Mind of the South* (New York: Vintage Books, 1991), xlviii.
3. Tracy Thompson, *The New Mind of the South* (New York: Free Press, 2013).
4. Boaventura de Sousa Santos, *Epistemologies of the South: Justice Against Epistemicide* (Boulder, CO: Paradigm Publishers, 2014) and *The End of the Cognitive Empire: The Coming of Age of Epistemologies of the South* (Durham, NC: Duke University Press, 2018).
5. Santos, *Epistemologies of the South*, ix.
6. Randall Collins, *The Sociology of Philosophies: A Global Theory of Intellectual Change* (Cambridge, MA: Belknap Press, 1998).

Bibliography

Cash, W. J. *The Mind of the South*. New York: Vintage Books, 1991.
Collins, Randall. *The Sociology of Philosophies: A Global Theory of Intellectual Change*. Cambridge, MA: Belknap Press, 1998.
O'Brien, Michael. *Intellectual Life and the American South, 1810–1860: An Abridged Edition of Conjectures of Order*. Durham: University of North Carolina Press, 2010.
Santos, Boaventura de Sousa. *Epistemologies of the South: Justice Against Epistemicide*. Boulder, CO: Paradigm Publishers, 2014.
Santos, Boaventura de Sousa. *The End of the Cognitive Empire: The Coming of Age of Epistemologies of the South*. Durham, NC: Duke University Press, 2018.
Thompson, Tracy. *The New Mind of the South*. New York: Free Press, 2013.

ABOUT THE AUTHORS

Linda Martín Alcoff is a professor of philosophy at Hunter College and the CUNY Graduate Center. She was president of the American Philosophical Association, Eastern Division, in 2012–2013. Her books include *The Future of Whiteness* and *Visible Identities: Race, Gender and the Self*. She is half white and half Latina, grew up in Florida as an immigrant from Panama, and today regularly eats both *arepas* and grits.

Arnold L. Farr is a professor of philosophy at the University of Kentucky. He is also founder and president of the international Herbert Marcuse Society. His books include *Marginal Groups and Mainstream American Culture*, with Yolanda Estes and Clelia Smyth, and *Critical Theory and Democratic Vision: On Herbert Marcuse and Recent Liberation Philosophies*. He was born and raised in South Carolina.

Kim Q. Hall is a professor of philosophy at Appalachian State University. She is a coeditor of *The Oxford Handbook of Feminist Philosophy* (forthcoming) and guest editor of a 2015 special issue of *Hypatia* on *New Conversations in Feminist Disability Studies*; she is working on a book titled *Queering Philosophy*. Hall is originally from a one-stoplight town in rural southern Virginia. When she decided to major in philosophy, some members of her family worried that she had been brainwashed by liberal Yankees.

Devonya N. Havis, a native Mississippian, is an associate professor of philosophy at Canisius College in Buffalo, New York. She teaches in the areas of ethics, contemporary continental philosophy, critical philosophy of race, and Black women's thought, and her essays have appeared in venues such as *Hypatia*, *Philosophy and Social Criticism* and *The Cambridge Foucault Lexicon*.

Ladelle McWhorter was born and raised in Alabama. She took her undergraduate degree in Alabama at Birmingham-Southern College and her graduate degrees at Vanderbilt University. Author of *Bodies and Pleasures: Foucault and the Politics of Sexual Normalization* and *Racism and Sexual Oppression in Anglo-America: A Genealogy*, she has taught at the University of Richmond since 1992.

Michael J. Monahan is from a part of Indiana that is west of Louisville, Kentucky. Not the deep South, to be sure, but when he moved to California, his new peers were happy to point out that he sure did talk funny. He is past vice president and current treasurer of the Caribbean Philosophical Association and is an associate

211

professor of philosophy at the University of Memphis. He is the author of *The Creolizing Subject: Race, Reason, and the Politics of Purity*.

Mariana Ortega is originally from Managua, Nicaragua. She is an associate professor of philosophy at Penn State University and the author of *In-Between, Latina Feminist Phenomenology, Multiplicity and the Self*. She is the founder and director of the LATINA/X Feminisms Roundtable, a forum dedicated to discussion of Latina/x and Latin American Feminisms.

Lucius T. Outlaw (Jr.), long a lapsed Black Baptist, was born and raised in Starkville, Mississippi, where race matters became an abiding perplexity. He earned degrees in philosophy from Fisk University and Boston College, and has taught at Fisk, Morgan State University, Haverford College, and Vanderbilt University, where he is a professor of philosophy. He is the author of *On Race and Philosophy* and *Critical Social Theory in the Interests of Black Folks*.

Lindsey Stewart was born and raised in Louisiana and is an assistant professor of philosophy at the University of Memphis. Her research focuses on developing Black feminist conceptions of political agency, with special attention to the intersection of sexuality, region, religion, and class. Her book *The Politics of Black Joy* is forthcoming from Northwestern University Press.

Shannon Sullivan is a Texan who appreciates big hair and has lived most of her adult life north of the Mason-Dixon line. She currently and very happily lives in Charlotte, North Carolina, where she is a professor of philosophy and health psychology at UNC Charlotte. She is the author or editor of nine books, including *Good White People: The Problem of Middle-Class White Anti-Racism* and *White Privilege*.

Shiloh Whitney was raised evangelical in rural Alabama. She is now an associate professor of philosophy at Fordham University in New York City. She completed her BA at the University of Alabama in Huntsville, and her PhD at McGill University in Montreal, Canada. Her work can be found in journals such as *Hypatia*, *Philosophy and Social Criticism*, and *The Southern Journal of Philosophy*.